O'CASEY'S SATIRIC VISION

O'Casey's Satiric Vision

" . . . to plough is to pray, to plant is to prophesy."
—DRUMS UNDER THE WINDOWS

B. L. Smith

The Kent State University Press

80-26131

Copyright© 1978 by The Kent State University Press
All rights reserved
ISBN: 0-87338-218-8
Library of Congress Catalog Card Number: 78-10853

Library of Congress Cataloging in Publication Data

Smith, Bobby L
    O'Casey's satiric vision.

    Includes bibliographical references and index.
1. O'Casey, Sean, 1880-1964—Humor, satire, etc.
2. O'Casey, Sean, 18801964—Political and social
views.   I. Title.
PR6029.C33Z86   822'.9'12   78-10853
ISBN 0-87338-218-8

For Deborah, Lee, Sara, and Arwen who would be Sean, and for Sean who is.

Contents

Acknowledgments

Grateful acknowledgment is due to Macmillan, London and Basingstoke; Macmillan Publishing Co., Inc., New York; and the Macmillan Company of Canada for permission to quote from O'Casey's autobiography (*Drums Under the Windows, Inishfallen, Fare Thee Well, Rose and Crown*, and *Sunset and Evening Star*). Grateful acknowledgment is due to Macmillan, London and Basingstoke; and St. Martin's Press, Inc., New York, for permission to quote from O'Casey's *Collected Plays*, 4 volumes, *Three Plays* (*Behind the Green Curtains, Figuro in the Night*, and *The Moon Shines on Kylenamoe*), *The Drums of Father Ned, Under a Colored Cap*, and *Blasts and Benedictions* (selected and introduced by Ronald Ayling). Grateful acknowledgment is due to Macmillan, London and Basingstoke, for permission to quote from *The Bishop's Bonfire* and *Feathers from the Green Crow* (introduced and edited by Robert Hogan; originally published by the University of Missouri Press, Columbia, Missouri). Grateful acknowledgment is due to George Braziller, Inc., for permission to quote from *The Green Crow*.

Chapter 1, essentially intact, appeared in *James Joyce Quarterly* as "O'Casey's Satiric Vision" (vol. 8, Fall 1970), and I thank editor Thomas F. Staley for permission to republish. A section of chapter 2 was published in the *Ball State University Forum* as "Satire in O'Casey's *The Plough and the Stars*" (vol. 10, Summer 1969) and I am grateful to Professors Merrill Rippy and Frances M. Rippy for permission to republish that essay. Portions of chapter 3 appeared in *Arizona Quarterly* as

"From Athlete to Statue: Satire in Sean O'Casey's *The Silver Tassie*" (vol. 27, Winter 1971), and I thank editor Albert F. Gegenheimer for his permission to republish that material. Portions of chapter 4 were published in *Renascence* as "Devils, Dogmatists, and Dancers: Satire in O'Casey's *Cock-a-Doodle Dandy*" (vol. XIX, Winter 1967), and I am grateful to Professor John D. McCabe for republication permission. "The Hat, The Whore, and the Hypocrite in O'Casey's *Bedtime Story*" appeared in *The Serif: Kent State University Quarterly* (vol. 4, June 1967). I am grateful to Dean H. Keller, editor, for republication permission.

I am not including a bibliography, selected or otherwise, for two reasons: first, my notes clearly indicate my sources and my debts; second, and more important here, *Sean O'Casey: A Bibliography*, compiled by Ronald Ayling and Michael J. Durkan, published by the University of Washington Press (1978), is readily available.

I appreciate the two Summer Research Fellowships and the continued research assistance provided by Kent State University's Research Council and by the English Department. Special thanks to Professor Bernard Benstock: we have shared O'Casey and other Irish things for more than a decade.

Finally, and most important, I am deeply aware of thirty years of help, love, and life provided by my wife Nancy.

1

PreRumble

From its beginnings, satire has been a darkly, occasionally a deadly, serious art. Since the satiric barrage of the phallic processionals and the stinging missiles of old comedy, the satirist has traditionally seen the world as the battlefield for the continuing war between good and evil. Whether he posed as a down-to-earth realist speaking to his deaf fellows or as a *divine* despairing of man and society, the world he viewed was a chaotic and self-destructive one. His goal, in little, was to attack evil; in large, to restore order.

His traditional targets have been topical and immediate; his solutions, symbolic and far-reaching. Satirists who attack vulgarity and destructive pride are not overly tolerant of such weaknesses and have sought to destroy rather than to understand them. Whether the primary sources be the old comedies of Aristophanes, the comic mirrors of Ben Jonson, or the missiles of Alexander Pope and Jonathan Swift, the satiric artist is not profoundly sympathetic toward those he must destroy. In most cases, the surface evils and vices are seen as symptomatic of the near transcendental blackness in the human race that gives rise and support to corrosive evils. It is recognition and desire for justice that make us unhappy with Volpone's prison sentence and delighted with the fates of his avaricious victims; it is recognition that permits us to rejoice in the symbolic and continuing victories of Dol, Face, and Subtle. The satirist's vision is more often bleak and pessimistic than joyful and affirmative.

Nonetheless, it is a mistake to see the satirist as a sober didactic pedant who has eyes only for his adversary and no time for a victory celebration. For him, as for all men, a sense of humor is a sense of perspective: he evokes and takes part in laughter, the laughter being simultaneously a joy and a weapon against evil. It is a mistake to distinguish arbitrarily between the satirist and the humorist,[1] the satirist and the comic artist—or the satirist and the historian, for that matter. The satiric vision is a dual one that sees things as they are and as they ought to be. The one who is given the vision seeks to transform the lesser into the greater world—using laughter, fear of ridicule, and common sense, together with the vast array of other weapons at his command.

The complexities of satire are clearly revealed in the continued efforts of its masters (Horace, Juvenal, Pope, John Dryden, Swift, Jonson, et al.) to define it. It is perhaps as often defined as its sister art-technique, comedy. Like comedy, it remains essentially fluid and must be redefined for every age, and like comedy, satire is both genre and technique. Its boundaries, as noted by Northrop Frye, range from pure denunciation sans humor to the humor of pure fantasy.[2] Its world, then, can be Cloudcuckooland, Lilliput, or Nyadnanave; London, New York, or Dublin. Its arsenal includes the entire range of language and imagination—from the stated to the implied, from the specified to the general, from the feared to the hoped for. The power of the word and the magic of language are the satirist's weapons: the subtleties of innuendo, irony, and wit; the directness of invective, caricature, and lampoon; and the structural artifices of burlesque, parody, and allegory. The Irish satirists who rhymed rats to death, who raised telltale blisters on the skin of their victims, who cursed a land with barrenness, are the ancestors of the more modern satirist whose chief power lies in the half-remembered conventions and traditions of satire and in the everpresent fear of ridicule and laughter innate in the hearts of those who would destroy others for personal gain, those whom the gods have made mad, and those whose only strength is in the titular dignity of office. These targets of satire, whether topical or archetypal, are rendered absurd or grotesque by the satirist, whose persona's mask of innocence should remain intact whether he is a shipwrecked sailor, a boy on a raft, a court-appointed wiseman, or an Irishman in exile.

It comes as no great shock to those who know his work that Sean O'Casey was a satirist; what might seem surprising, at first, is that O'Casey's satiric vision gives both continuity and unity to the kaleidoscopic variety of his work. From what seems to be incidental satire in *The Shadow of a Gunman* to the sustained satiric barrage of *The Bishop's Bonfire* and *Behind the Green Curtains*, O'Casey is engaged in a quest for an ever more effective vehicle of satire. It is more than superficially informative to note that O'Casey's first three major plays *(The Shadow of a Gunman, Juno and the Paycock, The Plough and the Stars)* are called tragedies; his next is experimental tragicomedy *(The Silver Tassie)*; then, he enters the morality play world *(Within the Gates, The Star Turns Red)* which gives way to the frankly fantastic *(Red Roses for Me, Purple Dust, and Cock-a-Doodle Dandy)*.

Though never to be dismissed as incidental or ornamental—not even in his Irish tragedies—O'Casey's satire is developmental and does not emerge as fully mature until near the end of the transitional period, *Purple Dust* and *Red Roses for Me* clearly anticipating in theme and technique the satiric onslaught so manifest in *Cock-a-Doodle Dandy, The Bishop's Bonfire*, and *The Drums of Father Ned*. Like satirists before him, O'Casey, with his probing revelations and his methodical dissections, earned himself the enmity of the establishment—the establishment being, for him, Church, Business, and Politics. But, unlike many satirists before him, O'Casey's satiric vision includes ample room for joy and laughter, for having a good time, and for loving life in the process.

O'Casey, the satirist, is not Jonson's Tribulation Wholesome, nor Mark Twain's Philip Traum, nor John Bunyan's Pilgrim. He does not beat his breast and lament the plight of the world; he does not cynically wait for it to destroy itself; and he certainly does not plan to keep his face straight and lead mankind toward salvation. O'Casey, again unlike many of his predecessors, is almost consistently optimistic: he is a reformer who knows that personal involvement and personal action are the only real avenues toward personal wholeness; he also knows that before a society can be whole, its individual members must be so. Except in his worst plays (*The Star Turns Red* and *Oak Leaves and Lavender*), O'Casey shares this revelation through the antics of a gallery of delightfully comic, thoroughly human, frequently capricious people. His comic genius is clearly evident in his Captain Boyles, Joxer Dalys, Fluther Goods, and their descendants.

As satirist, O'Casey offers something vital to replace that which he seeks to destroy. He is neither a universal cynic nor a "demolition expert," as Kenneth Tynan labels George Bernard Shaw. He is sensitive, perhaps "abnormally sensitive to the gap between what might be and what is."[3] What he offers in lieu of the mental rigidity, moral apathy, and automaton living which he seeks to destroy is life itself—life as it can be when no longer controlled by a dead past, by "business as usual" standpatters, or by those who consider mortification of the flesh as a prerequisite to joy. O'Casey's concern is not with the past nor the future, but with the here and now. This is the world he seeks to correct, to save from its own foolishness. "After all," as Shaw notes in his *Quintessence of Ibsenism*, "the salvation of the world depends on the men who will not take evil good-humoredly, and whose laughter destroys the fool instead of encouraging him."[4] O'Casey's writing identifies him as a man much concerned with what Shaw calls "the salvation of the world."

O'Casey did "not take evil good-humoredly"; like Mark Twain, he saw laughter as the human race's "one really effective weapon" against evil and against "colossal humbug." Among the few things that are consistent in O'Casey's canon are his penchants for directing laughter against the ridiculous and against the distorted ugliness of any system (religious, economic, political, etc.) that dehumanizes or destroys the people involved in it. Whether the victims are involved by choice or not, O'Casey views the systems themselves as manifestations of "curable idiocy" and seeks to initiate the cure. Hence, he directs his healing satire at such systems whether they are innately evil or simply seem so due to the manipulations of the mannikins who control them and their victims. Furthermore, and equally important, O'Casey has a lot of fun and provokes a great deal of amused laughter while his shots are enroute to and through his targets.

O'Casey's people, from those in his earliest to those in his latest plays, are involved in desperate, sometimes fatalistic, struggles against tradition, materialism, religion, nationalism: against forces which, in their uses of human beings, would lessen or obliterate the joys of life. O'Casey's healthy rebels declare their independence with Avril *(Purple Dust)*, who says, "I'm fed-up carrying things about to get this foolish old house in order." They recognize with the workman that "there is sweet music in the land, but not for th' deaf; there is wisdom too, but it is not in a desk it is, but out in th' hills, an' in the life of all things rovin' round, undher th' blue sky."[5]

In his own terms, O'Casey held that man is responsible for the "chassis" of the universe, and he attempted from 1924 to 1964 to answer Juno's exclamation, "Ah, what can God do agen the stupidity o' men!"[6] The answers vary from the drunkenness and joy of Joxer Daly and Jack Boyle *(Juno and the Paycock)* to the political involvements of Ayamonn and Red Jim *(Red Roses for Me* and *Star Turns Red)* to the dancing and cavorting of the Cock and Maid Marion *(Cock-a-Doodle Dandy)*. Only partial answers are gained by those who try to see into Heaven through the wrong windows of drink and abandon; a prophecy of order restored is implicit in the actions of the young people in *The Drums of Father Ned*, who would replace the hate and hypocrisy-laden government of their fathers; momentary victories are won by Nannie *(Nannie's Night Out)* and the young whore *(Within the Gates)* who, in affirming their joy of life, dance to their deaths. On the other hand, nothing but distress and continued anguish are gained by O'Casey's cowards, who are content to thump their craws and say, either in a whine or a self-assured bellow, "I am what I am." O'Casey's villains are generalized rather than specific. They are businessmen, quarrelsome Irishmen, newly powerful politicians, officers of the church, army personnel, and domineering parents. They are, in short, all those who would (by choice or through ignorance) halt change or deny the joys of life to the living. They are those who affirm the status quo and are respectable members of society because they do not dare do otherwise. Those who have the most to lose are rarely enamored of any apostle of change. Since O'Casey equates change with progress and sees both as inevitable in any social order that is alive, he is disliked and attacked by all who have an aversion to change, by all who see nothing wrong with the way the world is now, and by all who are suspicious of laughter.

The world in his drama is rarely restricted to the three walls on the picture-box-stage, but extends to include the audience in a specific theatre and to include the world outside the theatre. This is true in his first and his last plays and in most of those in between. The wars he uses, while specifically and historically accurate, are artistic microcosms of the chaos that most modern men inhabit. The device of the microcosm, when not implicit in the action on stage, is made explicit in the title or in the language of his drama. For example, *Oak Leaves and Lavender* is subtitled *A Warld on Wallpaper* and *The Drums of Father Ned* is subtitled *A Mickrocosm of Ireland*. His tenement dwellers in *The Shadow of a Gunman* and *Juno and the Paycock* are first of all human beings. Their involvements and their obviously human desperation are not restricted to tenement dwellers in Dublin any more than the pretensions and fears ridiculed in *The Plough and the Stars* are restricted to those on stage who did and did not participate in the Easter Rising of 1916.

Just as O'Casey uses the same stock characters (parasite, strong women, oul' butties, drunkard) over and over, so does he use the same themes in successive plays. The themes, like the characters who work them out, are extended, clarified, and examined from several different viewpoints. So it is that Bessie Burgess and Fluther Good in *The Plough and the Stars* are richer, more fully developed artistic creations than their prototypes, Nannie in *Nannie's Night Out* and Joxer Daly in

Juno and the Paycock. O'Casey uses the war metaphor in all of his first six plays except *Kathleen Listens In*. The war that begins pretty much as setting in *The Shadow of a Gunman* becomes an active destructive agent in *The Plough and the Stars* and a malignant ritual in *The Silver Tassie*. Also, the themes of the earlier plays are more fully developed in the succeeding ones. For example, in *The Plough and the Stars*, the viewer is bludgeoned with the idea that the vanity and immediate excitement of untempered patriotism and sense-less war destroy the most basic and most meaningful human relationships—those between friends, those between husband and wife, those between mother and child. In *The Silver Tassie*, the impersonal chaos of war destroys these same human relationships and reduces human beings to less than living things. The same human relationships are disrupted and destroyed as in *The Plough and the Stars;* in addition, the golden boy of Act I becomes the half-life who suffers "the horrible sickness of life only from the waist up" with his "body dead from the belly down."[7] This is what is left of Harry Heegan, the legendary hero of Act I who could break a chain by flexing his biceps. Harry's war has destroyed beauty, joy, and human potential. Harry's comment as he leaves the dance, "The Lord hath given and man hath taken away,"[8] echoes Juno's "Ah, what can God do agen the stupidity o' men!" Fur-thermore, it restates O'Casey's contention that man himself is responsible for the chaos of his society, and that man himself must restore sanity and order, if they are to be restored.

O'Casey's target in his earliest and latest satire is mankind—more specifically, the stupidity and the passivity of mankind that destroy individuals or prevent them from living life as it should be lived. In O'Casey's vision, organized religion, nationalistic organizations, and politics are all mad games played by mad men. In any conflict of these forces, civil or universal, it is individual human life that is destroyed or impaired; it is individuals who make up mobs, even when the mobs are called armies; ultimately, there is no panacea and individuals must shoulder the responsibility for their own well-being rather than blame their miseries on those in power or wait for an outside miracle to relieve their suffering. Individuals do elect representative politicians, and this is the hope of the young in *The Drums of Father Ned*, and the fear of the young in most of O'Casey's earlier plays. As he phrases it in "Come to the Fair,"

> It isn't the politician who makes the community, but the community that makes the politician: the politicians are but the looking-glass in which the citizen sees himself.[9]

Man's search for an all-inclusive answer, for an outside miracle to solve his everpresent problems in the world that is very much with us, might (as it has in the past) lead him into an organized, long-established religion. Such religions, as O'Casey confided to Rod Nordell, frequently "lead people into metaphysical puzzles that delude them from the sordidness of the world which needs to be dealt with."[10] O' Casey's objections to organized religion are well known, but the fact that he was opposed to them as repressive and restrictive forces, not as faith, is too little known. In his drama, as in his essays, O'Casey's satire is consistently directed against repressive forces, however impressive their names may be. His own devotion to Russian Communism and its promises did not protect its inelastic advocates who, according to O'Casey, "drive me mad. They know nothing but what they read in their little pamphlets." O'Casey himself was, of course, a communist "long before Russia came out with it,"[11] but his much repeated theme that man must make his own miracles and must right his own world is proof enough, as many American critics need to know, that he did not find communism per se the answer to all of man's ills. Neither did he find Catholicism per se the cause of all man's ills.

His communists (Covey, *The Plough and the Stars;* Ayamonn, *Red Roses for Me;* Jack, *The Star Turns Red*) provide more than passing evidence that faith and membership and memorized dogma—however sincere—are insufficient. The three miracles in *Red Roses for Me* are man-made miracles that reaffirm for O'Casey that commitment to action is necessary for the transformation of the world from what it is to what it might be. O'Casey's earliest plays (before *The Shadow of a Gunman*) were turned down by the Abbey "because they were full of propaganda," according to A.E.[12] O'Casey's propaganda efforts in behalf of Communism *(Star Turns Red)*, like those in behalf of a war-torn England somehow united by an Irish butler in a holy war against Fascism *(Oak Leaves and Lavender)*, are bad drama: both are hate-filled and splenetic attacks, both depict the essential strength and wisdom of the communist doctrine, and both trace a steady progression from despair to hope and from disillusionment to prophecy of inevitable victory. Both plays fail, in part, because O'Casey was unable to preserve even the illusion of detachment.

In the later play, O'Casey's comic genius is overwhelmed by the circumstance of the blitz of London, a crumbling nation, and the apparently unstoppable massive strength of Germany's military. The call to arms that his play is does provide, of course, slapstick and farfetched laughter, but his main thesis is that the bumbling, stumbling Prufrocks, in the face of crisis, are able to unite and defend themselves heroically against the military barrage hurled by Germany. His attacks on tradition, ritual, organized religion, and the old who would deny the young, while present, are at best glancing blows. He does demonstrate, to the dismay of many, that fools remain fools whether they are united or not, and whether England is at peace or at war.

I don't share the current critical stance that sees *Red Roses for Me* as a mere propaganda vehicle, though it does make it quite clear that O'Casey's commitment is to Labor, not to Nationalism, and says as clearly as *Drums under the Windows* that Nationalism is no better avenue than organized religion to the kind of new world that Ayamonn Breydon envisions in the shilling. The miracles wrought are wrought by man acting, not by man talking and not by man waiting. O'Casey, the satirist, is effective in his portrayal of Dublin and Dubliners who wait for their due. He presents, as Joyce did before him, the sterility and death that await those bound, by tradition and duty, to the old ways. O'Casey's hindsight in *Red Roses for*

Me goes far to explain his separation from the Citizen Army, his opposition to the Rising of 1916 as clearly presented in *The Plough and the Stars,* and his total disillusionment with the bloody civil wars from which the terrible beauty was ultimately born. Even during his last decade, O'Casey's commitment was to Labor, to action, and to what he saw clearly as the Red Star of Ethical Humanism.

Of O'Casey's "Colored Plays" (*Silver Tassie, Star Turns Red, Purple Dust, Red Roses for Me,* and *Oak Leaves and Lavender*), only *Purple Dust* does not deal directly with war. His basic target in *Purple Dust* is the rationalistic English mind, with its incumbent faith that empire, heritage, and culture will somehow muddle through. The decaying mansion is a museum to such bumbling: its residents (Stoke and Poges) are living embodiments of Gray's country churchyard, and their aims are to glorify England by putting it back together as it was in the good old days—to put it together in a kind of living museum somehow immune to the ravages of time and season and mutability. They, their mansion, and their project are, of course, doomed from the outset. Stoke and Poges, with their mercenary values, are hopelessly outmatched by the realistic Irishmen led by O'Killigain, so the impotent Englishmen lose their women, their investment, and—unless they are more fortunate than fleetfooted—their lives. They are unfit for the better world that's coming, for they do not desire to live in a vigorous and meaningful way.

The specific incidents of the dissections of Stoke and Poges are those of farce comedy: a huge grass roller gets out of control when the ineffectual Poges attempts to maneuver it as the salesman from simple Ireland told him he could; the roller crashes through a wall; a cow, also bought from a simple Irish salesman, sends Stoke and Poges scurrying for protection when they mistake it for a bull (their enterprise is, in part, like that in *John Bull's Other Island*—courtesy of G. B. Shaw); the innocent cow is shot dead; the workmen methodically destroy the mansion's ceiling, walls, door frames, and heirlooms (there are no family jewels, of course, and not an Englishman in residence who can even build a fire); Stoke falls from a spirited horse and his "lassie o' th' house went off with O'Killigain riding naked through the locality!"[13]

The Irishmen in *Purple Dust* are close kinsmen of Synge's tramps and tinkers: existence and the necessities of life are not their prime concerns, nor are they conspicuously nationalistic. They revel in freedom and joy and life. Their pride is natural and they relinquish neither freedom nor identity to work for their symbolically deaf and blind English employers. They know, as the old codger knows in a later play, and as the employers do not know, that

> there is sweet music in the land, but not for th' deaf; there is wisdom too, but it is not in a desk it is, but out in th' hills, an' in the life of all things rovin' round, undher th' blue sky.[14]

Purple Dust is wayward comedy with heavy satire a major ingredient. Youth and life win out, as they must in O'Casey's work, over old age and death. O'Casey utilizes setting, sound, and the threat of rain and inevitable flood to establish the atmosphere and mood of the play. When the rain comes, it does not dampen the spirits of O'Killigain and Avril, nor of O'Dempsey and Souhaun; rather it is a healing and life-giving rain which will wash away the purple dust of a dead past and send the dabblers in antiquity out of a land which is not theirs: *Purple Dust* "hits, of course, at the adoration of the old, outworn things, and leans towards new thought and young ideas."[15]

O'Casey's "Colored Plays" come almost in midstream of his dramatic canon: preceded by the masterful Irish plays and followed by plays too easily discussed as rehashes or reruns, they are seldom given the attention that they merit. *The Silver Tassie* is a first-rate play—effective, moving, and innovative. As the first of the colored plays, it establishes directions and guidelines concerning plot, setting, and character. *Cock-a-Doodle Dandy*, which immediately follows the colored plays, is also excellent drama. The dimensions, the themes, and the hilarious manipulations of materials are directly attributable to the experiments—successes and failures—which preceded it. In all of these, O'Casey—whether he said he wrote tragicomedy, morality play, a sad play, or a tragedy—was first and foremost a satirist. The targets of his satire were consistently man-made evils that could be cured by man: the men responsible range from repressive religionists (Father Domineer, Purple Priest, Bishop Mullarkey) through repressive militarists (Kian [anagram for Cain], Hitler and his fascists, the Auxiliaries and the Black and Tans, to good men who have lost their way (Sailor Mahan, Manus Moanroe), and all are punctuated by the antics of the delightful Fluther Goods, Joxer Dalys, and Angela Nightingales; the essential goodness of Bessie Burgesses, Juno Boyles, and Mrs. Breydons; and the operative wisdom of the Cocks, Father Neds, Feelim O'Morriguns and Codger Sleehauns.

Basically, O'Casey's satiric world is a wasteland world whose deformity and sickness are personified by the halt, the lame, and the blind who parade there. The lack of vitality and fear of change are readily apparent in the Binningtons, McGilligans, Fillifogues, Domineers, and Murphys who control the world. His greatest monsters are those who have eyes yet see not, those who have ears yet hear not. The comic war with machines (*End of the Beginning, Silver Tassie, Purple Dust*) is a continuing one: those who cause, perpetuate, and suffer from the wars seek meaning in rituals, processionals, gaudy costumes, plastic saints, new pianos, and social decorum. The meaning they seek, in all cases, lies elsewhere.

An escape from and an antidote to the social poisons of the world are discovered by limited numbers of O'Casey's people—by the Cock, Marion, Lorna, and Lorleen, who are driven out of the society they have sought to help (*Cock-a-Doodle Dandy*). They leave singing. Folly-ridden society triumphs, but the outcases are triumphant in the sense that they, like Synge's tramp and Nora Burke, are free. Again, in *The Bishop's Bonfire*, Father Boheroe, who preaches that merriment is a kind of worship, and the old codger, who has a "vilely venemous tongue," are ostracized while the Prodical continues to drink and vow temperance, as did the delightfully funny and remarkably efficient Fluther Good in *The Plough and the Stars*. Foorawn dies for love. All escape, at a price, and a sick society remains victorious and unchanged. It is unchanged because it lacks the essential vitality to accept or to cope with changes. Its down-and-outs, standpatters, and business-as-usual villains and victims are as frightened of laughter as they are of change. In short, as O'Casey paints them, they fear life itself.

In "The Power of Laughter: Weapon Against Evil," O'Casey states specifically what he has so long preached in his plays and essays—that those who deny or condemn laughter as evil are themselves to be feared, that laughter reveals the greatest dangers in those areas where it is forbidden:

> Laughter tends to mock the pompous and the pretentious; all man's boastful gadding about, all his pretty pomps, his hoary customs, his wornout creeds, changing the glitter of them into the dullest hue of lead. The bigger the subject, the sharper the laugh. No one can escape it: not the grave judge in his robe and threatening wig; the parson and his saw; the general full of his sword and his medals; the palled prelate, tripping about a blessing in one hand, a curse in the other; the politician carrying his magic wand of Wendy windy words; they all fear laughter, for the quiet laugh or the loud one upends them, strips them of pretense, and leaves them naked to enemy and friend.[16]

In O'Casey's world, heroism and effective action are not dead, as is clearly demonstrated in *Cock-a-Doodle Dandy*, *The Drums of Father Ned*, and *Purple Dust*. They are possible, as they frequently are not in the wasteland worlds of much other modern literature. As O'Casey notes in "The Lark in the Clear Air Still Sings," "Life will never want for heroes, mostly unhonored and unsung, but always there and ready to act."[17] O'Casey's love for mankind and his enthusiastic optimism are in conflict with and lend depth to the confused state of "chassis" and anarchy that continue to exist at the final curtain of most of his drama. As a dramatist and as a satirist, O'Casey loves the world he reveals in his own version of the Steel Glass and he preaches to the pessimists that, "We have no reason whatever to be ashamed of our humanity; we have many good reasons to be proud of it."[18] He mocks mental apathy, complacent acceptance of the status quo, and moral cowardice. He insists that those who have eyes to see and ears to hear must find both sorrow and joy in life.

O'Casey's art (drama, autobiography, essay, letter, short story, etc.) is frequently didactic in that he has a point to make and will not be put off. His heroes are the young and the strong—gifted with song, dance, and an appreciation for the joys of life. The group that follows the Cock (*Cock-a-Doodle Dandy*), the group that marches to the drums of Father Ned (*The Drums of Father Ned*), and the gifted couple in *Time to Go* have much in common. Their gifts can cure a sick society and save its people from the fate of Joyce's Dubliners in "The Dead." They have counterparts in several of O'Casey's plays after *Red Roses for Me*. In that play Ayamonn Breydon is close to the standard pharmakos: his virtues and goals and values make him an easily discernible Christ in worker's wardrobe. It is his fate to be destroyed by the society that he is part of and would save. Later, in *Cock-a-Doodle Dandy*, the fools of Nyadnanave are also left to their own devices as the young in spirit are driven out. In *Time to Go*, after the miracles—like those in *Red Roses for Me*—fail to bring about any lasting change, society is abandoned as hopelessly lost by Kelly and the Widda Machree. In *The Drums of Father Ned*, the beat of the human heart establishes the tempo of the drums and the young recognize the enemy to be "what is old and stale and vicious." The young combat the hate-drenched values of the establishment—of Fillifogues, Binningtons, and McGilligans—and the young win. "The Dead March" and "Boots and Saddles" become the rally music for a united Ireland. Doonavale, unlike Nyadnanave, is not abandoned by the young: they will win the election so "That mobled minds may all new courage grow,/And Miser'd hearts be merry."[19]

O'Casey's didacticism is more than offset by his humor and his capacity to present even the straightest preachment in brilliantly funny episodes. Moreover, the antihero, not the hero, is perhaps his most significant contribution to the theatre: the antics of Joxer Daly, Captain Boyle, Fluther Good, together with those of Bernadette Shillayley (*The Drums of Father Ned*), Angela Nightingale (*Bedtime Story*), and the saucy vital wenches of *Cock-a-Doodle Dandy* under-line the basic themes of those plays. All are creatures of instinct who manage to survive in the chassis of modern civilization. O'Casey's plays are about human life and the foibles and tragedies that are necessarily a part of that life.

As satirist, he uses laughter as a weapon against all who would destroy social order for selfish gains and all who would perpetuate the chaos of social disorder for personal profit. O'Casey, as a man, viewed laughter as a weapon against evil, surely, but also as "wine for the soul . . . a great natural stimulator, a pushful entry into life"; he recognized in laughter the power of healing and the means to what Shaw calls "the salvation of the world." Laughter, like dance, is one of the joys of life and is more indicative of real life than breathing is, "and once we can laugh, we can live."[20] The aims of his satire are to strip away the fearful facade of regimented powers of repression, to reveal and destroy the ugliness concealed by those facades, and to establish a meaningful social order in lieu of the "chassis" perpetrated by the stupidity of men. These aims he would further and ultimately realize through the power of laughter.

From *The Shadow of a Gunman* through *The Drums of Father Ned*, the vision of this Irish satirist expands from the limited scope of Ireland's troubles to the universal scope of human society. His continuing experimentation in technique and his ability to use what he learned from those experiments led ultimately to the mature satiric vision of such later plays as *Cock-a-Doodle Dandy* and *The Drums of Father Ned*. His last three plays (*Behind the Green Curtains, Figuro in the Night*, and *The Moon Shines on Kylenamoe*) represent an obvious encore by the prolific O'Casey and are, in effect, recapitulations of themes, characters, and techniques long familiar to his readers and viewers.[21] Within the "Mickrocosm" of O'Casey's "warld on wallpaper," his satire is alternately destructive and curative, his aims being to destroy the source of infection and to replace "chassis" with some semblance of joyful order. In his "Colored Plays," fore and aft, the green crow wears his colored cap and marches to the tune of his own drummer as he urges those who have hearts to pay heed to the shout in the street.[22]

2

The Irish Plays

When *The Shadow of a Gunman* was first produced at the Abbey Theatre in April 1923, the spectators were reminded by a program note that any gunshots heard were a part of the script and that members of the audience were to remain seated. The setting has frequently been described as realistic, and William A. Armstrong has meticulously equated the play's events with history and with passages from *Inishfallen, Fare Thee Well,* the fourth part of O'Casey's autobiography.[1] The curfew, the raids, the Black and Tans, and the ambushes of the play are based on historical fact—reason enough for Seumas's comments, "Oh, Kathleen ni Houlihan, your way's a thorny way!" and ". . . Kathleen ni Houlihan is very different now to the woman who used to play the harp an' sing . . . , for she's a ragin' divil now. . . . "[2] The world of O'Casey's Irish trilogy, the world in which his characters strut and cower, brag and fear, live and die, is a mad world, a world of very real and immediate death, a world ruled by ruthless uniformed men whose raids are inevitable; it is, as O'Casey notes, a world where "the angel of death is a biting bitch."[3]

It is clearly not O'Casey's intent to glorify the insurrection, nor to romanticize those who die bravely for creed or nation. Rather, the madness generated by the chaos of war acts as a backdrop for and catalyst to the action onstage. The dramatist's chief concern is with the people in the tenement, especially those who are unwillingly invaded by the madness that reigns outside their tenement walls. The tenement is an isolated world set in a chaotic and mad universe. The madness, throughout the action of *The Shadow of a Gunman*, is a kind of touchstone which reveals to viewers and readers the relative values and the deep flaws in the human character. It is this touchstone which ultimately reveals the true characters of those on stage: by it we know Grigson, Seumas, Donal, and Minnie; by it we know the world they inhabit. As Seumas Shields notes in the second act:

> I wish to God it was all over. The country is gone mad. Instead of counting their beads now they're countin' bullets; their Hail Marys and paternosters are burstin' bombs—burstin' bombs, an' the rattle of machine-guns; petrol is their holy water; their Mass is a burnin' buildin'; their De Profundis is "the Soldiers' Song", an' their creed is, I believe in the gun almighty, maker of heaven an' earth—an' it's all for "the glory o' God an' the honour o' Ireland." [*SOG*, p. 131]

Seumas describes the insanity that ultimately engulfs the world in *The Silver Tassie* to the extent that the howitzer becomes a god demanding sacrifice and the soldiers become willing priests and protesting victims. The insanity increases as we move through the Irish trilogy and into the assorted microcosms of O'Casey's world at war in *The Silver Tassie*. Seumas, for all his superstition and for all his cowardice, does see clearly.

In *The Shadow of a Gunman* or "On the Run," O'Casey wrote about a world he knew firsthand and was part of. The acts of heroism, cowardice, and foolishness in this "Tragedy in Two Acts," give us our first glimpses of a parade of O'Casey characters as a gallery of the satirist's targets that are recurrent in his plays through the final curtain.

Man's penchant for hypocrisy, for seeming to be what he is not, is satirized—sometimes bitterly, sometimes lovingly. Adolphus Grigson with his refrain of "Here's the fust today" becomes the first of a long and continuing parade of O'Casey's delightful drunks who find courage, self-respect, and independence in their cups. Grigson proves his manhood by reading the scriptures to his wife and thereby putting her in her place. In what is perhaps the funniest scene of the play, he brags that "Adolphus Grigson wasn't born in a bottle!" that "Dolphus Grigson's afraid av nothin', creepin' or walkin', . . . that Grigson's no soft thing" [SOG, pp. 138-39]. Mrs. Grigson speaks of her ineffectual husband in a series of Freudian puns which characterize him before he enters the action. Her chief concern about her fumbling husband, despite her protestations, is the lateness of his arrival, for it is after one o'clock, after the curfew, and the raids of either the Black and Tans, or the Auxiliaries, are everpresent dangers. She asks, "Do the insurance companies pay if a man is shot after curfew?"

As the madness tears its way into the tenement in the persons of the dreaded Auxiliaries, the boisterous drunken Grigson becomes a snivelling coward, seeking refuge in his Bible, which is his sole authority, except for his bottle. The Auxiliary throws his Bible on the floor, confiscates his bottle, forces him to offer up a prayer for the Irish Republic and to sing "We Shall Meet in the Sweet Bye an' Bye." Upstairs, after the danger has passed, Grigson tells the story quite differently, mentioning his own nonchalant courage and the manner in which he backed the soldiers down—all these possible, he notes, "If a man keeps a stiff upper front" [SOG, p. 155]. Grigson's comic role is, without explication, exceedingly funny. When he is recognized as a burlesque of the stage Irishman and a cornucopia of the many fears and hypocrisies that are as common in Ireland as elsewhere, when it is recognized that his quicksilver changes from braggart to coward and from he-man to fumbling husband are not out of character, he is recognized as one of O'Casey's many satiric triumphs. Grigson and Seumas, despite the relative youth of the latter, become the "oul' butties" of O'Casey's later drama.

The cowardice of Seumas parallels that of Grigson, as does his ability to retell his adventure in such a way that he emerges heroic. For Seumas, too, the Bible is talisman; for him, too, his plaster saints, his true poetic gift, and his congenital slovenliness help him to maintain some semblance of security. He blames others with his own most blatant faults, clings to superstition (the tappin' in the wall), to pat answers, and to the time of day for perspective.

Seumas's courage is like that of Grigson. Both are basically creatures of instinct who cling to whatever is at a given moment and adapt readily whenever circumstances change. Seumas—natural poet, braggart philosopher, and devoted Catholic—is revealed in terms of relationships to Grigson and Davoren. For example, in one exchange between Seumas and Davoren, the essential religions of both are talismans and words only:

> Seumas: You're one of the brave fellows that doesn't fear death.
>
> Davoren: Why should I be afraid of it? It's all the same to me how it comes, where it comes, or when it comes. I leave fear of death to the people that are always praying for eternal life; "Death is here and death is there, death is busy everywhere."
>
> Seumas: Ay, in Ireland. Thanks be to God I'm a daily communicant. There's a great comfort in religion; it makes a man strong in time of trouble an' brave in time of danger. No man need be afraid with a crowd of angels round him; thanks to God for His Holy religion!
>
> Davoren: You're welcome to your angels; philosophy is mine; philosophy that makes the coward brave; the sufferer defiant; the weak strong; the . . . . [SOG, pp. 132-33]

When the discourse is interrupted by a volley of shots, both men reveal very real fear of death. Their "stiff upper fronts" wilt as readily as Grigson's when they are threatened. Earlier in the exchange between the religious Seumas and the philosophical Davoren, Seumas observes quite specifically what becomes the major theme and action of *The Plough and the Stars*.

> . . . I look at it this way:
> You're not goin'—you're not goin' to beat the British Empire—the British Empire, by shootin' an occasional Tommy at the corner of an occasional street. Besides, when the Tommies have the wind up—when the Tommies have the wind up they let bang at everything they see—they don't give a God's curse who they plug.
>
>   . . .
>
> It's the civilians that suffer; when there's an ambush they don't know where to run. Shot in the back to save the British Empire,

an' shot in the breast to save the soul of Ireland. I'm a Nationalist meself, right enough—a Nationalist right enough, but all the same—I'm a Nationalist right enough; I believe in the freedom of Ireland, an' that England has no right to be here, but I draw the line when I hear the gunmen blowin' about dyin' for the people, when it's the people that are dyin' for the gunmen! With all due respect to the gunmen, I don't want them to die for me. [*SOG*, p. 132]

In addition to setting the stage for *The Plough and the Stars*, this passage at least anticipates an answer to Davoren's question that ends Act I: "And what danger can there be in being the shadow of a gunman?" Further, it anticipates the death of Minnie and goes far to destroy whatever semblance of heroism there is attached to the actions and death of Maguire. O'Casey's true heroes go not on maneuvers with the IRA nor on practice marches with the Irish Citizen Army. Nor do they do battle with the Black and Tans or the Auxiliaries. They stay at home and combat the real fears and problems of human existence that are everpresent in the Dublin slums.

O'Casey also satirizes the fear of gossip, a fear that is apparently universal; in *The Shadow of a Gunman*, the fear is ironic and especially ludicrous as Davoren, the presumed gunman, warns Minnie of it, and as Seumas, who shares his apartment with Davoren, warns his young tenant, "The oul' ones'll be talkin', an' once they start you don't know how it'll end" [*SOG*, p. 129]. The fear of gossip is made ludicrous and ironic by the much greater danger outside the tenement walls—the immediate danger of raids and death. Minnie Powell fears neither gossip nor death, so she says little of either. Minnie thinks she dies a heroic death, but she dies for a false idea, a shadow that disappears in the bright light of truth. Her shadow of a gunman is as false and as unreal as Davoren's philosophical totems and as ineffectual as Seumas's half-baked religion, but for her the shadow is real. In his presentation of Minnie, O'Casey emphasizes the human hypocrisy of the other characters, whose talismans are discarded, ignored, or blasphemed in time of danger or whenever fear takes over. Minnie, despite or perhaps because of her youth and her innocence, is true to her ideal, but her ideal remains false. In several ways, she in her naivete and commitment anticipates Mary Boyle's equally immature, "a principle's a principle."

O'Casey here subscribes to a pattern that is consistent in his canon. The talkers of brave deeds and miracles and manhood are rarely the doers. When confronted in reality with that which they so easily manage in their rhetoric, they crumble, wilt, or withdraw. On the other hand, those like Juno Boyle and Bessie Burgess who accomplish heroic or miraculous deeds make little talk about them.

O'Casey satirizes the poetic temperament of Shelley's disciple, who desires and expresses desire for great heroic and creative activity at the same time he relishes his own inactivity, gives way to his own lethargy, and is revealed as a sincere coward—a charge, by the way, that cannot be levied against either Seumas or Grigson. They, like Fluther Good in *The Plough and the Stars,* are never out of character, whatever they say or do. Despite Davoren's poetic exile and his protestations, it is Seumas who is the poet. It is he who readily quotes Shakespeare; it is he who warns Davoren against the uselessness of poetry for the working man; it is he who defines the limits of a poet's greatness:

> If I was you I'd give that game up; it doesn't pay a working-man to write poetry. I don't profess to know much about poetry—I don't profess to know much about poetry—about poetry— I don't know much about the pearly glint of the morning dew, or the damask sweetness of the rare wild rose, or the subtle greeness of the serpent's eye—but I think a poet's claim to greatness depends upon his power to put passion in the common people.

Davoren replies:

> Ay, passion to howl for his destruction. The People! Damn the people! They live in the abyss, the poet lives on the mountain-top; to the people there is no mystery of color: it is simply the scarlet coat of the soldier; the purple vestments of a priest; the green banner of a party; the brown or blue overalls of industry. To them the might of design is a three-roomed house or a capacious bed. To them beauty is for sale in a butcher's shop. To the people the

end of life is the life created for them; to the poet the end of life is
the life that he creates for himself; life has a stifling grip upon the
people's throat—it is the poet's musician. The poet ever strives to
save the people; the people ever strive to destroy the poet. The
people view life through creeds, through customs, and through
necessities; the poet views creeds, customs, and necessities
through life. The people. . . . [*SOG*, p. 127]

Davoren's holier-than-they response to Seumas's definition
of "a poet's claim to greatness," together with his frequent
invocations to Shelley and his frequent quotations from
Prometheus Unbound, mark him as O'Casey's stage poet. As
such, he is the polar opposite from O'Casey's notion of what a
true poet should be. Seumas's definition of a poet's greatness
as "the power to put passion into the common people" is much
closer to O'Casey's vision of what a poet should be—a vision
that is much expanded in *Within the Gates, Red Roses for Me,*
and *The Drums of Father Ned.* For O'Casey, as for his
American idol Walt Whitman, the poet's place is with the
people, and he is of the people. The mystery of color, the
might of design, and beauty—however rhapsodic Davoren
is—are dead whenever they are isolated from the lives of
people. O'Casey's poet figures mature in succeeding plays
until ultimately they become satirists rather than objects of
satire, leaders of action rather than recipients of action, people
rather than stock characters.

O'Casey's "Always the Plough and the Stars," begins "The
artist occupies a perilous place in life, for he is the most
expendable of men." If he separates himself from life, he is
comic. He must cope with the everpresent danger of not
getting "enough dough to live"; he must struggle against the
notion that an artist is not a human being; he must somehow
escape, if he is to be an artist, both "self glorification, and the
glorification of the crowd." In Sean O'Casey's opinion, "The
artist's place is to be where life is, active life, found in neither
ivory tower nor concrete shelter; he must be out listening to
everything, looking at everything, and thinking it all out
afterward."[4]

Davoren, in the sequence of events, moves from his role playing gunman to recognition of his cowardice and his complicity in Minnie's death. His self-imposed and self-declared separation from life and from people—"Damn the people"—makes the stage poet a poltroon, a ridiculous figure, and a burlesque of a true poet. It is to his credit that Davoren ultimately recognizes and knows himself, "We're a pair of pitiable cowards to let poor Minnie suffer when we know that we and not she are to blame" [*SOG*, p. 151]. It is not to his credit that by his pretense as playboy, as shadow of a gunman, he is clearly accountable for Minnie's romantic commitment to a false idea, for her attempt to protect him, for her arrest, and for her death.

Davoren, at best, is O'Casey's embryonic poet, gifted with clarity of vision, but little else. He lacks the essential ingredient of the artist, experience in real life. He can learn much from Seumas, as noted earlier, though he surpasses Seumas in perception. He recognizes both the courage and the innocence of Minnie, but does not recognize in her the ingredient absent in himself, the independence and the knowledge of life that permit her to dance the Hooley, to dismiss Donal's wild flowers as weeds, and to say as he warns her of gossip, "An' do you think Minnie Powell cares whether they'll talk or not? She's had to push her way through life up to this without help from anyone, an' she's not goin' to ask their leave, now, to do what she wants to do." Minnie sees life in terms of her own experience. Donal Davoren cannot; instead, he isolates himself from human experience, seeks solitude, and believes the poet to be a scapegoat-savior who can save the people only by being scorned or destroyed by them. He is, at best, the first step toward the men of the people who battle for and sometimes die for the ideas they express in O'Casey's later plays. Unlike Davoren, they are a part of life and promote the improvement of life.

Minnie's death has real artistic value in that it affords the viewer with yet another touchstone by which to test the professed values of those in the tenement—especially the

values of Mrs. Grigson, Seumas, and Davoren. For Mrs.
Grigson, the dead Minnie ceases to be the deceitful little hussy
who needs a "coolin' an' deserves whatever happens to her"
and becomes "Poor little Minnie." Seumas earlier proclaimed
Minnie "A Helen of Troy come to live in a tenement." At her
death he proclaims his own innocence, "Is it my fault; am I to
blame? . . . She did it off her own bat—We didn't ask her to do
it." Davoren insists that he and Seumas are "a pair of dastardly
cowards" and that shame is his portion now as he recognizes
himself as "poet and poltroon." All of these observations occur
after the danger is past. They do not, in any case, reflect any
real or significant change. Davoren voices his recognition of
his own cowardice, but were the scene replayed, he would
still be a coward. The observations following Minnie's death,
after the departure of the murderous Auxiliaries, re-emphasizes a basic theme of this play, voiced earlier by Seumas: "—
an' as for bein' brave, it's easy to be that when you've no cause
for cowardice . . . " [SOG, p. 130]. Neither the raids nor the
quotations from *Prometheus Unbound*, neither the assorted
talismans nor Minnie's death effects any real changes within
the walls of the Tenement.

The basic methods of satire employed include the verbal
irony implicit in all the dialogue between Seumas and Davoren, the irony of character of those who loudest proclaim
their courage and soonest seek refuge in time of danger, and
of course the dramatic irony which reveals courage in the
romantic girl who goes to her death for a shadow that has no
substance. O'Casey's juxtaposition of stock characters permits
a clearer view of both Seumas and Davoren, and his burlesque
of the IRA's true relationship to those in the tenements clearly
establishes the people's separation from the political conflict.
The Auxiliary soldier's rapid departure from Seumas's room
when he hears that whiskey has been confiscated in another
room underlines Davoren's earlier comment that "A man
should always be drunk . . . when he talks politics—it's the
only way in which to make them important" [SOG, p. 106]. It
also indicates something terrifying about the bully's dedication to duty, to cause, and to country.

The plot line of *The Shadow of a Gunman* is as carefully contrived as any in the well-made-play tradition. The letter, for example, is not lost sight of, though its function in the play is at best a mechanical one. The letter, as Mrs. Henderson states, "is as good a letter as was decomposed by a scholar" [*SOG*, p. 116]. Its jargon and meaningless circumlocution, together with the fact that its author and Mrs. Henderson are greatly impressed by it, add comedy as well as perspective to the play.

A bit of paper on which Davoren typed his and Minnie's names is confiscated by the Auxiliaries and is, of course, smeared with her heart's blood, blood which obliterates Davoren's name and thereby protects him, just as Minnie, by taking the bombs, had protected him earlier. Whether he knows it or not, Davoren has nothing to fear, though he will probably continue to be afraid. Seumas's insistence on knowing the time of day and his concentration on the tapping on the wall lend thematic as well as mechanical structure. O'Casey, as his guides (architects of the well-made play, and Henrik Ibsen and Dion Boucicault) direct, leaves no loose ends as he puts his characters through their paces.

During its three nights on the Abbey Stage, *The Shadow of a Gunman* was performed before ever larger audiences, anticipating the future success of O'Casey's drama on that stage and a kind of rebirth for the Abbey Theatre itself, which was rapidly falling into economic ruin. O'Casey's share of the £93 total receipts was less than £4, hardly enough to pay his bills.[5] These facts have their place in literary history; the important thing is that O'Casey had for the first time adorned a public stage with his combination of riotous laughter and grim tragedy; that he had insisted for the first time that man look within himself for courage, faith, reason for being; that he had used his satiric scalpel to strip naked the follies, fears, and vices of man.

Following O'Casey's disappointment in his share of the ticket sales for *The Shadow of a Gunman,* he vowed to

> go forward. He had put his hand to the plough, and he wasn't the one to look back. He would start a new play that very night.

So he had, and he called it *Cathleen Listens In,* a jovial sardonic sketch on the various parties in conflict over Irish politics—Sinn Fein, Free State, and Labour. It was a short one-act work, and was performed after a major play had ended [in the Abbey Theatre on 1 October 1923]. Another experience for Sean! The audience received the little play in dead silence, in a silence that seemed to have a point of shock in its centre. Not even a cold clap of a hand anywhere. They all got up from their seats, and silently filed out of the theatre.[6]

Thirty-eight years after the writing of *Kathleen Listens In: A Political Phantasy in One Act,* O'Casey noted:

> there are two things connected with this play that may add just a little interest: it was written specifically to show what fools these mortals were in the quarreling factions soaking Ireland in anxiety and irritation after the Civil War. I imagined that satire might bring some sense to the divided groups so busy practicing envy, hatred, malice, and all uncharitableness: it didn't do it. The second item of interest was (or is) that the audiences received it in dead and embarrassed silence. . . .[7]

This "jovial sardonic sketch" has more historical and bio-graphical than literary value. It shows O'Casey's early interest in fantasy as a satiric vehicle and indicates, as does "The Seamless Coat of Kathleen,"[8] his unhappiness with the various factions who sought to claim Ireland, or to rape her if she did not acquiesce. As O'Casey says of his satire intended to "bring some sense to the divided groups":

> . . . it is a "phantasy," done after my first play at the Abbey [*Sha-dow of a Gunman*], showing this form was active in my mind before the "major" realistic plays were written, tho' most critics maintain that phantasy began after I left Dublin. This, of course, is what they want to believe, and so, God be with them.[9]

This "political phantasy" used several devices of the moral-ity play, including the reader's awareness of responsibility, consequence, and final judgment—an awareness not shared by those most involved in the pursuit of Kathleen's favors. Jimmy the Workman, the Man in Kilts, the Free Stater, the Republican, the Business Man, and the Farmer all vie for the young Kathleen's hand. She is weak, sick, and ultimately on her deathbed as the doctor tries to save her from the devastating noise made by her suitors. "She's very weak," he says, "but she'll pull round after a bit, if she gets perfect quietness: A whisper may prove fatal—she'll need perfect peace and quietness for the rest of her National life."[10]

The satire is not subtle, and virtually all the vested interests in the new Free State are represented, from the Orange Man who beats the big drum over the boundary question to Jimmy the neophyte Socialist who threatens strikes and walkouts and promises houses for all workers. In one delightful scene, O'Casey satirizes the Free Staters' Oath so violently opposed by Republicans and Labor:

FREE STATER. Now let us all take a solemn an' sacred oath.

REPUBLICAN. I won't, I won't, I won't; I'll not take no oath for nobody, so help me God![11]

He parodies the old Irish line of status quo, tradition-bound, solid citizens as two men urge, or rather command, the newly powerful Miceawl O'Houlihan (who sold his cow to buy a house) to throw out his poppies and his English flag and to grow shamrocks, to sing "The Soldiers' Song" before and after meals, and to read a chapter of Mitchel's *Jail Journal* nightly. The door is slammed in their faces as they chant their litany:

1ST MAN. We think what we thought, we say what we said, we stand where we stood seven hundhred years ago; the world may change but Ireland'll never alther.

2ND MAN. As it was in th' beginning,' is now an' ever will be, world without end, amen.[12]

Miceawl is a rather fearful spokesman for progress and for keeping up appearances. He does not want to be called Mick anymore, and is confused by all who want to educate Kathleen. He finds his "house is hardly worth livin' in. . . . The inside's in a shockin' state!" primarily because every group in Ireland insists on aiding in furnishing and redecorating it. One group, "That rowdy Dawn o'Liberty Fife an' Drum Band is afther puttin' the finishin' touch on it." It is a band which

Tomaus says has "too many bandmasters in it! Playin' an'
playin' the one tune, till everybody was fed up with it."
Miceawl has formed his own brass band and his "heart's bruk
tryin' to keep them together . . . every member . . . wants to
play a defferen' tune, an' the big drummer only wants to hear
himself."[13]

In this severally veiled allegory, Ireland is represented by
the cow which has been sold too cheaply, by the house which
is a shambles, and by the sickly Kathleen. The young Kathleen
has all of the pretensions long associated with newly arrived
bourgeoisie, pretensions parodied by O'Casey in *Juno and the
Paycock* and in virtually all of his plays after 1950. Kathleen
says to the first two who come to court her,

> Oh, for God's sake go away, an' done be annoyin' me. I have to
> practice me Fox Trots and Jazzin' so as to be lady-like when I
> make me deboo into the League o' Nations.[14]

Jimmy threatens to go on strike, to go to Russia, because as he
asks,

> What's the good o' lovin' Kathleen, when she won't take any
> notice o' you? Others can hold her hand for hours, an' bring her
> for walks, but whenever she sees me, she passes me by with her
> nose in the air—just because I can't play the bloody piano![15]

The various forces—all as embryonic in Ireland as the Free
State itself—in their striving to possess or to give advice
concerning the cow, the house, and Kathleen, are responsible
for the chaos and, in O'Casey's view, for the ultimate destruction of all three.

The various groups are further parodied by the endearing
names they call Kathleen and by the gifts they offer her. The
Republican calls her "Me own sweet, little red little rose" and
offers her a "picture I painted of herself in 1916 in everlastin'
oils." The Free Stater calls her "Me own fair Little brown
cow" and offers her "a Manual on the Government of a house
accordin' to a Constitution." To the Farmer, Kathleen is "Me
clusther o' little brown nuts" and he offers her "a bag o' self
raisin' flour." The Business Man promises his "sweet little

beautiful pulse o' me heart" that he will crown her with silver and gold and give her "a little clockwork motor car that'll run all around the room." Jimmy, the worker, vows to "love her more than an increase in wages," but threatens either to strike or to leave if he isn't given due consideration.

The satire, like the "phantasy" in *Kathleen Listens In,* is obvious and funny. Without Solomon to guide them, the suitors willingly and willfully tear Kathleen in as many directions as they tear the seamless coat in O'Casey's short story. Each suitor sees his Kathleen in terms of his goals and his needs. As characterized by her suitors, she is less attractive than either the cow sold too cheaply or the demolished house, both of which also represent Ireland. O'Casey's satiric phantasy does identify the factions tearing the new nation to pieces, and his play does illuminate—from our vantage point, we do have half a century of hindsight—the Irish political system. The Abbey audience did not recognize O'Casey as Solomon and continued to demand full ownership of Kathleen. Their representatives, the Abbey theatre audience "Like the Arabs . . . folded their tents (minds) in the night, and silently stole away."[16]

Whatever else it is or was, *Kathleen Listens In* is topical satire that cannot be ignored in any serious study of Sean O'Casey's development as a satiric artist. The foolishness, follies, and insolence of Everyman intent on having his own way are presented in the restricted scope of a national teacup, and the chaos continues within that teacup as the curtain concludes the action of the play. Moreover, as O'Casey stated, the play clearly establishes his early efforts to write satiric fantasy, efforts largely ignored by those who emphasize the early works as "realistic."

Gabriel Fallon played the role of the Man in Kilts. As he recalls the Abbey audience's response to *Kathleen Listens In:*

> . . . as soon as the curtain rose . . . the laughing began, but before long it was obvious that it was sectional laughter. I laughed when your party got a rap; you laughed when it was the turn of mine. Towards the middle of the piece the laughter began to lose something of its earlier substance; then it started to fall off,

flicker, and finally to die out completely. The curtain came down in what was worse than silence—a few thin apologetic hand-claps obviously intended for the players. There were no calls for author. We knew that the author had been in front. When the theatre emptied we couldn't find him. He told me afterwards that he had run out of the place mortified at the play's reception. After walking the streets for a few hours . . . he returned to his tenement room and . . . sitting down at his typewriter he . . . set down the opening lines of *Juno and the Paycock*.[17]

Juno and the Paycock, O'Casey's third Abbey play,

> . . . was, from the Abbey Theatre point of view, an emphatic success, and Yeats halted in his meditations to tell Sean that he had given new hope and new life to the theatre. The house had been booked out for the first week, and the run of the play was extended for a week longer.[18]

Juno and the Paycock netted £25 for O'Casey and won the Hawthornden Prize (£100) as the best work of the year by a new writer. Lady Gregory, one of the founders of the Abbey Theatre, a versatile playwright herself and long since O'Casey's champion, recorded in her Journal that *Juno and the Paycock* was ". . . a wonderful and terrible play of futility, of irony, humour, tragedy." After the performance she told W. B. Yeats, "This is one of the evenings at the Abbey which makes me glad to have been born."[19]

The action of this "wonderful and terrible play of futility, of irony, humour, tragedy" takes place during a two-month period in 1922. The time is that of the bitter and deadly Irish Civil War that erupted almost immediately following the creation of the Irish Free State, Yeats's and O'Casey's terrible beauty. The war and its madness here, as in *The Shadow of a Gunman*, are outside the tenement and outside the lives of the characters, outside except as they are represented in the mutilated person of Johnny, who lights candles, hides, and makes selfish demands throughout the play. The backdrop of the play begins with the announced death of young Tancred and ends with the execution of Johnny, his betrayer. Though the madness of the Irish Civil War reigned in Ireland in 1922, it is essentially meaningless to O'Casey's characters, who live their lives much as they would without the disturbance. It is meaningless, that is, except for its occasional deadly interruptions of their lives.

The satire of the play hinges on the ludicrous but painful reduction of the Boyles to a ridiculous level as they assume they have been freed from poverty by the legacy. The presumed release from poverty leads them, especially Captain Boyle, to the same excesses enjoyed by Paul Morel (*Sons and Lovers*) and Stephen Dedalus (*A Portrait of the Artist as a Young Man*) when they win substantial prizes. Both enjoy the holidays and extended luxuries of spending, giving, lending. Both enjoy—for the first time in their lives—being among the "Haves." The Boyles are among O'Casey's first newly arrived members of the bourgeoisie. Captain Jack Boyle dons respectability like a mantle. In his strutting, his respectability, his new attitude toward church and fellow slum dwellers and self, he is delightfully funny. Ultimately, of course, his new pose, like the ostentatious new furniture and the gramophone, is ridiculous. O'Casey knew from long and painful experience that poverty itself is not ridiculous and does not render its victims ridiculous. He also knew that joy and the temptation to spend were the immediate response to promised money. His awareness of poverty, including the shame and rage of never having enough, is most effectually portrayed in "Mrs. Casside Takes a Holiday," chapter two of *Inishfallen, Fare Thee Well*. O'Casey had sold *The Story of the Irish Citizen Army* for "Fifteen Pounds," had to wait for the check, had difficulties cashing the check, and had to endure the suspicions of those who refused to cash it. All the while, his beloved mother lay dying, needing food and warm clothes and medical attention. The Boyles are, of course, lifelong victims of the same kind of poverty. With the promise of release, they begin to purchase, to borrow, and to promise. The release from poverty is no more ridiculous than poverty itself. Neither is ridiculous. As the Boyles mimic the taste and the ways of life of those more economically solvent, as they flaunt their newfound good fortune by acquiring gaudy, ostentatious and unnecessary material possessions, and as they strut proudly and take pride in the new which but emphasizes the old, they do become ridiculous because pretense is ridiculous. As George Meredith, Shaw, O'Casey, and others have noted, poverty has a bareness that cannot be concealed behind a facade. The facade of his new found plenty leads Captain Boyle to take his own preening and assumed mastery of the household seriously. In short, he concentrates on shadow rather than substance—on what appears to be rather than what is. Insofar as he treats his own shadow with great respect, he is delightfully funny, but when he becomes so addicted to appearance that he rejects his family for "respectability," he is pathetic.

The rivalry of Joxer Daly and Juno Boyle for the attention and the time of the superficial and infinitely selfish Captain Boyle is made more painful by Juno's role as supporter and rock, rather than shrew. She is the mother for the entire household, a kind of universal mother, as her name implies. As she says to Johnny and Mary directly and as she demonstrates throughout the play, "I don't know what any o' yous ud do without your ma."[20] Her infinite common sense and goodness lend tragic as well as comic depth to the microcosm of the play. Joxer is the traditional parasite, fully equipped with an endless parade of maxims and platitudes that adequately represent his accumulated wisdom. He is always in perfect agreement with whatever is said by whomever he is with, and his replies are usually just off center and make the conversation, in some cases, oddly tangential rather than direct. His loyalty to his role is paralleled by Juno's loyalty to hers and, by contrast, lends grandeur to Juno's common sense and goodness. Just as Juno hides in her own home in order to confront the parasite, Joxer hides later to avoid Juno. Then, like the hiding Dapper in *The Alchemist*, he is forgotten. Unlike Dapper, he is neither stifled nor unconscious when his claim on Captain Boyle is threatened by news of the legacy.

Captain Jack Boyle, like the mythical Juno's husband, is also a thunderer; however, his thunderbolts cause confusion rather than lightning. The Paycock, like the pre-Homeric Zeus, is ridiculous and cowardly—essentially a selfish entity of many disguises, each one a false face.[21] Like his predecessor, Captain Boyle lies to his Juno, denies responsibility for his children, and is primarily concerned with personal satisfaction and immediate pleasures. Like Zeus, Captain Boyle is funny as he rants and prances and boasts. We laugh at his antics even while the facade is being stripped away. Captain Boyle, no less than Joxer and only mortally less than Zeus, is a parasite. Juno knows this, of course, long before the enlightened members of the audience recognize it. She tells us early in the play: "He wore out the Health Insurance long ago, he's afther wearin' out the unemployment dole, an', now, he's thryin' to wear out me! An' constantly singin', no less, when he ought always to be on his knees offerin' up a Novena for a job!" [*JAP*, pp. 5-6]. Boyle's refrains concerning the pains in his legs whenever a job threatens his leisure and his "I've a little spirit left in me still!" when Juno offers to feed him despite his laziness identify him in the same way that Joxer's platitudes identify himself.

Although Captain Boyle throws a large shadow in Act II, a shadow which he accepts as reality and treats with the greatest respect, he undergoes no real change in substance, as his "relapse" in Act III shows quite clearly. He, like Joxer, is still a parasite. The satiric value of his manifesto in Act I is not lost on an audience so recently shaken by Great Britain's demands that officers of the Irish Free State must take oaths of allegiance to the British crown. Coming as it does before any mention of the legacy, Captain Boyle's manifesto is part of the false front he builds to satisfy his own ego: "Today, Joxer, there's goin' to be issued a proclamation be me, establishin' an independent Republic, an' Juno'll have to take an oath of allegiance" [*JAP*, p. 27]. Joxer, of course, urges his oul' buttie to be firm.

With the promise of money and therewith the necessities of life, Juno can relax and relinquish at least nominal control of the family. Boyle senses this and, as Act I ends, he proclaims himself "done with Joxer . . . I'm a new man from this out" [*JAP*, p. 35]. Donning his new mask, Captain Boyle becomes

ludicrously pompous and authoritative concerning the responsibilities of money, man's true relationship to the church, and
his newly acquired, money-inspired authority on any subject.
In short, he becomes one of O'Casey's first caricatures of an
Ireland slum dweller who gains enough wealth to adopt the
religious, political, and social attitudes that he associates with
success and prosperity.

In this new role, Boyle reverses his earlier comments on the
church and its officers, and, like Seumas in *The Shadow of a
Gunman*, attributes his earlier heresy to an absent acquain-
tance. His listener is Joxer Daly, two days after Boyle has
promised Juno he was "done with Joxer":

> Comin' up the stairs who did I meet but that bummer, Nugent. "I
> seen you talkin' to Father Farrel," says he, with a grin on him.
> "He'll be folleyin' you," says he, "like a Guardian Angel from this
> out"—all the time the oul' grin on him, Joxer.
>
> . . .
>
> "Mr. Nugent," says I, "Father Farrell is a man o' the people, an', as
> far as I know the History o' me country, the priests was always in
> the van of the fight for Irelan's freedom."
>
> . . .
>
> "Who are you tellin'?" says he. "Didn't they let down the Fenians,
> an' didn't they do in Parnell? An' now . . ." "You ought to be
> ashamed o' yourself," says I, interruptin' him, "not to know the
> History o' your country." An' I left him gawkin' where he was.
> [*JAP*, p. 38]

The Paycock, with promise of money, realigns himself with
the church and flaunts a new-found pride in the history of his
country. Since his newly respectable status demands that the
Paycock eliminate any fear of gossip, he will beat and
ostracize the sinful Mary who, in addition to her other
encumbrances, doesn't show her father the proper respect. He
rejects her and her plight, in spite of the fact that he already
knows his prosperity is all facade and that "The Boyo that's
afther doin' it to Mary done it to me as well." Even in the face
of this fact, the Paycock continues to strut, to demand his
rights, to order new clothes from Needle Nugent, and to

demand honor for the shadow he casts on the wall rather than draw attention to that which he really is and is not.

The time-worn plot device of daughter wronged by someone who was just passing through re-emphasizes the poignancy of Mary's desire to escape the tentacles of poverty, an attempt she makes early in the play through reading what her father calls "nothin' but thrash . . . *The Doll's House, Ghosts,* an' *The Wild Duck*—buks only fit for chiselurs!" Her participation in the labor strike, her concern with the proper clothes to wear, and her immature repetition of "a principle's a principle" reveal the caustic and slyly irreverent O'Casey's attitudes toward her youthful adherence to her values. Johnny also utters "A principle's a principle," and he dies a traitor. Brother and sister underline O'Casey's contention that neither Ibsen nor Labor movements are "for chiselurs."[22] Both are "immature idealists" and both fall far short of being O'Caseyean realists. A realist, both for O'Casey and for Shaw, is a man strong enough to face truth as it is, even truth that might be painful or destructive.[23] The realist is willing to discard tradition, precedent, and history whenever they obscure truth or prevent happiness. O'Casey's young idealists are not equal to that task.

O'Casey's and Juno's common sense approach are reflected in their shared adherence to reality rather than to appearance. It is Juno who tells her husband, "I'm afraid we're runnin' into too much debt." It is she who remains loyal to Mary and makes the decision to leave Boyle and Joxer in the barren tenement; it is she who affirms during the funeral procession for Mrs. Tancred's son that "it's nearly time we had a little less respect for the dead, an' a little more regard for the livin'" [*JAP*, p. 58]. It is she who brings whatever order there is into the "chassis" of the Boyle home. The chaos of that family—the legacy in the bush, Johnny's execution as a traitor, Mary's pregnancy, and the Paycock's continued sense of self-importance—reflects in little the chaos of Ireland in 1922, a chaos which could give way to order only under the guidance of a firm hand. In O'Casey's opinion, there was no strong hand, and the people's choice, Eamon de Valera, was far from the answer.[24]

It is significant, I think, that much of O'Casey's satire is topical and incidental to the play. For example, recognitions of his obvious references to the Free Staters' oath, his running critique of the state of Ireland, and his asides on de Valera are not essential to understanding or appreciating his drama. What is important is that his people isolated in their tenements discuss only those aspects of Ireland's political chaos that immediately affect them; the raids, the death of a neighbor boy, young Boyle's wounds and his sacrifice for the glory of his country. For the characters in O'Casey's drama, the external chaos and resulting fear which frames their own world are essentially the same, whether it is the 1913 strike (*Red Roses for Me*), the Easter Rising of 1916 (*Plough and the Stars*), the time of the troubles *(Shadow of a Gunman)*, or the Irish Civil War of 1922 *(Juno and the Paycock)*. O'Casey distinguishes among the framing conflicts by his continual topical referents, but does not insist that either his characters or his audience make such distinctions. The chaos in the Boyle household would be essentially the same, whatever the state of the nation. O'Casey's citizens see themselves whether they look into the political, the economic, or the religious mirrors of their country. They see their own confusion, their own weakness, their own folly magnified—though it may seem neither magnified nor relevant to them.

Juno and the Paycock includes several processionals, all leading up to the final one, that of the repossessors who strip the barren tenement of its gaudy display. On the occasion of the first processional, that for Robbie Tancred, Juno states that life is for the living as Tancred's funeral processional interrupts the gaiety of the party in the Boyle rooms. The next processional, which includes the stripping of the Boyle's apartment and the arrest of young Johnny, culminates in the arrival of the police, who want Juno to identify her son's body. Juno then reveals her essential kinship to Mrs. Tancred as she repeats the same phrases and suffers the same pain that Robbie Tancred's mother had already endured:

> Maybe I didn't feel sorry enough for Mrs. Tancred when her poor son was found as Johnny's been found now—because he was a

Die-hard! Ah, why didn't I remember that then he wasn't a Diehard or a Stater, but only a poor dead son! It's well I remember all that she said—an' it's my turn to say it now: What was the pain I suffered, Johnny, bringin' you into the world to carry you to your cradle, to the pains I'll suffer carryin' you out o' the world to bring you to your grave! Mother o' God, Mother o' God, have pity on us all! Blessed Virgin, where were you when me darlin' son was riddled with bullets, when me darlin' son was riddled with bullets? Sacred Heart o' Jesus, take away our hearts o' stone, and give us hearts o' flesh! Take away this murdherin' hate, an' give us Thine own eternal love! [*JAP*, p. 87]

This kinship with Mrs. Tancred, the inefficacy of Johnny's constant candle burning before his saint, and the fact that a dead son is dead whether the Republic is up or down, lend universal depth to Juno's outcry, "These things have nothin' to do with the Will o' God. Ah, what can God do agen the stupidity o' men!" [*JAP*, p. 86]. The stupidity and short-sightedness of men, their penchant for looking backward toward church, history, and tradition, and their insistence upon looking at the shadow they cast rather than at what casts the shadow are the targets of O'Casey's satire here and elsewhere. He contends that the madness and chaos that reign outside the tenement are not separate from the chaos within, that it will continue until that within gives way to some kind of order.

Juno and the Paycock is a play about the confusion, chaos, and lack of discipline that reign within the tenement. In Act I, Boyle says, "Ah, I suppose it's just the same everywhere—the whole worl's in a state o' chassis!" [*JAP*, p. 20]. His reference is not to the civil war, but "Chiselurs [who] don't care a damn now about their parents. . . ." Methodically and consistently the cleavage between father and daughter is developed throughout *Juno and the Paycock* until Boyle orders her out of his respectable house.

The poignant ending of the play reveals Boyle reaffirming that "th' whole worl's . . . in a terr . . . ible state o' . . . chassis," as he has chosen an alliance with Joxer to the disrepute of sheltering his daughter. The hollow revelry of his uncomprehending conversation with Joxer in the crepe-paper-adorned and barren room is a suitable medium for his pronouncement as he discards the last of his borrowed money, "last o' the Mohicans," and symbolically ends his charade:

> The blinds is down, Joxer, the blinds is down!
>
>   . . .
>
> The counthry'll have to steady itself . . . it's goin' . . . to hell. . . .
> [. . .] No matther . . . what any one may . . . say. . . . Irelan' sober
> . . . is Irelan' . . . free.

We laugh at Joxer's platitudes, at Boyle's excuses, and at the excesses of both. The banter and laziness and drunkenness of the "oul' butties" are funny, very funny even when "the blinds is down." In fact, we might recognize that their excuses might not be their problem, but their solution to the problem, for the problem continues whether the Republic is up or down and whether the invading terrorists are Tommies, Tans, or Free Staters. Nor does the Trades Union have any lasting solution. Jerry Devine's commitment to Mary is as fleeting as Bentham's presence. It promises much and delivers nothing.

Ultimately in *Juno and the Paycock*, the problem is one of survival. How does one survive in poverty when the added terrors of gunfire, raids, and senseless executions are added to the already impossible task. The characters in O'Casey's play survive—if they survive—by instinct, by heavy reliance on the bedrock of Juno's human love and sense of responsibility, and by not becoming involved. Joxer and Captain Boyle, like their successors in *The Plough and the Stars*, survive by instinct. Juno's strength and human compassion anticipate those of Bessie Burgess in *The Plough and the Stars*. The rank and file tenement dwellers—Needle Nugent, Maisie Madigan, and their comrades in *The Plough and The Stars*—have no political or nationalistic commitments. They make the most of any given moment and they survive.

Here, as elsewhere, of course, the turmoil continues behind the final curtain. O'Casey had fulfilled his vow to "write a play that would bring all Ireland to the theatre."[25] Too many of those who entered the theatre (through no fault of O'Casey's) left believing that Johnny's heroism, the Paycock's devotion to escape, and the way of a lawyer with a maid are the prime concerns of this drama. Juno is certainly the most difficult and challenging role of the play. Her essential goodness; her devotion to Johnny, who is her dead son whether the Republic is up or down; her assumed responsibility to Mary; her concluding prayer, "take away our hearts o' stone, and give us hearts o' flesh! take away the murdherin' hate, an' give us Thine own eternal love!"—these are the values espoused by this play. The Paycock's role; his active participation in the ritual of being what he is not; Mary's and Johnny's immature espousal of "a principle's a principle"; Bentham's lack of knowledge and his pretense to all knowledge—these are among the objects of satire, satire intended to reveal truth and to reduce shadow to substance.[26]

The next play, *Nannie's Night Out*, was a predictable letdown after the high excellence of *Juno and the Paycock*. It is difficult not to share O'Casey's opinion of *Nannie's Night Out*, an opinion that kept him from including it in his collected works and led him to describe it in *Inishfallen, Fare Thee Well* as "a play no-one liked, except A.E., otherwise known as George Russell, who thought it O'Casey's best work; an opinion that didn't bother Sean, for he knew A.E. knew nothing about the drama and felt it a little less. . . ."[27] In this instance, O'Casey's judgments of both the play and the critic seem well founded.[28] The alternate endings printed in *Feathers from the Green Crow* tend to emphasize rather than eliminate the play's dramatic deficiencies.

Nannie's Night Out makes much use of the cacophony of disjointed conversation experimented with in the earlier plays. There is no real plot as such and the comic situation is hackneyed. Polly Pender, widow and keeper of the dairy store, is sought after in marriage by three oul' men. Their physical incapacities contrast violently with Nannie's frenzied song of life, as they brag of their physical stamina and great good health and of the agonies they've endured without complaint. All are old, nearer death than life, and all are cowards who urge Polly to give her money to the gunman who comes to rob her. They are the physical and spiritual fathers of O'Casey's "Down-and-Outs" in such later plays as *Within the Gates* and *Red Roses for Me.*

The atmosphere of boredom and petty incident is created by Polly's repetition of the egg story, by the lack of imagination in the blind, the halt, and the lame who propose to Polly, and by the ballad singer who alternately sings, begs, cajoles, and threatens. The atmosphere belies the true situation, for in the period of one day, Polly Pender is hit in the eye by a rotten egg thrown by an outraged customer, courted by three men, approached by a begging ballad singer, duped by a clever child who steals a doll, and visited by her bookie; furthermore, she is the victim of an attempted robbery, and she watches Nannie—the only vital person in the play—die in her shop.

O'Casey's satire here is bitter as he assesses the plight of the Irish Free State: an admirable little con-artist dupes the storekeeper; a hunchbacked boy (son of Nannie) is a tipster and a bookie; an Irish gunman is overcome and expelled by a drunken woman; and a ballad singer begs in order to support his wife and eleven children. In all cases, human need is ignored while the powers that be concern themselves with overwhelming questions. O'Casey's satiric thrust is quite clear in this exchange between Polly Pender and Oul' Joe concerning Johnny's crooked spine:

> JOE. He's a crabby lookin' little youngster.
>
> MRS. PENDER. He couldn't be anything else; he lives on th' streets. When he was three or four he fell down a stairs an' hurted his back. . . . It's a wondher they wouldn't do something for poor little kiddies like him, instead o' thryin' to teach them Irish.
>
> JOE. Oh, we've bigger things than that to settle first; we have to put th' Army on a solid basis, an' then, th' Boundhary Question has to be settled too—in comparisement with things like them, a few cripples o' chiselurs is neither here nor there.[29]

In O'Casey's enlightened view, Gaelic, the Army, and the Boundary Question combined are of less importance than "a few cripples o' chiselurs" so easily dismissed by Joe.

Nannie further indicts the Irish for their lack of manhood. In the alternate ending, she identifies the Irish Bobbies as a "gang o' silver button'd bouseys," far inferior to the British soldiers, for "Th' poor Tommies was men, th' poor Tommies was men!" The lack of vitality of the three oul' men of Ireland is well summed up in Polly's analogy as she berates them for aiding the gunman who came to rob her: "Comparin' Nannie with some o' yous is like comparin' a flywheel to a trouser's button—." In the alternate ending of the play, to belabor the point, Nannie takes oul' Jimmy's cane after she expels the gunman and dances off with it down the street, breaking windows as she goes.

Her vitality is the most striking and obvious force in the play. Nannie's refrain and resolution to die game, "to tear and kick and bite," and her wish that the ballad singer have "a short lif and a merry wan," help to emphasize the death and the deadliness of the world she dances through. Her song and dance are uninterrupted except for drink and death. There is a wide separation between this Irish Nannie and the oul' men whose songs are interrupted by coughing fits, whose lovemaking is trite and according to custom, whose conversation sparkles most when it is concerned with personal bodily ailments. Polly Pender, of course, resolves to remain "a bird alone."

Nannie's Night Out has some historical significance in that it satirizes the unimproved social conditions of the new Ireland, the ineptness of the Irish to meet responsibility, and the awe with which the living dead view anything that is as really alive as Nannie is. O'Casey tells a tale of the same woman on a marvelous drunken spree in *Drums under the Windows,* wherein she is called Mild Millie.[30] Here, too, he laments that such vigor and life and infinite potential cannot be salvaged and cannot find expression in any other way. O'Casey's spokesman for his social gospel is the virile but careless ballad singer, who must beg to feed his eleven children. He addresses those assembled to watch Nannie die:

Yous gang o' hypocrites! What was it made Nannie what she was? Was it havin' too much money? Who gave a damn about her? It

was only when she was dhrunk an' mad that anywan took any
notice of her! What can th' like o' them do, only live any way they
can?' Th' Poorhouse, th' Prison, an' th' morgue—them is our
palaces! I suppose yous want us to sing "Home Sweet Home,"
about our tenements? D'ye think th' blasted kips o' tenement
houses we live in'll breed Saints an' Scholars? . . . It's a long time,
but th' day's comin' . . . th' day's comin'. . . . Oh, it's cruel, it's
cruel![31]

O'Casey's Irish Period, which includes his first three mas-
terpieces (*The Shadow of a Gunman, Juno and the Paycock*,
and *The Plough and the Stars*), also includes *Kathleen Listens
In* and *Nannie's Night Out*. To ignore these short and less than
superior pieces is to do a disservice to the developmental and
repetitive patterns so basic to O'Casey's growth as a dramatist. With all their weaknesses, the two short plays do anticipate Sean O'Casey's later and more effective plunges into
fantasy and outrageous satire. The ebullient joy of Nannie and
her love of life are not unlike those same qualities in the more
fully developed Jannice in *Within the Gates* and the women in
Cock-a-Doodle Dandy. The fantasy and allegory in the later
plays had their beginnings in the midst of the Irish period—a
period acclaimed by most major critics as O'Casey's "realistic" period. I have no argument with the label, but suggest that
the playwright's own comments on realism—especially his
statement prefacing *Kathleen Listens In* in *Tulane Drama
Review's* publication of the play and his "Green Goddess of
Realism" in *The Green Crow*—should also be taken into
account.

The settings and the satiric jabs of the three Irish tragedies
clearly reveal O'Casey's attitude toward the destructiveness of
political conflict. Equally clearly, they identify those who
suffer and die, and they reflect the endless confusion that
begets, accompanies, and follows armed battle—whether the
battle is civil or not, whether the uniforms are gaudy or not,
whether the people are moved by the rhetoric of nationalism
or not.

The Troubles and the creation of the Irish Free State and
the Irish Civil War which provide the settings, substance, and

aftermath treated in *The Shadow of a Gunman, Kathleen Listens In,* and *Juno and the Paycock* are lesser Holy Wars than the Rising of 1916. The Rising, of course, preceded and begat the Troubles, the Irish Free State complete with the Boundhary Question, and the Civil War. The Rising, together with its other accomplishments, converted the General Post Office into a national shrine and added an impressive number of names to the lists that already included Wolfe Tone and Robert Emmet. Patrick Pearse, Joseph Plunkett and James Connolly likewise became the subjects of legend, myth and history—national martyrs for a nation whose martyrs are not to be tampered with.

In *The Plough and the Stars,* O'Casey tampered. His play is in no way a history of the Easter Insurrection, nor does it pretend to be. In history, however, as in the play, large segments of the Irish population were uninvolved in the Rising; in fact, many were unaware of it until reminded by inconvenience, threat, or violence. Not a few, then and there, were appalled by the destruction and the bloodshed of the glorious but hopeless revolution. The nationalists objected to O'Casey's tampering, as the 1926 riots in the Abbey Theatre and O'Casey's departure from Ireland clearly show. Wherever O'Casey spent Easter week and whatever his relationship to the Irish Citizen Army, the Easter veterans and their comrades had no desire to be mortalized in O'Casey's play.

In *The Plough and the Stars,* an uneven but beautiful play, O'Casey's characters are human and they are mortal. As their lives go on, they get thirsty; they respond to the emotional rhetoric of Patrick Pearse; they want recognition and promotion and uniforms to match. Rosie, the prostitute, is present in the pub where great thirsts are measured, where the warriors bring their colors and vow to fight to the death, where a child is abandoned in the intensity of the moment.

Further, and perhaps more important, O'Casey's slum dwellers—for whom deprivation is a way of life—do participate in the ritual looting and, despite the hilarity and fun and pretense indulged in by O'Casey's immature, overly serious communist and his "oul' Butties," the consequences of the

Rising are bloody and deadly. *The Plough and the Stars*
depicts the whole bag—the glory, the heroism, the selfless
courage together with the foibles and follies that are also
human. Here, as in *The Shadow of a Gunman* and *Juno and
the Paycock*, O'Casey is concerned with the wide gap between shadow and substance, between idealism and realism,
between rhetorical commitment and meaningful action.

In *The Plough and the Stars*, a bitter artist portrays the wide
variance between the pomp, parade, and splendor that men
take war to be and the deprivation, gore, and death that war
(even a holy war) really is. Here, as in his earlier plays, the
madness of war affects the fate of O'Casey's people; but here
it controls that fate, whereas in the earlier plays it afforded
only the setting and the circumstances for the human involvements of the characters. Sean O'Casey in this play
presents the attitudes of his dreaming, arrogant, vain Irishmen
as they prepare for war against Great Britain with much the
same attitude and many of the same activities that a home
team uses in preparing for the big game against a traditional
rival. It is important that the characters who participate in the
battles are secondary characters. Jack Clitheroe makes his
choice—after he knows he is commandant. He is not a hero,
either to his wife or to anyone in the theatre audience. Uncle
Peter, for all his splendor, does not fight—except when
provoked by the Covey. As the war's intensity increases,
O'Casey's tenement dwellers move from the excitement of the
rhetoric outside the pub to the abandon and new-found riches
to the horror of the last scene that leaves the men in custody,
Bessie dead, Nora insane, and the English still in charge.
O'Casey's characters learn, as he knew all along, that war itself
is neither festival, game, nor passing activity.

The first two acts of *The Plough and the Stars* present the
home team preparing for battle, wearing colorful uniforms,
marching off under beautiful flags, and being inflamed and
mesmerized by powerful rhetoric. The first uniform seen is
that of the Foresters, proudly worn by Uncle Peter: "green
coat, gold braided; white breeches, top boots, frilled shirt. He
carries the slouch hat, with the white ostrich plume, and the

sword in his hands."[32] As is usually the case in this play, the
Covey's response to the cowering Peter's regalia is the most
revealing one: "Isn't that th' malignant oul' varmint! Lookin'
like th' illegitimate son of an illegitimate child of a corporal in
th' Mexican army!" [P&S, p. 182]. Later the Covey says to
Bessie Burgess of the same uniforms and the continuing
preparations for war:

> When I think of all th' problems in front o' th' workers, it makes
> me sick to be lookin' at oul' codgers goin' about dhressed up like
> green-accoutred figures gone asthray out of a toyshop! [P&S, p.
> 202]

The next uniform that the audience sees is that of the Irish
Citizen Army, worn by Captain Brennan—"green suit; slouch
green hat caught up at one side by a small Red Hand badge;
Sam Browne belt, with a revolver in the holster." Brennan has
gone to Commandant Clitheroe's apartment with orders for a
reconnaisance attack on Dublin Castle. Prominently displayed
in Clitheroe's apartment is a portrait of Robert Emmet, the
Irish martyr who was executed by the British for leading an ill-
planned, ill-executed attack on Dublin Castle in 1803. Emmet's
forces consisted of 150 undisciplined, untrained men, many of
whom deserted before the march on the castle, many of
whom deserted enroute. Emmet was caught up in the same
kind of nationalistic zeal that nurtured the Easter Rising of
1916. He himself was further sustained by great faith in Irish
manhood and by the impotent promises of Napoleon to lend
aid to the Irish if they wished to escape British bondage. His
portrait in this initial scene, like Pearse's rhetoric that pervades
Act Two, helps to develop the locker-room atmosphere of the
first half of The Plough and the Stars.

Jack Clitheroe, standing in the room with Robert Emmet's
picture, accepts his orders and—as heroes in story books do—
rushes away from wife and hearth in his uniform and with his
newly discovered promotion to the rank of commandant. The
uniforms reveal at the same time the vanity of the peacocks
who wear them, the envy of those who do not, and O'Casey's
own bitterness that his good sense was overruled by Captain

White, the Countess Markievicz, and even Jim Larkin in their move to uniform the members of the Irish Citizen Army. Further, O'Casey, as secretary, was expected to get the money to pay for the uniforms. O'Casey argued correctly, but not convincingly, that the kind of fighting that such soldiers might have to do could best be accomplished by trained guerrilla fighters cloaked in the anonymity of civilian dress.[33]

In Act II[34] the soldiers, citizens, and laborers are spellbound by the rhetoric of a shadowy figure who inflames their nationalistic fervor. The orator is the historical Patrick Pearse, one of the principal planners of the Easter Week Rising, signer of the Proclamation of the Republic, and Commander in Chief of the Republican forces during Easter Week. His extended call to arms in this play is taken directly from his address at the grave of O'Donovan Rossa.[35] The overheard comments as used by O'Casey, and as responded to by the soldiers and by the customers, contribute to the atmosphere and lead ultimately to one of the basic thematic truths of this play, that "the vanity and excitements created by patriotism and war disrupt fundamental human relationships . . ."[36]—an especially true observation if the patriotism is a shallow one begotten on vanity by oratory, as it is for several of the characters who populate this play.

The tension that precipitates the violence of the last two acts builds throughout Act II, motivated by the words of Pearse as spoken by the shadowy figure:

> It is a glorious thing to see arms in the hands of Irishmen. We must accustom ourselves to the thought of arms, we must accustom ourselves to the sight of arms, we must accustom ourselves to the use of arms. . . . Bloodshed is a cleansing and sanctifying thing, and the nation that regards it as the final horror has lost its manhood. . . . There are many things more horrible than bloodshed, and slavery is one of them! [*P&S*, pp. 193-94]

Rosie, the prostitute, calls this "the sacred truth," and the usually sensible, settled Barman responds, "If I was only a little younger, I'd be plungin' mad into the middle of it!" These and the rhapsodic eloquence of Peter and Fluther indicate the effect of the speech. The cowardly Peter in full-dress Forester costume and Fluther Good, not to be outdone, become eloquent as the voice of the speaker and the malt whiskey move both to greater thirst and rhetorical splendor:

PETER [*splutteringly to Barman*]. Two halves . . . [*To Fluther*] A meetin' like this always makes me feel as if I could dhrink Loch Erinn dhry!

FLUTHER. You couldn't feel any way else at a time like this when th' spirit of a man is pulsin' to be out fightin' for th' thruth with his feet thremblin' on th' way maybe to th' gallows, an' his ears tinglin' with th' faint, far-away sound of burstin' rifle-shots that'll maybe whip th' last little shock o' life out of him that's left lingerin' in his body!

PETER. I felt a burnin' lump in me throat when I heard th' band playin' 'The Soldiers' Song', rememberin' last hearin' it marchin' in military formation with th' people starin' on both sides at us, carryin' with us th' pride an' resolution o' Dublin to th' grave of Wolfe Tone.

FLUTHER. Get th' Dublin men goin' an' they'll go on full force for anything that's thryin' to bar them away from what they're wantin', where th' slim thinkin' counthry boyo ud limp away from th' first faintest touch of compromization!

PETER [*hurriedly to the Barman*]. Two more, Tom! . . . [*To Fluther*] Th' memory of all th' things that was done, an' all th' things that was suffered be th' people, was boomin' in me brain . . . Every nerve in me body was quiverin' to do somethin' desperate!

FLUTHER. Jammed as I was in th' crowd, I listened to th' speeches pattherin' on th' people's head, like rain fallin' on th' corn; every derogatory thought went out o' me mind, an' I said to meself, 'You can die now, Fluther, for you've seen th' shadow-dhreams of th' past leppin' to life in th' bodies of livin' men that show, if we were without a titther o' courage for centuries, we're vice versa now!' Looka here. [*He stretches out his arm under Peter's face and rolls up his sleeve.*] The blood was BOILIN' in me veins! [*P&S*, pp. 194-95]

This scene anticipates in small what is happening to the mob outside as they yield up their senses to the flaming rhetoric of the Orator. The uniformed members of the mob are of the army led by and represented by Jack Clitheroe, Lieutenant Langon, and Captain Brennan. When these three enter the pub preceding the conclusion of the speech,

> Captain Brennan carries the banner of the Plough and the Stars, and Lieut. Langon a green, white, and orange Tri-colour. They are in a state of emotional excitement. Their faces are flushed and their eyes sparkle; they speak rapidly, as if unaware of the meaning of what they said. They have been mesmerized by the fervency of the speeches. [P&S, p. 213]

They, too, speak in the slogans of zealous patriotism as they describe Ireland as greater than a wife or a mother and repeat that "Th' time is rotten ripe for revolution. . . . Th' time for Ireland's battle is now— th' place for Ireland's battle is here."

The speaker, however, has not finished. His conclusion is calculated to make the Covey even thirstier and Fluther's blood boil even hotter, and to make the cheering sections cheer even louder:

> Our foes are strong, but strong as they are, they cannot undo the miracles of God, who ripens in the heart of young men the seeds sown by the young men of a former generation. They think they have pacified Ireland; think they have foreseen everything; think they have provided against everything; but the fools, the fools, the fools!—they have left us our Fenian dead, and, while Ireland holds these graves, Ireland, unfree, shall never be at peace! [P&S, p. 213]

One result of this final speech is a team emotionally ready for the Big Game. Brennan hoists the *Plough and the Stars,* vows "Imprisonment for th' Independence of Ireland!" Langon hoists the Tricolor and vows, "Wounds for th' Independence of Ireland!" Clitheroe vows, "Death for th' Independence of Ireland!" The three together chant, "So help us God." As Act II ends, the team is ready, and Commandant Clitheroe, having sealed his vow with a glass of port wine, clad in the full military regalia of the Irish Citizen Army, gives his troops their command to march in the practice raid on Dublin Castle.

The team is ready in November of 1915. The big contest, because of a postponement, began Easter Monday 1916. Another result of the speech was the momentary diversion and excitement for Fluther Good, the Covey, Uncle Peter, and the other tenement dwellers who had no intention of firing on anyone and no anticipation of being fired upon.

The last two acts unveil the reality and the ugly truth of war. The proud flags fall, uniforms are discarded, civilians loot, quibble, and die. Both teams are sure that their opponent is not being a proper sportsman. Fluther, as he hears the first artillery barrages, says, "Surely to God they're not going to use artillery on us? . . . Aw, holy Christ, that's not playing the game!" Captain Brennan doesn't play the game as he leaves Clitheroe to die, dons his civvies, and joins the noncombatants in the relative safety of Bessie's rooms. The British Sergeant Tinley complains of Irish ambushes and snipers, ". . . Dumdum bullets they're using. Gang of Hassassins potting at us from behind roofs. That's not playing the game: why down't they come into the owpen and fight fair!" The eerie repetitive chant, "Red Cr. . .oss, Red Cro. . .oss! Ambu. . .lance, Ambu. . .lance!" is part of the game and becomes more frequent and more thematic as the game nears the end.

O'Casey reveals in *The Plough and the Stars,* more directly than in either of his earlier plays, his antipathy toward war and its senseless shattering of human life. Here for the first time, war itself becomes an active agent in the drama. Its madness permeates the action of the play and no one is safe from its destructive forces. His invective and his outraged satire are directed not at the war itself, not at the British soldiers on sacred Irish soil, not even at the patriots at the barricades, but at the vanity and folly which lead men into uniforms, into parades, into demonstrations, and ultimately into disaster.

His vision of vain men in colorful uniforms and the consequences thereof is essentially the same as that expressed by Mrs. Gogan:

The Foresthers' is a gorgeous dhress! I don't think I've seen nicer, mind you, in a pantomime. . . . Th' loveliest part of th' dhress, I

think, is th' ostrichess plume. . . . When yous are goin' along, an' I
see them wavin' an' noddin' an' waggin', I seem to be lookin' at
each of yous hangin' at th' end of a rope, your eyes bulgin' an'
your legs twistin' an' jerkin', gaspin' an' gaspin' for breath while
yous are thryin' to die for Ireland! [P&S, p. 199]

O'Casey is not, as Mrs. Gogan is, a portender of doom who
gets his kicks by relishing the disaster of others, prophesying
death for all, and getting "a kind of threspassing joy to feel
meself movin' along in a mourning coach" at somebody else's
funeral. He satirizes in Mrs. Gogan the respectable woman
who giggles at naked pictures, gossips, swears that "any kid,
living or dead, that Jinnie Gogan's had since [marriage], was
got between the bordhers of th' ten commandments," and
who abandons her children for a row or a profit. Mrs. Gogan
is his creature of the Dublin slums who knows and is fascinated by Death. Her sensual pleasure as she describes its
horrors, her response to the death of her child who was "never
any other way but faintin'," her expressed gratitude to both
Bessie and Fluther, and her obvious delight with the lovely
shoes "with th' pointed toes an' th' cuban heels" are all facets
of her personality. Her devotion to the church and the rituals
of the church and her preoccupation with the beauty and the
gore of the deaths of other people are the opposite poles of
her personality that O'Casey combines in his own irreverent
but highly relevant way, as he portrays the plight of slum
dwellers and their talismans of respectability and redemption.

O'Casey's main satiric point developed throughout the
action of this play is that those who suffer most during any
war are the women and the children. More specifically, in the
Easter Rising, those who suffered most were the slum dwellers, the noncombatants, the wives and mothers. This point is
emphasized, in part, by the fashionably dressed, middle-aged,
stout woman who is almost fainting with fear, who pleads
with the Covey and Fluther for direction. She "was foolish
enough to visit a friend, thinking the howl thing was a joke,
and now I cann't get a car or a tram to take me home—isn't it
awful?" She testifies, "I'm so different from the others . . .";

she is afraid and says so, "I know I'll fall down in a dead faint
if I hear another shot go off anyway near me—isn't it awful!"
[*P&S*, pp. 225-27]. She and her class are inconvenienced, can't
find transportation, and are afraid of a war they took to be a
joke. In the meantime, Nora Clitheroe loses her baby, her
husband, and her mind; Bessie Burgess is slain in the most
unheroic and unromantic way possible; and Mollser dies of
consumption: the slum dwellers, especially the women and
children, suffer the real agonies of war, whether the war be an
Irish Civil war or an Irish revolution.

The war itself, despite history and despite the inspired
rhetoric, is not depicted as a holy war; the soldiers, as
presented by O'Casey, are not dedicated to any real cause,
but continue to fight because, as Nora says, "they're afraid to
say they're afraid." The moral inadequacy of the combatants
is testified to by the numerous incidents of betrayal that
follow the emotionalism unfettered by Pearse's rhetoric: Clitheroe sings "The Soldiers' Song" and abandons Nora to join
the troops after he knows of his promotion; later, he thrusts his
pregnant wife away from him and leaves with Brennan and
the wounded Lieutenant. He dies for the same reason that he
participates—"he is afraid to say that he is afraid"— just one
more indication of the vanity evidenced in his earlier separation from the ICA when he thought he didn't get a promotion,
the same vanity that led him to buy, polish, and adore the Sam
Browne belt that Mrs. Gogan says he slept with. He ought, as
Fluther notes, "to have a baby's rattle" [*P&S*, p. 167].

Giving way to the same kind of intoxicated emotionalism,
Mrs. Gogan abandons her consumptive daughter to attend the
rally, baby in her arms; then she abandons the baby in the pub
as she later abandons both Mollser and the baby to participate
in the ritual looting of the shops and bring home her new
belongings in the pram. But in reality, the war itself is neither a
big game, nor a joke, nor a bargain basement. O'Casey
depicts the reality of war in the destruction of basic human
relationships, in death itself, and in the madness of war as
reflected in the madness of Nora Clitheroe—wife, mother,
noncombatant, tenement dweller.

The only truly heroic actions are among those most affected by the war: Nora combats public opinion, the intoxication of patriotism, and the vanity of her husband as she attempts to search him out and take him home with her. Fluther Good, the man who operates according to instinct, flies into rage at the Covey's calculated insults, laughs at Peter Flynn's regalia, and, as demonstrated earlier, is momentarily sucked up in the vacuum of patriotism during the rally, before he goes home with Rosie. Nonetheless, it is he who dares to search for and bring back Nora Clitheroe from the madness of the barricades, and it is he who dares death again to arrange for the burials of Nora's stillborn child and Mollser. In his own participation in the looting, he is still the creature of instinct, and the war itself changes him no more than the imagined new wealth of Captain Boyle changes Joxer Daly.

Bessie Burgess, who is contemptuous of Nora for insulting her neighbors by putting a new lock on her door, who will "sing whenever she damn well pleases," is the "oul' orange bitch" who sings "Rule Britannia" as the madness of armed revolt reigns outside her doors. She participates in the looting and threatens physical violence to Mrs. Gogan, but it is Bessie Burgess who picks up the rejected Nora, goes for the doctor to care for Nora, sits up with Nora for three nights running, and ultimately dies trying to move Nora from in front of the window. In these noncombatants is seen what David Krause calls "the only kind of untainted heroism that O'Casey recognizes"—endurance.[37] Nora Clitheroe, Fluther Good, and Bessie Burgess have greater courage, greater charity, and greater human capacities than any uniformed patriot in the play. And, as O'Casey depicts them, they are morally superior.

The Covey specifically identifies himself with socialism and with the Labor Movement, questions the validity of Fluther's war wounds—as well he should—and offers his own platitudinous panaceas for the social, political, and economic ills of Ireland. These immature understandings and his ready reference book, Jenersky's *Thesis on the Origin, Development and Consolidation of the Revolutionary Idea of the Proletariat*, are treated with equally scathing satire. His answers to all problems are pat and emerge as ill-formed, adolescent enthusiasms without real understanding or meaning. He fulfills the role played by the Ballad Singer in "Nannie's Night Out" and by Mary Boyle in *Juno and the Paycock*. He is O'Casey's suggestion that the social problems and revolutions of the world are not games for "chiselers" any more than Ibsen is for children. The Covey, in his relative inexperience, is not as lacking in perception as some of his pat answers indicate. He notes early in the play amid the furor of preparation for the great demonstration that nationalism "is an accidental gatherin' together of mollycewels an' atoms." Following Mollser's death, he parrots another imperfectly understood truth, that "it's all because of th' system we're livin' undher" [*P&S*, p. 170, p. 249]. O'Casey could well have had a covey of Coveys in mind in 1958 when he said of the Communists, "They drive me mad. They know nothing but what they read in their little pamphlets."[38] In any case, the Covey is irascible and is the focus of the bickering within the pub during Act II. He bickers with Fluther Good, Rosie, and Peter, and is something less than an innocent bystander as the row erupts between Bessie and Mrs. Gogan. The bickering, in addition to its comic value, reflects the discordant factions in Ireland, and the Covey represents, in his caustic animosity and in his cynical denunciation of all this nationalistic "dope," something of the immature demands, frustrated aims, and disillusionment of the Labor forces in Ireland following the fiasco of the 1913 lockout. He is one of the suitors of Kathleen ni Houlihan in *Kathleen Listens In*.

Nora Clitheroe is rather obviously an Irish version of Nora Helmer in Ibsen's *A Doll's House;* she too is called by pet names. She is Jack's "little red-lipped Nora": she tries heroically to save her husband, who is as insensitive and as vain as Torvald; she, too, is blamed by her husband for her deception; she tries to improve the world around her, and early in the play, as quoted by Mrs. Gogan, describes the tenements as "Vaults . . . that are hidin' th' dead, instead of homes that are sheltherin' th' livin'." O'Casey's Nora, unlike Ibsen's, is ineffectual and is destroyed by that which she combats. It is she rather than the door that is slammed; it is she rather than her husband's hollow pride that is destroyed. As the play ends, she has gone with Mrs. Gogan to sleep in the dead Mollser's bed.

The card game played by the Covey and Fluther in Bessie's room with Mollser's coffin symbolizes for O'Casey the methods which shape the destinies of human beings; the players continue to shuffle, wager, and argue as the card game is interrupted by Bessie's commands that they be quieter, by Brennan's entrance in civilian clothes, by Nora's entrance and her eerie comments to her husband. They stop the game long enough to carry out the coffin as requested by Corporal Stoddart and would resume the game except for Stoddart's assurance that they are to be locked up—all the men are. They take the cards with them, for as Fluther notes, "I don't think we'd be doin' anything derogatory by playin' cards in a Protestan' Church." The card game goes on and on as does the violence outside, though the players have some difficulty keeping track of who played what card.

The game of chance and the abandoned cards—like the looting scenes themselves—reflect the total lack of order, the madness of society at war. It is a chaos to which Fluther Good is particularly suited, as is revealed by his many vows of temperance and by his answer to the Covey's urging that he "thry to keep a sup for tomorrow." Fluther responds,

> Spread it out? Keep a sup for to-morrow? How th' hell does a fella know there'll be any tomorrow? If I'm goin' to be whipped away, let me be whipped away when it's empty, an' not when it's half full! [P&S, p. 242]

The card game, the drinking, and the making of tea are rituals which give the only semblance of order to the chaotic world at war. This fact emphasizes the terror and the irony of the situation when the two British soldiers, both routinely performing their tasks, invade the apartment of the slain Bessie and drink the tea so recently prepared by Nora. Their professional and impersonal attitude is revealed in their matter of fact comments, "Oh Gawd, we've plugged one of

the women of the 'ouse," and "Whoy the 'ell did she gow to
the window?" Then they drink the tea and join their comrades
in song as the play ends. Life and the rituals of life do go on
even in the midst of mayhem.

Though *The Plough and the Stars* was ill received by many
of those about whom and for whom it was written, Lady
Gregory discovered it to be

> A wonderful play . . . [about] the forgiveness of sins, as real
> literature is supposed to be. These quarreling, drinking women
> have tenderness and courage showing all through, as have the
> men . . . and then comes what all nations have seen, the suffering
> that falls through war, and especially Civil War, on the women,
> the poor, the wretched homes and families of the slums. An
> overpowering play. I felt at the end of it as if I should never care
> to look at another; all others would seem so shadowy to the mind
> after this.[39]

This is the last of O'Casey's Irish plays, and it serves as a
fitting finale, as O'Casey includes the rawness of the slums,
the reality of war, and the true tragedy of discarded lives—
lives discarded even as Fluther and the Covey throw down
their cards. *The Plough and the Stars*, it seems to me, is the
best of the Irish plays, combining the humor, pathos, and
tragedy of the other four. The satire is further reaching and
more bitter as O'Casey seeks to identify to the world's eye the
factionalism and the adolescent grandeurs that caused and co-
existed with the bloodshed and madness of Easter Week. For
him, the Easter Rising was not a holy war, and those who
fought during Easter Week were no more heroic than those
who participated in the "murdhering hate" of the Irish Civil
War six years later. The dead and the survivors were victims
of both and of the global war depicted later in *The Silver
Tassie*.

The riots that erupted in the Abbey Theatre during the
fourth performance of *The Plough and the Stars* had been
anticipated by jeering, shouting, and booing during earlier
performances. The history of incidents leading up to the riot,
O'Casey's battle with his critics, and Yeats's heroism during
the riot are dealt with adequately in literary history and in

other critical appraisals of O'Casey as dramatist and Yeats as
Yeats, the fullest and best perhaps being David Krause's *Sean
O'Casey: The Man and His Work* and "Farewell to Inishfallen,
1926-27," chapter three of Krause's *The Letters of Sean
O'Casey*, Vol. 1. O'Casey captures in *The Plough and the Stars*
something of the fascination and horror of the Rising; he also
depicts what a large segment of Dublin's population was
doing during that week. So does James Stephens, in an equally
unhistorical way, in *The Insurrection in Dublin*. Stephens
wrote his text in 1916.

In the decade between Easter Week and the Abbey Theatre's production of *The Plough and the Stars*, memory and
eyewitness accounts and the emergence of the Irish Free State
had worked their wonders. The terrible beauty, defended by
cabbages and trumpets and fists, would not have her history
tampered with. O'Casey should have known better. The riots
and debates and his own disillusionment marked the end of
Sean O'Casey's Irish period. Like D. H. Lawrence's Paul
Morel, he turned to the quick of the town:

> It was bitterly cold, with a fierce, keen wind blowing, and soon it
> was sending sharp sleety hail and salty spray into his face, stinging
> it deeply—Ireland, spitting a last, venemous, contemptuous
> farewell to him. . . . He faced resolutely towards where the ship
> was going. Sweet Inishfallen, fare thee well! Forever![40]

3

The Colored Plays[1]

O'Casey's official separation from the Abbey Theatre and from Dublin did not go unheralded. The stormy riots during the performances of *The Plough and the Stars* together with their aftermath anticipate what is unfortunately the chief point of critical concentration in the life and works of Sean O'Casey—the Abbey's rejection of *The Silver Tassie*.[2] Critics of many colors have feasted on the battle between Yeats and O'Casey. O'Casey himself, never one to duck a battle, furnished the total correspondence concerning *The Silver Tassie* to St. John Ervine for publication in *The Observer* and to A. E. for publication in *The Irish Statesman*. A.E. did not publish the correspondence but warned O'Casey that Yeats might take legal action for the serious breach of copyright. O'Casey wrote "to the Press to say that he was indifferent to the threat, even if Dr. Yeats decided to lay the dispute before the League of Nations."[3]

The reading public—Irish, English, and American—was delighted with the battle, and it is unfortunate that O'Casey engaged in the hassle, which severed his relationships with Lady Gregory and reduced his relationship with Yeats to a cool, respectful, business arrangement. It is also unfortunate that Yeats, the Nobel Prize winner and virtual God of Irish Letters, should have assumed his pedantic and pompous role in the exchange.[4] The whole affair has been too much dealt with and has for too many years given critics something to write about besides the play itself. The overabundance of critical concentration on this episode and the mass of pages written during and about it do a very real disservice to the play that presumably caused it and to those sixteen plays which follow it.

In *The Silver Tassie*, as in all plays which follow it, O'Casey combines various techniques and types of drama to attain his artistic goal: to show individual man's involvement in various rituals of mankind, most of the rituals being at best meaningless and at worst totally destructive. The techniques utilized in *The Silver Tassie* are no more daring and, in several instances, are less effective than those in later works. From 1928 to 1942, the transitional period of his Colored Plays, O'Casey moves from the essential realism and naturalism of his Irish period into expressionism, symbolism, and the frankly fantastic, which became the established and effective techniques of the ten plays that follow *Red Roses for Me*.

In almost every instance, the kinship of O'Casey's drama to Old Comedy is obvious. His satiric attacks on church, crown, individual and public follies are not obscured by subtlety; the worlds of his drama become ever more fantastic until they are ultimately—except for costumes—virtually indistinguishable from the Cloudcuckooland of Aristophanes. Characterization, observed by Lady Gregory as O'Casey's strong point, remains his strong point as his characters continue their parade. His oul' butties and parasites and vital women, for all their memorable qualities, remain representative rather than individual personalities. His clerics, conspicuously absent from the plays of his Irish period, become ever more repressive as they become stronger and stronger. The Bishop in *Within the Gates*, for all his titular dignity, is ineffective in his efforts to deny life; Father Domineer in *Cock-a-Doodle Dandy* murders life; and Bishop Mullarkey in *The Bishop's Bonfire* would destroy any literary record glorifying life or the God who is a shout in the street.[5]

O'Casey's satiric laughter continues to strip away the pretentious well-fed demeanor of those in power and to reveal the sickness hidden by their facades of well being. The discovered sickness, like Mollser's, symbolizes a further-reaching and more deadly social ailment which can best be cured or destroyed by healing laughter. This much is constant in O'Casey's work.

Because of the Abbey's rejection, *The Silver Tassie* was first produced in London's Apollo Theatre on 11 October 1929. The violent world of O'Casey's earlier plays has been enlarged to include mankind literally rather than symbolically in the action of the Great World War. It is a destructive world which maims and kills, and its victims are no less dead than those of the Easter Rising and the Irish Civil War. The world and its war are responsible for the transformation, the deaths, and the mutilations that render the major characters of Act I virtually unrecognizable in the similar setting of Act IV. Act I portrays the central characters in the aftermath of a football victory, a victory toasted in long draughts from the silver tassie and by the hot young bodies of the victors and their followers. Harry Heegan is the golden boy, the athlete who has led his team to victory and has won for them permanent possession of the tassie. Due to the efforts of Sylvester Heegan, Simon Norton, and other admirers, the invincible Harry is becoming a myth during this own youth. They recall and embroider his athletic feats as they await his arrival. The emphasis on time, its inevitable passing, and man's obligations to it become thematic and of increasing importance as the play progresses. When Harry does arrive, he insists on replaying the football game with Barney, reliving the excitement of his victory, and basking in the enthusiasm of his followers. This intensity of the moment, this rage to live the moment for its own sake, makes it possible for Harry to suggest to his friend Barney that they "go to the spread and hang the latch for another night."[6]

Barney refuses this invitation to desert, partly because he could lose his pay and partly because he fears that the military powers would sentence him to permanent duty in the trenches. His is not an undivided devotion to duty, for he frankly fears reprisals. Mrs. Heegan, one of O'Casey's realistic Irish mothers, knows that her son can be shot at dawn for desertion; since she also knows that her government allotment would then cease, she urges Harry to return to duty, for "You've got only a few bare minutes to spare." He, in his exuberance, vows to "make the most of them, then."

Mrs. Heegan believes with Susie Monican that "the men that go with the guns are going with God," and she doesn't understand why his experiences in the trenches haven't given Teddy Foran "some idea of the sacredness of life!" When her son and his cronies actually board ship, Mrs. Heegan voices her ironic thanksgiving, "Thanks be to Christ that we're after managin' to get the three of them away safely" [ST, p. 34]. Act I ends with the football victory, the silver tassie, the allotment checks, and the bodies of all the young men intact. The victory wine has been consumed and the tassie placed on the altar beneath Harry's picture and his other athletic trophies. The madness and sickness suggested by Teddy Foran's drunken rage and the broken clutter he leaves "in a mad an' muddled heap like the flotsam an' jetsam of the seashore" anticipate and set the stage for the futility and the desperation of the succeeding acts. The flotsam and jetsam of the broken dishes anticipate that of the battlefield in Act II, that of the hospital ward in Act III, and that of another victory celebration in Act IV.

Neither the language nor the action of this first act can truthfully be described as realistic. The act itself is a victory hymn or a victory chant complete with altar and promise of sacrifice. The ritual itself is completed in the ensuing acts as the human sacrifice is completed. *The Silver Tassie* is "literally a hell' of a play" and, as Shaw contends, Yeats is extraordinarily wrong in calling Act I realistic:

> The first act is not a bit realistic; it is deliberately fantastic chanted poetry. This is intensified to a climax in the second act. Then comes a ruthless return for the last two acts to the fiercest ironic realism.[7]

Act I is part of an encompassing ritual, the ritual of human sacrifice.[8] The football victory, the victor's permanent possession of the tassie, the wine and the toasts, Harry Heegan's trophy display, and the altar which is to hold the tassie afford the setting as well as the action of this unit of the play. This segment of the play is complete in itself in that the football celebration is concluded: one phase of life is finished. The characters who reappear in later acts are totally changed by the incidents and the experiences of war.

The surrealistic setting of Act II mirrors the distortions and the horrors of war: the jagged, lacerated ruin of a monastery, the rubbish heaps that once were homes, the spiky stumps of trees that were once a small wood, the shattered shell-pocked earth, and the barbed wire fretwork that protects the men in the trenches. Above all this is a stained glass image of the Virgin and a life-size crucifix with an arm partially blown off by shell fire. The grotesque distortions of war are further emphasized by the ironic notation on the pedestal of the crucifix, PRINCEPS PACIS. The howitzer, the God and the altar of the scene, is marked HYDE PARK CORNER, and near the entrance to the Red Cross Station is chalked the notation: NO HAWKERS OR STREET CRIERS PERMITTED HERE. Barney is tied to the howitzer, and a cold rain is falling. The scene recalls Susie Monican's notion that "the men who go with the guns are going with God" and Mrs. Heegan's twin heresy that one can learn about the sacredness of life in frontline trenches. The whole scene is permeated by the terrifying silence of the battlefield: silence emphasized by the memory of the gaiety and noise of the celebration in the preceding scene.

The war is a highly stylized ritual involving the prophet of doom, ironic obeisance to the howitzer as God of War, ritualistic bitching, disappointing mail call, idiotic superiors, and, of course, the pomposity and arrogant cowardice of civilian visitors and the Staff Walla. The Croucher in his death mask is the prophet of doom, O'Casey's satiric inversion of the Biblical Ezekiel, who prophesied the granting of sinews, flesh, skin, and breath by God and who witnessed the transformation of the dry bones into a living and exceeding great army into whom the wind breathed the breath of life. In O'Casey's inversion, the Croucher

. . . prophesied, and the breath came out of them, and the sinews came away from them, and behold a shaking, and their bones fell asunder, bone from his bone, and they died, and the exceeding great army became a valley of dry bones. [*ST*, pp. 36-37]

The God who will bring Croucher's prophecy to pass is the howitzer before which the soldiers kneel in obeisance as battle begins. Led by the corporal, the soldiers chant their litany of thanksgiving and adoration:

CORPORAL: Let us honour that in which we put our trust.

SOLDIERS: That it may not fail us in our time of need.

CORPORAL: Hail, cool-hardened tower of steel emboss'd
            With the fever'd, figment thoughts of man;
            Guardian of our love and hate and fear,
            Speak for us to the inner ear of God! . . .

SOLDIERS: We believe in God and we believe in thee.

CORPORAL: Tear a gap through the soul of our mass'd enemies;
            Grant them all the peach of death;
            Blow them swiftly into Abram's bosom,
            And mingle them with the joys of paradise!

SOLDIERS: For we believe in God and we believe in thee. [*ST*, pp. 54-55]

The ritual of war includes, in addition to the prophet and his god, the ritualized bitching of the men who do the fighting as they curse the "god-dam rain and blasted whistling wind"; as they envy the shirkers safe at home curled up at ease, warm and dry, happy and safe at home; as they chant "But wy'r we 'ere, wy're we 'ere—that's wot we wants to know"; and as they hearken to mail call where one soldier receives a prayer book with a green plush cover with a golden cross, and another receives a "red and yellow coloured rubber ball" and a note from his Mollie, "To play your way to the enemies' trenches when you all go over the top."

The surrealism of the setting and the fantastic chanted poetry of Act II provide an adequate vehicle for O'Casey's rage against the "remediable idiocy of war" and for his own enforced belief that the young and essentially innocent are the ultimate victims. The meaningless patter of command and the painful idiocy of those in command are parodied in the Visitor and the Staff Walla, both of whom learned about the heroics of war from the silver screen, pulp magazines, and academic pep talks. The Visitor complains that the military authorities "won't let a man plunge." He lectures Barney, whose crime was stealing food, concerning the sacred trust of private property; he urges the Corporal to keep his exhausted men moving as much as possible; and he praises the worship service, "Splendid. Bucks 'em up. Gives 'em peace." After a two-minute visit to the field hospital that is overfull of wounded and dying, he notes his findings: "Nurses too gloomy. Surgeons too serious. Doesn't do." Then he urges the men to attend his lecture the following day. In short. the Visitor is a compendium of hypocrisies detested by O'Casey and is a character type immediately recognizable to most veterans of frontline and field-hospital service. O'Casey's contempt and that of the battle-weary soldiers who have been resting on the besieged battlefield for "twenty-nine days, twenty-three hours and twenty-three minutes" is summed up rather effectively in the first soldier's chant as the Vistor disappears into the field hospital:

> The perky bastard's cautious nibbling
> In a safe, safe shelter at danger queers me.
> Furiously feeling he's up to the neck in
> The whirl and the sweep of the front-line fighting. [*ST*, p. 43]

Just as the Visitor mirrors the cowardice and the security of the civilian political powers behind the scene, the orders read by the prancing Staff Walla reflect the idiocy and the chaotic minds in control of the military maneuvers:

BATTLE BRIGADE ORDERS, F.A., 31 D2
Units presently recuperating, parade eight o'clock P.M.
Attend Lecture organized by Society for amusement and mental development, soldiers at front.
Subject: Habits of those living between Frigid Zone and Arctic Circle.
Lecturer: Mr. Melville Sprucer.
Supplementary Order: Units to wear gas-masks.
As you were. [*ST*, p. 42]

The overcomplexity and ludicrous inanity of the military jargon summoning the troops to a meaningless lecture are further parodied in another set of orders:

> BRIGADE ORDERS, C/X 143. B/Y 341.
> Regarding gas-masks. Gas-masks to be worn round neck so as to lie in front 2½ degrees from socket of left shoulder-blade, and 2¾ degrees from socket of right shoulder-blade, leaving bottom margin to reach ¼ of an inch from second button of lower end of tunic. Order to take effect from 6 A.M. following morning of date received. Dismiss! [ST, pp. 51-52]

The pervading distortion and the unreal qualities of men and language depict the destructive and omnipresent force of the silent war, which functions as the only recognizable individual identity—except for the death mask of Croucher and Barney, who is being punished because:

> A Brass-hat pullin' the bedroom curtains
> Between himself, the world an' the Estaminay's daughter,
> In a pyjama'd hurry ran down and phon'd
> A Tommy was chokin' an Estaminay cock;
> An' I was pinch'd as I was puttin' the bird
> Into a pot with a pint of peas. [ST, p. 49]

The senseless chaos of war is not made up entirely of battles, visitors, and commanders. It also includes the increasing madness of individuals separated from familiar surroundings and their gradual decay as sensitive men are forcibly kept away from beauty and are forcibly imprisoned in a world of increasing ugliness. The end results of this madness, decay, and separation from beauty are the flotsam and jetsam of the battlefield. O'Casey wrote of his attempt to portray war and of one of this play's basic themes:

> I wished to show the face and unveil the soul of war. I wanted a war play without noise, without the interruptions of gunfire, content to show its results, as in the chant of the wounded and in the maiming of Harry; to show it in its main spiritual phases, its inner impulses and its actual horror of destroying the golden bodies of the young, and of the Church's damned approval in the

sardonic hymn to the gun in Act II. Yes, the play symbolically treats with the theme of human sacrifice.[9]

The nightmare world of Act II with its surrealistic setting and its chanted responses does much to capture the essence of the silent destroyer begat by the stupidity of men. The characters are all shades, grotesque moving figures devoid of individual identities. They represent that portion of mankind victimized by those who happen to be in positions of power. O'Casey's scream of protest against war actually begins in Act II, with the backdrop of the preceding act to afford contrast and perspective. The scream increases in volume and intensity from the beginning of this battleground scene through the sterile life of the hospital wards to the final ironic episode of another football victory celebration.

The fiercest kind of ironic realism, as Shaw noted, permeates the action of the last two acts. The fantastic chanted poetry, dreamlike movements, and surrealistic setting of Act II are at the same time replaced by and intensified by the sterility, efficiency, and order of the antiseptic hospital ward. The god, the picture of Mary, and the crucifix are symbolically present in the wooden crosspieces, which enable the wounded and the sick to pull themselves into a sitting position, in the statue of the Blessed Virgin which sits inertly on its pedestal, and in the sister who carries her rosary and her brass crucifix from bed to bed. The Visitor of Act II has his ideal realized in this hospital ward as Surgeon Maxwell bounces about cheerfully doling out life and death and interrupting his songs and bawdy stories frequently to flirt with Nurse Susie Monican. The cheerful facade of Surgeon Maxwell, who is a close kinsman of Act II's Staff Walla, combines with the antiseptic atmosphere and the morphia to further distort the haunting results of the war.

In addition to the maimed and dying soldiers, the hospital ward houses other casualties of war, among them Sylvester and Simon. They continue to function as chorus and to represent the society within which football victories are won and for which the young athletes go off to war. The sickness of war is the sickness of their society, as reflected in their presence in the hospital. On a literal level, they are obviously not war casualties, but on another, perhaps more meaningful, level, they and that which they represent are.

Another battle casualty is the Susie Monican of Act I. Gone is the rifle polisher who concealed her beauty and her beautiful body behind sombre ill-fitting dress, persecuted Sylvester and Simon with her tambourine theology, and maintained that Harry was different from those who would manhandle lassies; Susie has become a very attractive girl dressed to show her charms most effectively, a professional nurse who teases Surgeon Maxwell with her kisses, does her job efficiently, and considers Harry as Number Twenty-Eight, no different from any other patient in her ward. As she notes, "If you'd passed as many through your hands as I, you'd hardly notice one." The tambourine theologian of the first act, who functioned with her Old Testament rhetoric as a prophet priestess foretelling the doom of the hot young men of Act I, has become the Queen of Sheba, as Sylvester notes, and tends the ailing as she displays her charms. She is the priestess of life rather than death, and life goes on—infinitely poorer, perhaps, for the carnage and the desolation of battle, but it is life, and it is for the living: it is not for the half alive and not for the dead. In this play, life is for Jessie, Barney, Susie, and the insensitive, cliche-spouting Surgeon Maxwell—not for blind Teddy, half-paralyzed Harry Heegan, or for Number Twenty-Three, who will be kept alive by morphia for a few days more.

The increasing deterioration of Harry Heegan's body is accompanied by his own increasing bitterness as he loses hope. He shouts to Simon that he needs a miracle, not an operation:

> The last operation was to give life to my limbs, but no life came, and again I felt the horrible sickness of life only from the waist up. Don't stand there gaping at me, man. Did you never clap your eyes on a body dead from the belly down? [ST, pp. 64-65]

Later he says to Nurse Monican,

> In a net I'll catch butterflies in bunches; twist and mangle them between my fingers and fix them wriggling on to mercy's banner.

I'll make my chair a Juggernaut, and wheel it over the neck and spine of every daffodil that looks at me, and strew them dead to manifest the mercy of God and the justice of man!

. . .

To hell with you, your country, trees, and things, you jibbering jay!

Harry would become war itself and render unto the butterflies and daffodils the same mercy and justice shown to him by senseless war. O'Casey's own bitterness toward the church's sanction of and active involvement in the war ends Act III. A Sister of Mercy enters, paraphrases scripture, urges Harry to pray, and exits. And Harry does pray, accompanied by the choral response of the sisters' "Salve Regina,"

God of the miracles, give a poor devil a chance, give a poor devil a chance!

The answer to Harry's prayer is implicit in the carnival world of the last act, a carnival world complete with fantastically shaped paper hats, music for dancing, and a football victory to celebrate. The hollow gaiety of this frantic "tinkle-tinkle" world of paper hats is emphasized by the everpresent reminders from the hospital ward (the blinded Teddy and the wounded Harry) and by the list of honored dead. Barney's frantic clutching for the available charms of Jessie is thwarted by Harry Heegan, the wraith or spectre of the lusty football hero of the preceding year. The music is a foxtrot, but the real dance that everyone is involved in is the dance of death, the danse macabre. It is the postwar, cardboard, "let's-be-happy" world, the tinkle-tinkle world of artificial and frenetic gaiety depicted by D. H. Lawrence in *St. Mawr*, by Ford Madox Ford in *Parade's End*, by Ernest Hemingway in *The Sun Also Rises*, and by scores of other modern artists.

In O'Casey's wasteland, as in the others, there is neither direction nor communication. The effective and hilarious telephone incident helps to make this point. When the phone rings, Simon wants to "manipulate the thing in tranquillity"; he first hears "a kind of buzzing and roaring noise" and then doesn't "seem to be able to hear a damned thing." Sylvester correctly observes that "the stupidity of some persons is . . .

terrifyin'!" He can't operate the phone either. Mrs. Foran, as usual, has the last and the most perceptive word on the incident and on the world that it is a part of: "Curious those at the other end of the telephone couldn't make themselves understood" [*ST*, pp. 83-88].

Harry's answer is that a poor devil does not have a chance. His bitterness becomes tinged with self-pity as he notes with Coleridge's Ancient Mariner that "even creeping things can praise the Lord"; however, the Lords toasted by Heegan "are men puffed up with the pride of strength," and he, unlike the mariner, has gained neither new vision nor new understanding. His song of life and joy in Act I is caustically modified when Jessie urges Barney to take her back to the dancing:

> To the dancing, for the day cometh when no man can play. And legs were made to dance, to run, to jump, to carry you from one place to another; but mine can neither walk, nor run, nor jump, nor feel the merry motion of a dance. But stretch me on the floor fair on my belly, and I will turn over on my back, then wriggle back again on to my belly; and that's more than a dead, dead man can do! [*ST*, p. 82]

He is more, though little more, than a dead, dead man. When the silver tassie is brought to him, he toasts only himself, "for the shell that hit me bursts for ever between Jessie and me." His bitterness is shared by the blinded Teddy, who "seest not as man seeth," who sees—in lieu of the beauties and vibrances of life—nothing.

Harry's increasing kinship with Teddy is further clarified in the litany between them as the mad party, the danse macabre, goes on about them:

HARRY: I can see, but I cannot dance.

TEDDY: I can dance, but I cannot see.

HARRY: Would that I had the strength to do the things I see.

TEDDY: Would that I could see the things I've strength to do.

HARRY: The Lord hath given and the Lord hath taken away.

TEDDY: Blessed be the name of the Lord.

The litany itself is concluded after Harry observes Barney and Jessie seeking the comforts of the couch, and after he mangles and bruises the silver tassie he had won the year before.

> TEDDY: Come, Harry, home to where the air is soft. No longer can you stand upon a hill-top; these empty eyes of mine can never see from one. Our best is all behind us—what's in front we'll face like men, dear comrade of the blood-fight and the Battlefront!
>
> HARRY: What's in front we'll face like men! The Lord hath given and man hath taken away!
>
> TEDDY: Blessed be the name of the Lord! [*ST*, pp. 94-102]

Mrs. Foran speaks for the dancers as she urges Harry to play, "for there's nothing I love more than the ukelele's tinkle, tinkle in the night time." The real and symbolic presences of Teddy and Harry are constant reminders of the destructive madness of war and of society's continuing responsibility to its heroes. The relatively brief time between Act I and Act IV emphasizes the uncertainty and the lack of stability within any established society, just as it points up the short-lived memories of hero worshippers. The victory spectacle reaches a premature climax as the colored balloons are released; nostalgia and the bitterness implicit in the *ubi sunt* comments of Mrs. Foran and the other guests bring the cycle of the play and of the ritual full circle. O'Casey and his characters testify that life does survive "in the race after the destruction of its finest youth, but it survives in more vulgar, cruel, debased forms than before."[10]

The Silver Tassie is a morality play in which Harry Heegan, completely undistinguished except for youth and athletic prowess, is mutilated. His destruction symbolizes the inevitable ruin of the young and the beautiful by the madness that is war. This pacifist drama is a militant attack on war per se. It "assailed the spectator with a long, silent scream of protest; . . . it protested against man's inhumanity to man; . . . it protested against the remediable idiocy of war."[11] This same scream against exactly the same kind of destruction exists in O'Casey's earlier plays. Here it reaches a crescendo as he methodically presents the realities of war and its aftermath. By artful juxtaposition, controlled litanies, and functional silence, O'Casey cuts through the exterior shams and postures that men take war to be and gets at the horror that it is. He distorts what men take reality to be in order to get behind the facade and reveal what reality is. For the Sean O'Casey of 1928, a facsimile of life was no longer sufficient. He, like O'Neill, desired to bring "the inward outward through symbolic distortion."[12]

O'Casey's satiric mirror reflects the false values and false security and false religion in Act I that beget the black grotesque horrors of the battlefield in Act II. Just as the athletes and their trophies are displayed for pleasure and aggrandizement of those present in Act I, so are the wounded and dying displayed for the pleasure and aggrandizement of the Staff Walla and the Visitor in Act II, of Surgeon Maxwell and the Sisters in Act III, and of the revelers in Act IV. O'Casey's satiric bitterness reaches greater intensity in the panorama of the antiseptic "while there's life, there's hope" hospital ward, and ultimately reaches its peak in the final act wherein the mutilated and the dead must cede their world to the whole and the living. As the metamorphosed Susie says of Teddy and Harry in urging Jessie to go on with the dance and to take her part in life:

> No longer can they do the things we do. We can't give sight to the blind or make the lame walk. We would if we could. It is the misfortune of war. As long as wars are waged, we shall be vexed by woe; strong legs shall be made useless and bright eyes made dark. But we, who have come through the fire unharmed, must go on living. [*ST*, p. 103]

The football celebration, battlefield scene, hospital ward, and the final celebration function in sequence as microcosms of the way of the world. O'Casey's attack on war intensifies as Harry Heegan moves from pedestal to total nonentity to hospital ward to wheelchair in the sequence from Act I to Act IV. His absence from Act II points up the ability of war to erase identity, as does the numbering system in the hospital ward. The old men's function as chorus, not unlike the traditional Greek chorus, is one more example of O'Casey's willingness to use the old as well as the new in his efforts to achieve greatest dramatic impact. In this play, largely dismissed as an experiment in expressionism, O'Casey manages to incorporate the universality of the morality play in both setting and character, thereby anticipating and setting the stage for his next play, *Within the Gates*.

Set in Hyde Park, through whose gates pass the whole procession of human life, the play, like *Everyman*, presents man's symbolic quest from birth to death or from spring to winter. Most of the characters evidence a continuing decay and are crippled in one way or another; both they and the setting itself reveal the inevitable toll of time. One who reads the Down-and-Outs, the Attendants, the Evangelists, and the Arguers as the sole representatives of mankind must misread the play as O'Casey's call for submission to inevitable and restful death. Such a reading does not account for the Bishop, the Dreamer, and the Young Whore, whose combined experience and growth reveal the basic theme of *Within the Gates* to be a "cry for vigorous and effective life,"[13] the same theme so basic to virtually all of O'Casey's plays written after 1938, from *Purple Dust* through *Cock-a-Doodle Dandy*, to *The Drums of Father Ned*.

Within the Gates is, in many ways, a sequel to *The Silver Tassie*. The opening stage direction rather obviously recalls Harry Heegan:

> In the centre of the slope are a few wide steps leading to the top, where, a little to one side, stands a War Memorial in the form of a steel-helmeted soldier, the head bent on the breast, skeleton- like hands leaning on the butt-end of a rifle. Bushes allow the *figure to be seen only from the waist up*. The body and arms of the figure are shaped in a sharply defined way; the hat a wide circle; and the features are cut in long, sharp, and angular lines. The figure stands out grey against the blue sky and the green shrubs, and *seems to be shrinking back from the growing interests brought into being by new life and her thrusting activities*. [Italics are mine.]

The great economic depression that necessarily followed the
Great War serves as setting. The depression O'Casey focuses
on is the depression of the human spirit so evident in the
Down-and-Outs. In this sense, it is an effective morality play,
despite Gabriel Fallon's preference for "more play and less
morality, more work and much less art."[14] It is important, I
think, to remember through all the seasons of this play that the
war memorial stands as a grim reminder and tends to emphasize the sharpness of O'Casey's attack on the monoliths of
public opinion and organized religions that survive wars and
depressions unchanged. They continue to be operative and
restrictive in every arena of human existence, whether the
arena be Park, Dublin, or Nyadnanave.

The characters in *Within the Gates* are not individuals, but
morality play figures as their names and their actions indicate.
Each is a symbolic representation or a symbolic distortion; for
example, the Bishop is

> good-natured, well-intentioned, religious, and sincere; but he is
> timid, mistaking good-nature for the fire of the Holy Ghost, and
> life has passed him by. And he is not a character, but simply a
> symbol.[15]

He has a partial view of life, but takes it to be a total view and
the only correct one. The distortion necessitated by his human
limitations (hypocrisy, guilt, and fear of public opinion) is
both real and symbolic: he is obviously an unfit spiritual guide
for human beings destined to sing and laugh and dance. He
and all of the other characters, including the Dreamer, have
partial views. Their answers, like their dogmas, are incomplete. Jannice has no answer, but as a seeker she is less
fragmentary than those who refuse either to think or to relate
their philosophies to their immediate lives.

The Evangelists symbolize "those preachers who daub the
glories of God with mockeries."[16] They enter, as the stage
direction tells us, prowling forward "looking left and right for
sinners." One carries a banner with the red letters ONCE TO DIE,
the other a banner with black letters THEN THE JUDGEMENT.
One "has a lemon-shaped head, staring, stupid-looking eyes,

shrunken cheeks, surly lines round a wide mouth, and ears that stick out from the sides of his head." The other "has a big head, coarse face, heavy, hanging lips, and a small snubby nose. As he chants, he continually blinks his eyes. Both are shabbily dressed, and look for all the world, like sullen, long-forgotten clowns."[17] These physical descriptions, even without the warning litany of the two, make their spiritual value to O'Casey's people quite obvious. They, like the other spiritual advisers and like their closest kinsmen, the two attendants, are among the Down-and-Outs. They are fragmented personalities who lack a total view of life and have a tremendously restricted view of man's role and his destiny. Their placards and their movements symbolize their crippled condition just as the exaggerated limps of the attendants symbolize theirs.

The Atheist symbolizes "those who, trying to get rid of God, plant Him more firmly on His throne."[18] He had become the stepfather of Jannice and attempted to teach her his own fragmented view of life, which leaves neither time nor room for song. The Dreamer informs Ned, the Atheist, that he has led his step-daughter "from one darkness into another . . . man can study *or* worship God in dance and song and story" [*WG*, p. 124]. The loyal follower of the Atheist, the Man with the Stick, parrots his master, and both are engaged in a continuing stalemated argument with god-fearing public opinion as it is represented by the man wearing a Bowler Hat, the man wearing a Trilby Hat, the man wearing a Straw Hat, and—to be sure—such public servants as the Policewoman, the Nursemaids, the Guardsmen, and the Gardener. The continuing argument is static and much of the humor of *Within the Gates* results from its misunderstandings, its misquotations, its malapropisms, and its off-center focus. The arguers are not involved in any action; they just talk. Jannice, the Everywoman and protagonist of this play, must move around and through the foggy haze of their rhetoric in her active quest for a meaningful life.

The play begins on a note of joy and quickness quite similar to that in Chaucer's *Prologue* to the *Canterbury Tales*. It is springtime, the birds sing, the Earth is a maiden again, and the

warming sun is her quickening groom. "Our Mother the Earth
is a Maiden Again" is a song of joy and its theme is basic to all
of the play that follows. The young boys and girls who sing
the song represent trees and flowers and are, as their later
frolic around the May-Pole suggests, allied with the life force
so foreign to the Down-and-Outs.

The second scene opens with the People's song, their call to
the money makers, the businessmen, the politicians, and the
churchgoers who are "haggard and giddy with care, busy
counting your profit and losses," to bellow their goodbyes to
"the buggerin' lot n' come out to bow down the head 'n bend
down the knee to the bee, the bird, 'n the blossom. . . ." The
call to worship is, of course, unheeded by the hat-wearing,
newspaper-reading representatives of public opinion, by the
Bishop, and by Ned, the Atheist. The scene, set during
Summer Noon, reflects their jaded, not an appreciative,
interest in life and in the life force of Nature itself. This
jaded and somehow nastily lascivious interest is always seen in
relation to the Young Woman. Her religious instructors can't
keep eyes or hands off her knees. Jannice seeks peace
everlasting with the fragmented, knee-patting Salvation Army
Officer who tells her to beware of the Bishop and his kind of
help: "Never heed him, Sister. He would hide God's counte-
nance with a cloud of ritual. Come with me; the yoke is easy,
the burden light." The Bishop, despite the guilt and shame of
it all, looks consciously and appreciatively at Jannice's legs.
When she approaches him for help, he gives her only cliches
about motherhood, work, and thrift. When he pats her knee
and has his hand forcibly removed, he takes refuge in his
book, and refuses to aid her because, as he announced
initially, "Oh, my child, I'm afraid I can help only those I
know."

Jannice, whose growing theology is more fitted to the
immediate needs and experiences of life, and whose expand-
ing view is more complete than the Bishop's, tells him that a
priest of "the most high God" is "neither a man nor a stranger,"
that she's heard "the same old rot" about "mother, work, and
thrift" a thousand times before, that he hides behind his book

when facts frighten him, and continues, "Are you afraid to find a lie in what you think to be the truth, or the truth in what you think to be a lie?" She says to him of his disassociation from life, his sheltered condition, and his facade of Christianity:

> You and your goodness are of no use to God! If Christ came again, He'd have to call, not the sinners, but the righteous to repentence.
>
> . . .
>
> A tired Christ would be afraid to lean on your arm. Your Christ wears a bowler hat, carries a cane, twiddles his lavender gloves, an' sends out gilt-edged cards of thanks to callers. Out with you, you old shivering shame, an' go away into the sun to pick the yellow primroses!" [WG, pp. 160-64]

The Dreamer offers the Young Woman a song for her pleasures. ". . . Come, sweet lass, and let's transmute vague years of life into a glowing hour of love." As Jannice exits with the Salvation Army Officer "to hear more of the peace that seems far away," she says to the Bishop, "Good-bye, old man, who, saving yourself, had no time to save others," and tells the Dreamer, "I have not quite forgotten your sweet song, young singer!" The Dreamer offers Jannice his song for her merry kindness and tells her, "I am thinking, not of your need, but of my own," promising nothing but transient pleasure, whereas the Salvation Army Officer is "a real friend who offers peace as a child might offer a friend a new-blown daisy."

O'Casey's satiric jabs at the limited views of those who talk most are effective here. Neither the Bishop nor the Salvation Army Officer has the answer for Jannice; neither does the Dreamer. She learns from each. Unlike the Bishop, she must be involved in life; unlike the Salvation Army man, she must question and earn the peace she seeks rather than accepting it at face value as a gift; unlike the Dreamer, she must find a purpose in life other than song and dance. These must be integral to, but not the total essence of, her life. Her continu-ing quest has as its background the continuing stalemate between public opinion's representatives and the atheistic spokesmen. The increasing fervor of the Old Woman's attacks, the conflict between any two theologies represented, and the perpetual suffering and bitching of the Down-and-Outs complete the atmosphere of the world through which this play's Everywoman must make her way.

The muffled drum, with its superstitious associations with England in danger, and the song of the Down-and-Outs have become thematic by Scene II. The danger to England is obvious in the Park, in the depression and in the hopeless attitudes of the Down-and-Outs, in the dogmatism of the Atheist, in the equally dogmatic views of public opinion, and in the continuing fruitless quest for answers among those divergent groups who have all the answers. The Dreamer is quite specific in stating that his "Song of the Down-and-Out" is not a hymn for the unemployed, for

> They remain men in their misfortune. I keen those who whine through to-day and dread to-morrow; who would for ever furl the flag of life; who fear any idea common thought hasn't had time to bless; those who have a sigh for a song and a sad sigh for a drumbeat. [WG, pp. 133-34]

He prays: "Kill off the withered mind, the violently stupid, O Lord, who having nothing to give, have nothing to get!" He answers the old attendant who tells him that "death's only the gytewye to a fuller en' a nobler life" by a direct order: "Take that dead hand off me! . . . Be off, and die, and keep a holy distance from the quick and the lively."

His definition of the Down-and-Out and his prayer function as continuing calls for a more meaningful life. The Dreamer is a more mature version of O'Casey's poet figure, who first appears as the adolescent Donal Davoren in *The Shadow of a Gunman*. While his vision of life is less ethereal and less removed from life itself than Davoren's, it is not yet whole. He serves as a kind of touchstone for the Young Woman who, through continuing and varied experiences of life, recognizes the limitations of even the Dreamer's vision. Her rebel spirit, central to any hero created by Sean O'Casey, erupts in her refrain, "If I go, I'll go game, and die dancing!" As the play progresses, Jannice becomes more and more aware of the many facets of life and less and less convinced that any single creed or spokesman has all the answers. The process of becoming aware is, in a sense, the process of becoming alive.

Scene III is set on an autumn evening and Jannice methodically rejects one pressure group after another. In one of O'Casey's more decisive episodes, Jannice tells the debaters, representatives of public opinion, who argue about evolution versus *Genesis*, still without any real communication, "Why, the wisdom each of you has, taken together, would fit on a spoon." The four hat-wearing men, immaculate in their dress, retreat into their newspapers just as the Bishop earlier had retreated into his book. They, as public opinion, are the God which the Bishop serves, as described by Jannice in that earlier scene; the newspapers, with their banners of *Murder, Rape, Suicide, Divorce,* are the totems of their God. The offstage band accompanies them as they sing "London Bridge is Falling Down," and Jannice scornfully and mockingly prays to Lucifer, "who has caused all newspapers to be written for our learning," as she watches the spouters of public opinion pore over their daily gospel.

After telling the Bishop, God's grenadier, to go away, Jannice returns her attention to the newspaper readers who "look like a silent gang of monkeys searching for fleas," identifies them as "deaf and dumb perishers" and tempts them as she dances in and out among the "bunch of 'high minded toads" who turn the "dear joy of a sin . . . to a sting and a bruising" [*WG*, pp. 175-76]. As she collapses, they return to reading the gospel of the day. Jannice recognizes that both the Bishop and the Salvation Army Officer have the "same gloomy glimpse of life. Miserere, miserere, all the way to heaven!" She sings her carpe diem song to the tune of "Little Brown Jug" and continues her frenetic quest for a more complete answer. The Salvation Army Officer, O'Casey's device to emphasize the wide divergence within the Christian religion, offers her help when the rejected Bishop leaves. "The ritualist has left you in your need, but the evangelist is here to comfort and help you—if you will." His plea is followed by the hymn sung by his followers and the emotional appeal of the moment sways Jannice until the Dreamer calls her "to the deep kiss and clutch of love; to sing our song with the song that is sung by a thousand stars of the evening!" The Salvation Army men continue to sing about the sad "fate of the lamb who strays" as the curtain falls on Scene III [*WG*, pp. 189-202].

O'Casey's parody of the evangelical altar call is a biting one, but despite its invective spirit, the Salvation Army representative is no more a villain than the Bishop is. O'Casey's target is organized religion, not the Christian faith, and his specific targets are those within various sects who pretend to be able guides for humanity. The Bishop learns, as this morality play progresses, that his sister is wrong when she tells him, "A bishop should be in the midst of the incense, in the sanctuary, safe away from the sour touch of common humanity." He learns from Jannice that a priest of God must be neither a man nor a stranger and that he must be involved in life itself rather than separated and merely pretending to be involved. The Bishop, like Jannice, is in the process of beginning life; he is not, like the Down-and-Outs, in a static cocoon serving death and waiting for death.

Scene I ends with Jannice in the arms of the law, arrested for prostitution when she asked the gardener to marry her; Scene II ends with her going forth with the Salvation Army Officer "to hear more of the peace that seems so far away," after having her plea for help rejected by the Bishop; Scene III ends with her in the embrace of the Dreamer after having rejected public opinion, the Bishop, and the Salvation Army. At the end of Scene IV, Jannice fulfills her vow to die dancing and dies as her hand is guided by the Bishop in making the sign of the cross. The sequence is not happenstance, but indicates the Young Woman's frustrated progress in her pursuit of a vigorous and meaningful life. A spiritual journey, in the traditional sense, it is not.

The continuing frustrations of her quest in the wasteland world of no communication, of newspaper gospel, and of apathetic acceptance of inevitable and somehow rewarding death, lend credibility to her choice of the Dreamer's offer of immediate pleasure, song, and dance. The fact that she hesitates when the evangelical call is reissued indicates that she is aware that even the Dreamer does not have the final and complete answer, that no single pat answer can be wholly right. Up to this point in the play, however, the Dreamer's creed is more nearly correct in that it is less limited than the other creeds.

By Scene IV, the cycle of seasons and of Everywoman's life has progressed to the fourth stage, Winter, a time of cold and blackness. Just as the singing of "London Bridge is Falling Down" functioned symbolically in the third scene and the various responses identified the speakers with their views of life, so do the mournful sound of "The Last Post" and the comments of the spokesmen for public opinion identify their continuing roles in this final scene. The satiric conflicts up to this point have pitted Atheism against Christianity, evangelism against ritualism, legal dictates against instinct and passion, and the Dreamer's carpe diem philosophy against all organized and dictated ones. In this final scene, a new conflict pits the militant Guardsman against civilians in the continuing argument of "styted hypothenuse," ridiculous analogy, confusing the issues, and pat answers. O'Casey's satire of these is superficial, to be sure, but the fact that they are represented in the cross section assembled in The Park is indicative of their continuing roles in the lives of men and women represented in that microcosm.

It is difficult to say how much of this final scene is dictated by O'Casey's sardonic humor, but his presentation of the Bishop as a growing, searching man who is in the process of learning about life suggests that Jannice's marriage of religion and dreams does not represent a defeat for her. Rather, it is a victory. The Down-and-Outs recognize their condition, as their song indicates, but do nothing about it: "We challenge life no more, no more, with our dead faith and our dead hope." The Dreamer continues to hurl his challenge and his prayer,

Way for the strong and the swift and the fearless:
Life that is stirr'd with the fear of its life, let it die;
Let it sink down, let it die, and pass from our vision for ever.

The Bishop tells his archetypal sister, "Go home, go home, for Christ's sake, woman, and ask God's mercy on us all!" He is moved by Jannice's death and somewhat awed that she died making the sign of the cross. The play ends, not with engulfing blackness, but with the sky changing "to a bright gray, pierced with golden segments, as if the sun was rising, and a new day about to begin" [WG, pp. 230-31].

This morality play does not offer a pessimistic picture of man engulfed in and destroyed by the poverty of a great economic depression. The depression is background, part of the scenery, but the real struggle is Everywoman's struggle against despair, hopelessness, and apathy, against the kind of incurable decay portrayed so vividly in the Down-and-Outs. The struggle is also against the remedial hypocrisy worn like vestments by the Bishop. This morality play, like most others, involves no great intricacies of plot. The action is not cloaked in any air of mystery; there is no suspense, and about the third time Jannice voices her defiance and her vow to die dancing, no one should be in doubt as to the eventual outcome. The plot itself is a mechanical one, one that is not foreign to any viewer of melodrama. If the plot per se concerns only the unravelling of the not too deep mystery of Jannice's father, it is, as Robert Hogan suggests, too predictable.[19] Viewed, however, as a morality play, which it is, *Within the Gates* can hardly be condemned for having too few human beings, too little character development, or too little mystery, any more than *Everyman* or *Mankind* can be condemned for the same reason.

The basic action is the search of Everywoman for salvation; the oft-repeated theme is her continuing "cry for a vigorous and effective life." Her continuing frustrations, as already noted, reflect the virtual impossibility of a contrived answer, whatever authority the answerer claims to have. O'Casey calls not for an escape from life, but for an involvement in life. The answers, whether they come from self-ordained philosophers or from organized religion, should not "lead people into metaphysical puzzles that delude them from the sordidness of the world which needs to be dealt with."[20] Jannice's symbolic and satiric struggle is for meaningful existence in a sordid world.

O'Casey's obvious sympathies lie with the Dreamer, his poet figure, but he makes it obvious that the Dreamer does not really come to grips with the problems of life; he evades or ignores them. The Dreamer recognizes the need in every life for song and dance and rightfully hurls his imprecations at the Down-and-Outs, the Bishop, and the Arguers. The Dreamer is, as O'Casey says, the

> symbol of a noble restlessness and discontent; of the stir in life that brings to birth new things and greater things than those that were before; of the power realizing that the urge of life is above the level of conventional morality; of ruthlessness to get near to the things that matter, and sanctify them with intelligence, energy, gracefulness and song; of rebellion against stupidity; and of the rising intelligence in man that will no longer stand, nor venerate, nor shelter those whom poverty of spirit has emptied of all that is worth while in life.[21]

He, like the other characters, is a morality play figure whose vision, though inspired, is incomplete. Were his view not a partial one, Jannice would have completed her quest at the end of Act III when she answered his honest proposal "to transmute vague years of life into a glowing hour of love." The play does not end there, for the quest is not complete there. The Dreamer, like the law and organized religions, offers only a partial answer.

Within the Gates presents a view not in sympathy with the various contemporary "messages of misery, of hopelessness, of the futility of life"—sombre messages "hailed as profound meditations, incontrovertible, showing life buttoned up into every-lasting woe."[22] The play was banned in Boston by the Wesleyans and the Jesuits for its "sympathetic portrayal of immorality" and its portrayal "of the utter futility of religion as an effective force in meeting the problems of the world." O'Casey describes the play as "a cry for courage, decency, and vitality in life," and attacks the outrageous weaknesses and misconceptions of the Catholic and Wesleyan churches, essentially the same weaknesses and misconceptions already

satirized in *Within the Gates*.[23] This satiric morality play, with
its sustained use of the expressionistic techniques and its
attempt to return song and dance to the stage, is an important
document in the history of the modern theatre. With its attack
on mechanized ready-made creeds and its insistence upon
active participation in life, it is, likewise, an indispensable
touchstone in any serious study of the attempts and attain-
ments of Sean O'Casey.

As satirist, O'Casey had a specific goal in mind. The goal in
this play is to rip away the ostentatious facade, however
impressive it may be, and to reveal the concealed truth. He
reveals the truth about a Bishop who hides from life, the truth
about soothsayers who do nothing but prattle, the truth about
the public whose opinion is God and whose totem is the
newspaper. He also reveals the truth about evangelical religion, the very existence of which is predicated on the inadequacy of the Bishop's faith. Each of these believes his partial
view to be whole and correct; all talk at cross-purposes; not
one has the total answer, as the Down-and-Outs exemplify.
Their very condition of being Down-and-Outs is due to their
own dependence on ready hand-me-down answers. The
babbling world of The Park is a world of much noise, but little
sense, where no one is interested in any except his own version
of truth.

For those who missed O'Casey's artistic manifesto in *The
Silver Tassie* and *Within the Gates,* "The Green Goddess of
Realism" clearly defines the position he held by 1937. It is his
declaration of independence and his official ultimatum to the
powers that be as it rather specifically denounces the picture-
box stage and the guises of Realism per se. His manifesto was
anticipated by the techniques and the intents of *The Silver
Tassie* and *Within the Gates,* both of which are illuminated
distortions of life rather than calculated slices of life, and both
of which present allegorical rather than concrete pictures of
that which is.

O'Casey, by 1928 and certainly by 1933, had become more
concerned with the continuing significance than with the
momentary effect of a situation, more involved in creating the

essence of experience than in portraying a reproduced description of experience. He, like his expressionistic forebears and contemporaries in Germany, France, and the United States, was searching for the inner meanings of a given experience for humanity as a whole. He believed, as they did, that

> Everything else is "facade," showing a "bourgeois" attitude that is to be destroyed with its superficial judgements of right or wrong. Once the bourgeois mask is torn away the link with eternity given to every human being will be revealed.[24]

O'Casey, the rebel, is foremost even within his new medium; he did not appreciate those who allied him too closely with the Expressionistic movement, any more than Shaw appreciated those who compared him (usually unfavorably) to Shakespeare. O'Casey protested as late as 1958 in an interview with Rod Nordell that he did not know the difference between impressionism and expressionism and that when he wrote *The Silver Tassie*, he thought he was writing some kind of ritual.[25] Again, on 24 March 1960, in a letter to Ronald G. Rollins, he denied that he "consciously adopted expressionism, which I don't understand and never did."[26] Whether O'Casey adopted the techniques consciously or unconsciously, they do exist in his plays and he does acknowledge his debt to Eugene O'Neill's *Mourning Becomes Electra* in his prefatory comment to *Within the Gates*.

Furthermore, the devices and techniques of both expressionism and stream of consciousness are effectively used by O'Casey in "I Wanna Woman," "The Star Jazzer," and "The Job," three of the four short stories appearing in *Windfalls* (1934).[27] The first of these treats precisely the same feelings of fear and guilt that torture the Young Woman in *Within the Gates*. These fears and guilts are stirred periodically by Jack Avreen's remembering Lochner's painting of the crucifixion, which he had removed from above his couch so that the painting would not interfere with his methodical seduction of an Irish Catholic girl who is supposed to visit him. The same guilts and fears are further amplified by sign-carrying evangelists and by hymn singers in Picadilly Circus, where Avreen goes to work off his frustration on a high-class whore. Though the point of view in "I Wanna Woman" is essentially omniscient, the imagery and sound patterns are stream of consciousness. The figures are not individuals but representative morality figures in the mob scene at Picadilly Circus which, like The Park in *Within the Gates,* is a microcosm.

O'Casey's irony and satiric bent are also operative in "The Star Jazzer," which utilizes essentially the same techniques to portray the mechanical nightmare world of the Dublin slums. The journey is not through the Circus nor through Hyde Park, but is up and down—up and down ten flights of stairs in the rhythmic ritual of washday. The woman's temporary escape from her slum world into song and dance is, so far as she is concerned, temporary madness, and she is frightened by it. Except for the temporary respite afforded by her midnight madness, she is one of the Down-and-Outs and will never again escape from the prison of her bed and her washtub. These stories demonstrate O'Casey's facility with the new techniques as well as his ability to write effective short stories. They also indicate that his experiments in form and his search for more effective expression continued despite his obvious disappointment with the decision of the Abbey directors concerning *The Silver Tassie.* As he describes them, "the three short stories were an effort to get rid of some of the bitterness that swept into me when the Abbey Theatre rejected *The Silver Tassie.*"[28] That the three stories work better as fiction than they did as therapy is not debatable.

O'Casey's next plays, *The End of the Beginning* and *A Pound on Demand,* were first published in *Windfalls* in a subsection entitled "Falls in An Idle Wind." As he describes them in his "Preface," "two One-Act Sketches were written when funds were low, to bring in a little money, but no attempt was made to market them, and so they shiver among the unemployed."

The End of the Beginning is a delightfully funny farce; it is O'Casey's recapitulation of an old folk tale claimed by virtually every European nation. O'Casey's additions and alterations are indicative of his wit and his ability to distort even a folk tale about a fool to reveal new and perhaps more meaningful patterns of behavior. The folk tale, as recorded by George Webbe Dasent,[29] involves one surly petulant husband and his sweet affectionate wife, who offers to harvest the hay so that her husband can keep the house to suit himself. The husband's only chores are to churn butter, to feed and milk the cow, and to cook dinner. He manages, during the complexities of housekeeping, to let a pig turn the churn over, to kill the pig accidentally, to run a keg of ale out onto the floor, not to feed and not to milk the cow, not to prepare dinner, to leave the baby unattended, and to be stuck in the chimney while the cow on the other end of the rope is suspended midway between roof and ground. His hungry wife returns from the field, cuts the rope with her scythe to release the cow, and discovers her husband head down in a porridge pot.

O'Casey's fool, Darry Berrill, is obese, obstinate, bald, and totally inept at any physical task. Any one of these traits would render him a stage fool; taken all together, they render him a laughingstock from the moment the curtain rises until the play is over. His buddy, Barry Derrill, is his exact opposite: slender, easy-going, heavily mustached, and quite well coordinated. His near blindness and his relationship with Darry identify him as the other half of the inseparable comic duo.

Lizzie, Darry's wife, is at least as efficient as her folk-tale equivalent. She is, however, less trusting and less devoted to her husband. She knows him. She also knows and has much to say about Alice Lanigan:

> The Alice Lanigan that's on the margin of fifty, n' assembles herself together as if she was a girl in her teens, jutting out her bust when she's coming in, 'n jutting out her behind when she's going out, like the Lady of Shalott, to catch the men—that's the Alice Lanigan I mean.
>
> . . .
>
> . . . she has a kid who has never had a pat on the head from a father.[30]

These additions, plus the various machines and paraphernalia of modern living (mower, town hall clock, alarm clock, razor blades, and the mysteries of electricity), render the folk tale virtually unrecognizable and leave in its stead a moral-making farce.

Barry is a comic Cassandra who persistently warns of impending doom, is ignored, and then is instrumental in, if not directly responsible for, each succeeding disaster. His recurrent warnings and his refrain, "You're not going to expedite matters by rushing around in a hurry," the efficient whirring of the mowing machine in the background, and the methodical tolling of the town hall clock impose a kind of order on the several incidents that occur. Other well-made-play devices used by O'Casey include the frame afforded by Lizzie's prayer, "God grant that it won't be the end, an' that when I come back, I'll at least find the four walls standing," and her return to the chaos within the four standing walls. Further, Darry remains obstinate and inept and refuses to accept responsibility for his own failings—whether he does not mow the hay, does not keep time to the music, does break the clock, or does effectively demolish everything within the four walls of the house. He greets his wife, who has mowed the hay and freed the dangling heifer, with the final ironic lines of the play,

> Now you see the result of havin' your own way! Why the hell didn't you hold on to the rope when you took it off the heifer, so that I wouldn't come down with a bump?
>
> . . .
>
> —my God, woman, can you do nothin' right!

The satire in *The End of the Beginning* is superficial and only incidental to the slapstick humor as the two buddies merge their talents and methodically wreck the house. O'Casey's attitude toward the reducing fad and the misuse of the gramophone are secondary to the spectacle of the huffing Darry doing his physical jerks and to the memory of his wife's viewing his naked body practicing the physical jerks before the mirror. That both men suffer wounds and are reduced to total helplessness by routine housekeeping tasks reaffirms O'Casey's admiration for efficient Irish women and his contempt for those inept individuals who insist on giving advice to others.

This play and *A Pound on Demand* were written just prior to their publication in *Windfalls* (1934). *The End of the Beginning* was produced in the Abbey Theatre in February 1937, but *A Pound on Demand* was not produced until January 1947, in the American Repertory Theatre. Robert Lowery, in his "Premieres and Casts of Sean O'Casey's Plays," has identified at least two, perhaps three, "premieres" earlier than the 1947 date—"October 16, 1939 at the *Q* Theatre in London," and two 1936 performances described by O'Casey in a letter to Gabriel Fallon: "one, by Irish Literary Society, & the other by Darrington Grammar School, Durham, at One Guinea per performance. . . ."[31]

A Pound on Demand is a sketch involving the maudlin drunkenness of Sammy Adams, who has money on deposit through the Government Post Office, and the parasitic Jerry, who wants desperately for Sammy Adams to withdraw a pound. The sketch is crammed with incident, and the juxtaposition of drunkenness and civil authority constitutes the central conflict of the sketch. For O'Casey, the treatments of the efficient postmistress and her policeman beau are remarkably kind. The postmistress quite correctly refuses to honor the request for a pound on demand and the policeman officiously but understandingly sends the two drunks toward home despite Samuel's proclamation overheard by the huge policeman:

> . . . Poleeish to the right of me, 'n to the left of me, 'n nothing left of them in the end but silver buttons for souvenirs!
>
> . . .
>
> . . .We often plastered the roads with policemen, 'n left them thryin' out how they were going to get themselves together again![32]

The stoutish woman represents outraged public opinion, and, like her counterparts in *The Plough and the Stars* and *The Silver Tassie*, is as much the target of O'Casey's satiric jabs as the two buddies are. She and they make ridiculous demands on the postmistress, are offended, and make hollow threats. Civil authority, despite the threats, presents a united front in the persons of the postmistress and the policeman. The demands are not honored, the incident concludes, and presumably the policeman and his girl resume their flirtation as the curtain concludes the sketch. The realistic technique, as used in this drunk scene, is similar to that used by O'Casey during his earliest years of writing. The devices of farce and the well-made play once again testify to O'Casey's debt to Boucicault and his apprenticeship in the Old Merchants' Theatre. While Guy Boas describes these two plays, along with *Shadow of a Gunman, Juno and the Paycock,* and *The Plough and the Stars,* as a complete self-contained unit of O'Casey's work, a literature of their own which presents "an urban and more robust version of the peasant world of Synge,"[33] they bear essentially the same relationship to the Irish period, actually, that *Kathleen Listens In* and *Nannie's Night Out* bear to the expressionistic or the transitional period. *A Pound on Demand* and *The End of the Beginning* recall the essentially realistic techniques, the stage Irishman, and the isolated humor of the Irish period in much the same way that *Kathleen Listens In* and *Nannie's Night Out* anticipate the expressionistic technique, thematic use of music, and distortion for the sake of clarity to be found in the major plays written after *The Silver Tassie.*

Written by his own account in 1937-38,[34] O'Casey's *Purple Dust* displays the same artistic combination of expressionism and realism, the same blending of morality play and farce so evident in other plays of the transitional period. *Purple Dust* has been damned by four decades of critical and theatrical opinion uttered in Ireland and England, but praised over the same period by O'Casey's enthusiastic American readers and viewers.

These extremes of critical opinion were somewhat anticipated by the "pre-rumble" of circumstances surrounding the play's initial production. After O'Casey had already commissioned George Jean Nathan to bring about production of *Purple Dust* in New York, he received an unsigned letter from a London Theatre Club requesting an option on the play. O'Casey, of course, refused. A second signed letter "came along to say that the play had been in rehearsal for some time, and would O'Casey kindly give formal permission to the production by the Theatre." Following his second negative response, a third letter informed O'Casey that "James Agate had been invited to see the play and give his views on it in the coming issue of the *Sunday Times.*" Agate, of course, "denounced the play as a worthless one; more, that it was an attack on England when England was helpless and unable to reply!"[35] O'Casey's consequent rage did have some justification, and this justification was compounded considerably by his earlier much publicized feud with Agate over the merits of *Within the Gates* and the demerits of a critic who found *Within the Gates* beyond his understanding. O'Casey's "The Cutting of an Agate" concludes characteristically, "The truth is that . . . the play *Within the Gates* is beyond him, and—to whisper the fact to the world rather than confine it between four walls—I am not a damn bit surprised."[36] One interesting result of O'Casey's exchange with James Agate was that critic's unqualified praise of a very bad play, *The Star Turns Red*, a play which Agate termed "A Masterpiece," "a *magnum opus* of compassion."[37] Agate apparently discovered the wasp's sting to be painful and offered this review in exchange for peace and as a presumed retraction of his earlier statements concerning the "pretentious rubbish" written by Sean O'Casey. Ironically, it is the rationalistic English mind such as Mr. Agate's that is the basic target of O'Casey's satire in both *Within the Gates* and *Purple Dust.*

Purple Dust depicts Great Britain as a crumbling old Tudor mansion ill-prepared to withstand the natural elements and doomed to fall before the force of wind and rain despite the efforts of Cyril Poges and Basil Stoke to hold it together with paint and gaudy furniture. These two inept and impotent stage Englishmen owe their names to Stoke Poges, Thomas Gray's melancholy country churchyard; they owe at least their germination to Shaw's comments in his "Preface for Politicians" and much of their development to Broadbent and

Doyle in Shaw's *John Bull's Other Island*. Among Shaw's other memorable and pertinent phrases in the preface is his confession that "it takes an Irishman years of residence in England to learn to respect and like a blockhead. An Englishman will not respect nor like anyone else."[38]

One basic theme of *John Bull's Other Island* is that Englishmen, like their country, will muddle through somehow and that their most stirring accomplishments are somehow muddled successes. Tom Broadbent is the stage Englishman ancestor of O'Casey's two blockheads—Stoke and Poges; he, like they, spouts all the traditional cliches concerning efficiency and modernism, and possesses the lethargic sense of humor associated with the stage Englishman since Shaw. To complete his play, Shaw leaves the impression that Broadbent will inevitably represent the Irish in Parliament. While not at home among his constituents, he will be very much at home in Parliament. Broadbent, unlike these O'Casey inspired descendants, does maintain, despite his gullibility and foolishness, a kind of dignity. O'Casey's Englishmen, however, are gulls and fools from the moment they enter the stage until the prophetic flood symbolically removes them from the stage.[39]

The decaying mansion in *Purple Dust*, despite the Oxford background and the financial wizardry of its owners, will crumble and fall into a heap of purple dust. O'Casey views the remnants of England's glory—"the Yeomen of the Guard and the cuirassed horsemen standing under the archway of the Horse Guards centre, and the bearskin of the Household Regiments"—as quaint album momentoes, as "part of an open-air museum."[40] All these will pass despite the efforts of Stoke and Poges to hold them and to glue them back together as they break apart. O'Casey portrays the Old House as the inevitable victim of the ravages of time and change; the disintegration of the manor is only superficially contributed to by the two Englishmen who try to put it back together as it was in the good old days so that they might enjoy it and bask in its reflected glory. Inevitable change, here as elsewhere in O'Casey's canon, brings with it inevitable progress as life triumphs over death.

The central conflict in *Purple Dust* is between the half-remembered tradition and unknown history of a dead past and the demands for life in the present. For O'Casey, the battle is between death and life, and death is overmatched from the outset, for Death's spokesmen are fools who combine the follies of the antiquarian, the bad taste of the nouveau riche, and the ridiculous posture of those whose total worth is measured in money. The Englishmen's opponents are the realistic Irish workmen led by O'Killigain, and the impotent Englishmen lose their women, their investment, and—unless they are more fortunate than fleetfooted—their lives. They are not fit to survive in the better world that's coming, and they, like the other relics of England's open-air museum, must make way for progress, and for those who are fitted to live.

Those who do live must have eyes to see and ears to hear; they must have voices to sing and feet to dance; further, they must desire to live in a vigorous and meaningful way. They must not lapse into the drowsy shadowland between life and death, as did the Irish at Liffey Bridge following the second miracle in *Red Roses for Me*. By inclination and by definition they are opposed to revering tradition, to "Thricking th' rotten beams into a look o' sturdiness with a coat o' white and black paint, an' they for a long a dismal swellin' even for the gnawin' beetle an' th' borin' worm." They are opposed to the clergy's trying "to keep a sensible check on the lower inclinations of the people," especially when those lower inclinations are the natural desires to sing, dance, and live. In this play those who live are dramatically opposed to Stoke and Poges, their hypocritcal reverence for a dead past, and a repressive religion that these two represent.

Purple Dust exemplifies the inevitable defeat of Poges and Stoke in a series of ludicrous incidents. The result of each incident is further destruction of the mansion and further illumination of the follies and false pride of the proprietors. Within O'Casey's canon, the nearest parallel to the destruction per se is in *The End of the Beginning*. There, too, total destruction results from the frenetic activities of the fault-finding fools—Darry Berrill and Barry Derrill. Their frenzied efforts, like those of Stoke and Poges, are to set a house in order. Neither pair knows what order is, and neither will accept guidance or responsibility. Darry's pride, like that of Poges, anticipates the painfully funny demise of his great plan. Order in the comic world can be established only when the Stokes, the Poges, and their antiquarian dreams cease to exist.

As noted earlier, the Tudor Mansion in *Purple Dust* is a microcosm of the British Empire on the verge of collapse. Though a one-to-one relationship is improbable, Poges bears a striking resemblance to O'Casey's version of Neville Chamberlain, a hopelessly naive, ineffectual old man who accepted Hitler's word and returned to England singing songs of peace:

> Mr. Chamberlain came home waving the talismanic umbrella. Is it peace, Jehu? It is peace! Herr Hitler has met an old man in the half-way house, and has promised to be good; has promised to go over the hills only. . . . We need have no fear. He will level Moscow. He won't harm us. He as much as told Mr. Chamberlain so.[41]

The trusting old man with his faith in reputation and his devotion to Empire is remarkably similar to the essence of Poges as his motives and methods are dissected on stage. The specific incidents in the dissection are those of farce comedy: a huge grass roller gets out of control when the ineffectual Poges attempts to maneuver it as the salesman from simple Ireland told him he could; the roller crashes through a wall; a cow, brought by another Irish salesman, sends the heroes scurrying for protection when they mistake it for a bull; the cow is later shot dead; the workmen methodically destroy the mansion's ceiling, walls, door frames, and the heirlooms of the house; Stoke falls from a spirited horse and his "lassie o' th' house went off with O'Killigain riding naked through the locality!"[42]

The Irishmen are capable of direct action; they combine the marvelous romanticism and the effective realism of O'Dempsey and O'Killigain with the sardonic humor and irreverent attitude toward modernity of the yellow-bearded electrician and the postmaster. O'Casey's Irishmen here are not of the Dublin slums, but of a rural world far removed from suffering and privation. They are close kinsmen of Synge's tramps and tinkers. Existence and the necessities of life are not their prime concerns, nor are they conspicuously nationalistic. They revel in freedom and joy and life. Their pride is natural and they relinquish neither freedom nor identity as they work for their English employers. It is not they who are out of their element.

Just as the majority of the Irish laborers are expert salesmen, the Irish girls are also superb con-artists who combine their particular talents with the foolish desires of old and virtually impotent men to amass tidy personal incomes and valuable collections of trinkets. The Irish laborers condemn the pretentions of the girls who claim descent from the Duke of Ormand and try "to be something else beside themselves." The same Irishmen are quite pleased with the artistry of the girls, each of whom has a cash settlement of £500 per year from her Englishman. It is important to the comic world of this satire that the Irishmen do not make moral judgments nor damn the girls for their whoredom, but that Poges and Stoke do condemn the girls as sluts and harlots. The condemnations are as ludicrous as the presumed matches between the lusty vital wenches and the cold hapless Englishmen, as ludicrous as January-May marriages always are in the comic world.

Poges and Stoke do not see clearly nor hear well. They are lost in the magic of their own sounds and seek to create their own Eden. Their Eden will consist of the world of the refurbished Tudor mansion in the simple rustic setting of old Ireland, a pastoral world wherein they can enjoy peace and dignity, wherein they can "forget the vile world and all its ways." Poges sees rustic Ireland as the land where peace was born, a land of simple ignorant Irishmen who will respect his native superiority and stand in awe of his glory as reflected by the Tudor mansion and its wonderful past. The pastoral never-never land is to be an Eden without a serpent to mar or jeopardize its perfection and everlasting peace. Unknowingly, they have the serpent on their payroll in the person of O'Killigain, whose very name, however Irish it be, suggests his true relationship to the sadly materialistic Stoke and Poges. To further damn their pastoral project, O'Casey endows the businessmen with the friendship of Reverend George Canon Chreehewel, who encourages Poges:

> . . . You have a very beautiful house here. An old house, but a fine one. It is almost a sacred thing to keep an old thing from dying, sir; for whatsoever things are just, whatsoever things are honest, whatsoever things are pure, whatsoever things are lovely and of good report, are invariably found close to, and, sometimes, intimately enclosed in the life and being of ages that have passed, and in the life of men and women who have gone away before us.
>
> POGES [gratified]. I wholeheartedly agree with you, reverend Sir. I feel it. I know it.
>
> CANON. With all its frills, its frivolities, its studied ceremonial, however gaily-colored its leisure may have been, the past had in it the core of virtue; while the present swirl of young life, I'm saying, with its feverish sthrut of pretended bravery, its tawdry carelessness about the relation and rule of religion to man, with all its frantic sthretching of pleasure into every second of life, contains within it a tawny core of fear that is turning darker with every chime of the passing hours! [PD, pp. 85-86]

Canon Chreehewel urges his moneyed friends to "assist the clergy to keep a sensible check on the lower inclinations of the people," to recapture the discipline and virtue of the past, and—"Help us to curtail th' damned activity of the devilish dance halls!"

The battle lines are clearly drawn: Poges, Stoke, and Canon Chreehewel are the defenders of tradition, history, and a dead past, just as they are the perpetrators of sterility. The work-men and the girls, aided considerably by wind, flood, and Sean O'Casey, represent life, enthusiasm, joy, freedom, and virility. The "gouty doughty Basil Stoke," the leader of the opposition, as known by Avril, is:

> A toddler thricking with a woman's legs; a theif without the power to thieve the thing he covets; a louse burrowing in a young lioness's belly; a perjurer in passion; a gutted soldier bee whose job is done, and still hangs on to life! [PD, pp. 15-16]

The young lioness, by mutual agreement, prefers O'Killigain. Against the virulent dreams of the Englishmen, the Irish worker promises fruitful love; O'Dempsey will show Souhaun "wondhers of a manly manner" and assures her that: "With firm fed men an' comely, cordial women there'll be laughter round a red fire when the mists are risin', when the roads an' fields are frosty, an' when the nights is still." In the Tudor manor, there is no fire until an Irishman builds it, nor is there fuel nor axe. There is a telephone and a desk and one electric light, and there will be a bathroom, "if we can fit one in without injuring the harmony of the old house." The choice for the girls is clearly between death and decay on the one hand and life and joy on the other, as the laborers urge the girls to leave the mansion of "creakin' grandeur an' poor witherin' talk; salt food without a dhrink to go with it; an' a purple dhryness turnin' timidly to dust!" [PD, p. 106]. In short, the invitation is to leave the world of the dead and half-dead and go forth into the land of the living.

The Englishmen are complacent and secure enough in their solvency that they make fun of the poetic pleas of O'Killigain and O'Dempsey: "Spit out what's here, an' come where love is fierce an' fond an' fruitful. Come, lass, where there's things to say an' things to do an' love at the endings!" They attribute the amusing madness of the workmen to the demented state of all Ireland, which must be due to the climate. It is "amusing up to a point, but hardly reassuring," as Stokes notes, and "it isn't exactly comfortable to be living in a community of crazy people. . . . It may even become dangerous." Poges complacently continues to write his business letter, to try to buy shares in a cement company, and to be certain of his holding power for the amours of Souhaun. When the girls do leave the palace of money with their nest eggs and promissory notes in hand, they are accused of taking money under false pretences; Avril speaks for both concerning the accusation, and in doing so repeats the essential character of the mock-Eden created by the Englishmen:

> I gave more than I got, you gilded monkey. It's winnowed of every touch of life I'd be if I stayed with th' waste of your mind

much longer. . . . Th' thrinkets I wormed out of you are all here, an' here they stay, for the wages were low for what was done for you. [*PD*, p. 165]

Poges and Stoke see their escapist's world as one which will "make us young again. We'll be as lively as goats in no time." It is, as the play demonstrates, a world without communication, without hope for the future, and without joy in the present. It is a ludicrous make-believe world where the inhabitants wear gaudy costumes, mimic country dance styles, and adore real and imagined relics of bygone days. Very early, O'Killigain recognizes their mansion as a morgue and chooses to "let the dead bury their dead"; he notes that "old things are perishing" and encourages the workers to cease working, "for it is waste of time to try to butthress up a tumbling house." The alternative is the real world and, as he tells Avril, it is to be found "where I have found it often, and seek to find it still":

> With the bittherness an' joy blendin' in a pretty woman's hand; with the pity in her breast; in th' battlin, beauty of her claspin' arms; an' rest beside her when the heart is tired. [*PD*, p. 18]

His gospel is that "there never can be evil things where love is living," that life should be lived as it is rather than adored as it was, and that a pretty girl is evidence that God is smiling. He agrees with O'Dempsey that

> there is sweet music in the land, but not for th' deaf; there is wisdom too, but it is not in a desk it is, but out in th' hills, an' in the life of all things rovin' round, undher th' blue sky. [*PD*, p. 100]

The chief targets of O'Casey's satire in this colored play are ignorance, confusion, and pomposity as personified in the figures of Stoke and Poges. He also attacks the hypocrisy of Poges the businessman, who would "cash in on splintered bodies" and the gullibility of the little man who wishes to cast a large shadow. The pastoral tradition is parodied in the impotent quest of the Englishmen and in the complete victory won by O'Killigain and his laborers. O'Casey's techniques remain those of the anatomy and the burlesque. The satiric wit is no more controlled here than the action itself. The wayward comedy is basically a farce but, owing to the poetic language and O'Casey's sheer exuberance, it carries the satire effectively.

I cannot agree with Gellbert that "the humor is puerile" nor that the "romanticism is . . . enshrined in long, wallowing passages of purple sub-Synge song."[43] Nor is Jacques Barzun accurate in assessing *Purple Dust* as "a sadistic persecution of bungling Philistinism."[44] It is a wayward comedy with heavy satire a major ingredient. Youth and life win out, as they must in O'Casey's work, over old age and death. O'Casey utilizes setting, sound, and the threat of rain and inevitable flood to establish the atmosphere and mood of the play. When the rain comes, it does not dampen the spirits of O'Killigain and Avril, nor of O'Dempsey and Souhaun; rather it is a healing and lifegiving rain which will wash away the purple dust of a dead past and send the dabblers in antiquity out of a land which is not theirs. Just as *Purple Dust* "hits, of course, at the adoration of the old, outworn things, and leans towards new thought and young ideas,"[45] it is also a part of O'Casey's continuing attempt to eliminate the blind followers and adherents to old forms of the so-called drama of realism and to create new forms of drama that

> will take qualities found in the classical, romantic, and expressionistic; . . . blend those qualities together; breathe the breath of life into the new forms and create new dramas.[46]

The Star Turns Red is an oddity, even in the canon of the versatile Sean O'Casey. On one level, like *Oak Leaves and Lavender*, it is a bitter attack on the dehumanization wrought by Fascism. The attack takes the form of a no-holds-barred propaganda piece presenting on the one hand the White Good Communist and on the other the Black Bad Fascist. For the receptive reader, there is no real choice between the two; from the outset, it is obvious that the clenched fist of communism must smite the evil out of existence at the earliest opportunity. On this level, the play is akin to *Within the Gates* in that it is a morality play demonstrating the optimistic gains of Good against entrenched Evil. Like *Within the Gates*, this play is also expressionistic rather than realistic in its presentation of materials.

The Star Turns Red makes further use of the Great Lockout of 1913 and presents in unmistakable clarity the great leader of that Lockout, Red Jim Larkin. On this level, the play should continue O'Casey's war against the miseries and the evils of poverty by pitting the forces of labor against those of capitalism. The association of communism and labor is not a difficult one to make, and O'Casey—like Shaw—viewed poverty as the gigantic foe, the black Apollyan; the demon that must be killed. In "A Whisper About Bernard Shaw," O'Casey quotes and agrees with Shaw, his "Seer, saint, and sage [who] was usually to be found teaching through a laugh among the community publicans and sinners." Shaw wrote:

> In the guise of plays, I contended that poverty should be neither pitied as an inevitable misfortune, nor tolerated as a just retribution for misconduct; but resolutely stamped out and prevented from recurring as a disease fatal to human society.[47]

O'Casey—like Shaw, a "born communist"—viewed communism as the ultimate weapon against the gigantic foe, poverty, and as the true religion. He makes this abundantly clear in his "Hymn to the Red Star":

> Morning star, hope of the people, shine on us!
> Star of power, may thy rays soon destroy the things that err, things that are foolish, and the power of man to use his brother for profit so as to lay up treasure for himself where moth and rust doth corrupt, and where thieves break through and steal.
> Red Mirror of Wisdom turning the labour in factory, field and workshop into the dignity of a fine song;
> Red Health of the sick, Red Refuge of the afflicted, shine on us all.
> Red Cause of our joy, Red Star extending till thy five rays, covering the world, give a great light to those who still sit in the darkness of poverty's persecution.

Herald of a new life, of true endeavour, of common-sense, of a
    world's peace, of man's ascent, of things to do bettering all
    things done;
The sign of Labour's shield, the symbol on the people's banner;
Red Star, shine on us all![48]

The Star Turns Red, however, does not examine the capitalism versus labor conflict, nor does it go very deeply into any
examination of communism. O'Casey seems content to reveal
and attack the horrors of fascism. While the drama is touted to
be social protest drama, proletarian literature, and a historical
examination of the forces at work in the 1913 fiasco, it is none
of these. While satire is clearly the most effective weapon for
social reform, there is virtually no satiric examination of
motives or powers in this play. O'Casey does pay lip service to
his muse in his parody of bourgeois tastes and standards and
in his treatment of the traitors to labor's cause, but the
effective weapon of laughter is not directed at either poverty
or fascism nor at their causes, despite the fact that these
should be his chief targets if the play is what he says it is.
    Language, gesture, and movement are as highly stylized as
the settings for the various acts. They do help to establish
mood and to reveal character. The action, like the rhetoric, is
frequently strained and artificial enough to seem a parody,
but the parody never quite comes off despite the Christmas
Eve setting. The labor movement (envisioned by O'Casey as
Whitman's *En Masse*) led by Jim Larkin, who sought shorter
working hours and "the right of men to live and die like men,"
is not portrayed effectively. O'Casey's bitterness at the defeat
in March of 1914 is clearly evident in the play written a
quarter of a century after the fact. Larkin assumes heroic
proportions, but his loyal followers include only the idealistic
Jack, the mature Michael, the one-man-gang Brannigan, and
the ineffectual Brown Priest. Larkin is overmatched in his
battle against the combined uniformed forces of the church,
fascism, capitalism, and the traitors within the labor
movement.

Despite those overwhelming odds and the methodical mur-
dering of both Michael and Jack, the setting and the singing of
the "Internationale" cause the drama to end on an optimistic
note. In the final scene, which presumably establishes this air
of optimism, even the most devoted reader's credulity is
impossibly strained by the awkward verse dialogue, by the
mass conversion of Kian and the soldiers to his dead brother's
ideology, and by the clenched fist of the weeping Julia.

As bad as it is, this play includes redeeming graces which
keep it from being altogether trite. Joybell, the self-centered,
uniformed Catholic flag-waver, speaks a kind of Orwellian
parody of the English language and, despite his monk's habit,
is forced by the teasing of Julia toward some rather decisive
action. The calculated teasing action backfires on the sadistic
trio of Julia and the old couple as they ridicule Joybell's
celibacy. Julia's repeated enticing, "How would you like to
cuddle me in a lonely wood with the darkness falling?" "Go
on—hug me! Give me a kiss hot enough to melt the bones in a
girlie's body!" and the taunting of the old people ultimately
make Joybell so mad with passion that he seizes and kisses
Julia "madly till she is breathless and frightened." The harm-
less joke has turned him into an animal, so far as Julia is
concerned. His reply to her taunting is couched to answer any
questions yet remaining in the minds of the laity: "I'll make
you giddy, you pretty little bitch! I'll press you till you break
in two! I'll tear off every stitch you ever had on, so I will!"

This episode, I presume, is responsible for Boas's description of Joybell as half-priest, half-imbecile,[49] a true but
perhaps misleading label. For a brief moment, the comic and
the pathetic elements are in suspension, but when Joybell
punches the old man in the eye and leaves, the social comedy
resumes as the trio bickers and blames each other for what has
happened. The old woman—who begins by defending Julia
as "a fully respectable girl, without a glimmer of guile in
her"—joins her husband two minutes later and orders Julia out
of her home: "Go home quietly to your own place, with your
dressed-up indecency. If you don't I'll leave the mark of my
fingers on your paint-patterned face!"

O'Casey's usually direct attack on the church is here an attack by suggestion and innuendo. Both the Purple Priest and Joybell have affectations of speech: Joybell utters meaning-less syllables and needless repetitions, and he frequently stammers and stutters; his superior, the Purple Priest, uses an inordinate number of sibilants and occasionally lisps.[50] Julia, who will not forego her party for her father, for Jack, nor for the Red Cause, enters in her dance dress and is greeted by the Purple Priest with what is potentially the most obscene line in O'Casey's canon—"I see before me a poor daughter of Eve dressed for a folly that will fondle sin with a busy finger. . . ."[51] As the Priest of Catholicism, Capitalism, and Fascism, he conceals motives as well as deeds behind his platitude,—"To a priest, the first step to heaven is obedience, the second is obedience, and the third step is obedience. Let what is to do be done!" The Lord Mayor, ally of the Purple Priest, affects the lisp of his canonical counterpart, but his lisp is lost entirely in a moment of real emergency. Unlike the Purple Priest, he is not as evil as he is ineffectual. His good deeds are calculated political investments. The tea provided for the poor does more to feed the pomp and vanity of the Lord Mayor himself than it does to eliminate the hunger of those who accept his gift.

Public opinion is here as elsewhere in O'Casey's drama a fearful and fluctuating barometer, ever seeking for stability and self-aggrandizement. The bickering old man who has been decorated by industry wants to maintain the status quo, to depend on the church and the police for protection, and to dress up like Father Christmas and dispense charity to the poor. The Lord Mayor, official representative of the people, revels in the comforts of his luxurious home, affects a more pronounced lisp when things are going his way, and has a devoted wife who can say, on the eve of pitched battle:

Oh, we don't mind the workers organizing; we like them to organize; we encourage them to organize. . . . But only in safe and sensible and secure and Christian and Catholic Unions.[52] [STR, p. 339]

The members of the public here are not unlike the public opinion mongers in *Within the Gates.* They, too, recognize the church and the police as ultimate authorities and would suffer any punishment to maintain the status quo. Julia, accused of immodest dress and of being a "sex-hilarious lassie eager to pillage him [any sensible man] bare of all his holy hesitation," moves the Most Respectable Man to say, for instance, "If the way of a maid with a man can't be controlled, it'll have to be stopped altogether." Public opinion reflects the complacency and the fear, the pomposity and the emptiness of its worshippers. It and its adherents are subject to the same quicksilver realignments, the same tongue clucking, and the same inactivity as their fellow worshippers in *Within the Gates.*

These same attitudes are also apparent in those laborers who wander in and out of the opulence of the Lord Mayor's house, doing nothing but waiting for a miracle to occur, in those who stand meekly aside from their revolutionary tasks when confronted by a priest, and in all who see change as a necessary evil. These readily observable traits led O'Casey to remark in 1919, "Trade Unionism may give the worker a larger dinner plate—which, heaven knows, he badly needs—but it will never give him a broader mind, which he needs more badly still."[53]

The Star Turns Red is not good drama, a fact recognized by O'Casey, who barely mentions it in his many pages of rapture concerning the hope and salvation of man through the auspices of International Communism, and who does not include it in his *Selected Plays.* As suggested earlier, its main flaw as either morality play or social protest drama is its unequivocal concentration on the evils of fascism, evils readily admitted by virtually all English and Russian readers and playgoers in 1940. The juxtaposition of Lenin's portrait with that of a bishop clearly establishes the lines of battle; so does the juxtaposition of the factory smokestacks and the church's cross. O'Casey manipulates these same themes much more effectively in earlier and later drama. The death of the idealist in this play and the use of his corpse as a rallying point for the labor forces emphasizes the necessity of his choosing loyalty to his brotherhood over personal safety, but the use of his body also emphasizes the less palatable doctrine that the end justifies the means. O'Casey's humanistic creed, his demand for life, and his opposition to regimentation in any form are as artificial in this drama as the optimistic note on which the play ends.

The same materials used for this play, the 1913 Lockout and the immediate consequences up to the Easter Rising of 1916, are used in O'Casey's next—and far better—play, *Red Roses for Me*. As Pat M. Esslinger has ably pointed out, the two plays have much in common.[54] The idealism of Jack, his choice, and his ultimate destruction parallel the more effective course followed by Ayamonn, the combination poet-idealist-worker. Both plays end on notes of hope for mankind. *The Star Turns Red* fails; *Red Roses for Me* does not, because the hatreds in the earlier play of brother for brother and of countryman for countryman are complete. O'Casey does not allow for human lethargy, laziness, and other frailties. It fails

> because O'Casey ignores what W. H. Auden presents in "Musee des Beaux Arts," and what O'Casey himself knows so well, the fact that at every nativity at least one camel would be scratching its backside against a tree.[55]

The transitional period (1928-1942) concludes with *Red Roses for Me*, a play utilizing the same combination of expressionism and realism evident in the *Silver Tassie*, the play which marked the beginning of a new era for Sean O'Casey. The numerous similarities in technique and theme make these plays more than arbitrary mechanical markers for this period in the development of O'Casey's satiric arsenal. *The Silver Tassie* pits individual man against the impersonal destructive machine that is war, and records the destruction of life, limb, personality, and identity by that machine. O'Casey's WAR functions as protagonist in at least one act and is omnipresent in the one ominous tone of the overall action; it, like Steinbeck's BANK, is a monster created by but not controlled by men. Whatever its aims, be they materialistic or idealistic, WAR ultimately is a destroyer of life, of individuality, and of hope. New lives must be built in its aftermath, preferably on new foundations, but sometimes on the shaky foundations left partially intact by the destruction of war.

In *Red Roses for Me*, man is pitted against another destructive monster, created but not controlled by him. He can be an unknown victim of the combined forces of capital, church, public opinion, and civil authority—all being components in the system—or he can gain identity and perhaps gain life itself by creating a new force, in this instance, labor. The goals of labor, if they become unclear or distorted, result in a broadening and weakening union with nationalism, religion, and personal aims. The result is a new monster and the ultimate effect can be defeat, such as that which ended the General Strike of 1913-1914 or that portrayed on the battlefield in Act II of *The Silver Tassie*.

Red Roses for Me premiered at Dublin's Olympia Theatre in 1943, O'Casey's first Irish premier since *The Plough and the Stars* in 1926.[56] The time of the play, "A Little Time Ago," recalls the time of the General Strike of 1913-14—a time when its author was very much involved in Larkin's Labor Movement and very much at home in Dublin. The O'Casey of 1913 knew the Dublin slum conditions and the appalling wage scales first hand. He also knew a representative few of the 28,000 people who lived in dwellings condemned as unfit for human habitation by the Commission of Inquiry, and he probably shared the British opinion stated in their recruiting slogan for World War I—"The trenches are safer than the Dublin slums." As is frequently recorded, the immediate aims of Jim Larkin's 1913 strike were thwarted when such Irish leaders as Arthur Griffith, Patrick Pearse, and Tom Clarke used the strike and its aftermath as a vehicle for nationalism, for glory rather than for improved living conditions, for a holy end rather than a material beginning. This, together with the powerful opposition, defeated the strike; then the laborers, after six months of deprivation, returned to work—actually grateful to have jobs under any conditions.[57]

O'Casey nursed this bitter defeat for a quarter of a century before reducing it somehow to a splenetic attack on fascism in *The Star Turns Red*. His bitterness is more effectively masked

and refined in *Red Roses for Me,* which Robert Hogan asserts
is about thirty-seven times better drama than the first Red
play.[58] The central character of O'Casey's second red play is
Ayamonn Breydon, who is in many controlled ways the
idealistic, politically involved, and younger Sean O'Casey. As
David Krause observes, "Ayamonn Breydon is a freely drawn
self portrait" in this most autobiographical of O'Casey's
plays.[59] Mrs. Breydon incorporates the strengths and virtues of
Susan Casside and is one of a series of O'Casey's tributes to his
beloved mother. She is from first to last concerned for the
needs of others: she goes to aid a dying neighbor, she rescues
the young atheist from the crowd, she helps Ayamonn re-
hearse for his role in *Henry VI,* Part III. Further, she is always
wise, always concerned for her son, and ultimately comes to
share his vision of what the shilling could mean for the
workers.

It is fitting that Mrs. Breydon, ideal mother, should have an
ideal son, a proletarian hero incorporating "The sum total of
the virtues of the working class." Breydon's zeal for the arts
(literature, painting, and theatre) and his total commitment to
the cause of the strikers led Robert Hogan to describe him as
"a combination of Red Jim Larkin, Jesus Christ, and the
president of the local Browning Society."[60] Taken all together,
it seems a heavy burden for a 22-year-old Dublin Protestant to
carry, but O'Casey demands more. Preceded by an impressive parade of poets and singers in O'Casey's earlier plays,
Ayamonn Breydon is far in advance of Donal Davoren
(*Shadow of a Gunman*) who sought refuge and separation
from the responsibilities of life. Davoren is O'Casey's embryonic poet, who recognizes, too late for Minnie Powell, that he
is a coward, that he is not capable of action, and that he is a
poltroon. The dreamer in *Within the Gates* is another fine
talker and he is always willing to talk, talk, talk, but little else.

Ayamonn Breydon, on the other hand, demonstrates the
essential truth of Seumas Shields's contention (*Shadow of a
Gunman*) that a poet's greatness is in his "power to put
passion into the common people." The poet's vision and
commitment are such that he must act and lead others to
act. Ayamonn's gifts are such that his fellow strikers choose

him as spokesman, as leader of their strike. O'Casey's mature
poet dons Shakespearean costume over his working clothes;
he knows and demonstrates the power as well as the beauty of
the word; he makes his poetic powers an integral part of his
answer to the demands of life. As idealist and poet, he views
Shakespeare as "part of the kingdom of heaven in the nature
of everyman," and vows, "Before I'm done, I'll have him
drinking in th' pubs with them."[61]

Ayamonn's ability to fuse art *and* life, to accept the ideal
and the real, and to recognize the beautiful *and* the ugly make
him O'Casey's mature poet. As such, he is able—at the same
time—to love and to hate Kathleen ni Houlihan, to revel in the
glories of Shakespeare and to move the "Down-and -Outs" to
sing and dance, to confront the mob which attacks Mullcanny
and to lead the strikers against the armed civil authorities. In
short, he uses his "power to put passion into the common
people." He is (as was Walt Whitman's ideal poet) a whole
man. His perception is quicker and deeper than that of
ordinary men, and he is more vitally and meaningfully
involved in life than they are.

I am convinced that this is an accurate reading of Ayamonn's role. It is, however, a role that he is thrust into in the
midst of *Red Roses for Me*. When the curtains part for the
beginning of the play, Ayamonn falls far short of being the
ideal proletarian hero, despite his attire: the Shakespearean
costume complete with "a big hump between his shoulders,"
his "heavy black, working corduroy trousers" and his heavy
hobnailed boots. When someone knocks at the door, Ayamonn assumes that a neighbor has come to borrow. His first
line in this—his play—is "Damn her for a troublesome fool!"
[*RRFM*, p. 131]. As the act continues so do his irritation and
his anger. He dismisses the concerns of Brennan as those of
"an old fool," is critical of the actor playing the role of Henry
VI, also an "old fool," and quarrels with his mother. However
Christlike he becomes by Act IV, he is less than a prophet in
his declaration, "there'll be no strike," and he is less than a
prophet in his response to Mrs. Breydon's warning that
Mullcanny will "meet with a mishap, some day, if he doesn't
keep his mouth shut." Ayamonn's one word response is,

"Nonsense." His greeting as Brennan arrives is: "Now what th' hell do you want?" His positive traits include his stated concern for his mother's health, his enthusiasm for the arts, especially his desire to paint, and his strong attraction to Sheila—though even that is less important than hearing the singer's rendition of his song.

O'Casey was 33 years old when the 1913 strike began, and some critics of *Red Roses* would clearly be more comfortable if Ayamonn were 33 instead of only 22. Most scholars are so intent on the heavy responsibility carried by Ayamonn, the martyred strike leader, that they choose to ignore the less graceful and less acceptable qualities emphasized by O'Casey in the first and in much of the second act of this play. Ayamonn responds to the request of his fellow workers, effects the transformation in the Liffey scene, and in the process, he too is transformed.

A close reading of his lines will demonstrate that they, too, improve. He becomes less pretentious, less presumptuous and more mature. In the first act, it is not dramatically convincing for the intense young man to say to Sheila, "Oh, Sheila, our time is not yet come to be serious in the way of our elders. Soon enough to browse with wisdom when Time's grey finger puts a warning speck on the crimson rose of youth. Let no damned frosty prayer chill the sunny sighs that dread the joy of love." In short, when Ayamonn becomes a man of action, he becomes a mature poet, a leader of men in crisis, and he has better lines. Ayamonn's lines in Act IV are few and he is on stage only briefly. To Rector Clinton, he says, "I come but to go. You got the cross of daffodils?" To Inspector Finglas, he defines the symbolic shilling: "A shilling's little to you, and less to many; to us it is our schechinah, showing us God's light is near; showing us the way in which our feet must go; a sun-ray on our face; the first step taken in the march of a thousand miles." To the men and women who call for him he replies, "I go with you!" To his mother and to the Rector, he says, "For the present—goodbye!" In the last bit of stage business, the last time the audience sees the living Ayamonn, he pauses, "turning to give a last look at the inspector." These are the only lines spoken by Ayamonn in the final act [*RRFM*, pp. 210-13.]

Ayamonn is a fictive voice, a persona, of Sean O'Casey, just as Johnnie Casside is a fictive voice in the autobiographies. By the time he has emerged as mature poet and leader of men and women, Mrs. Breydon and Rector Clinton have assumed the task of speaking the truths that Ayamonn dies for. They address them to Inspector Finglas, Dowzard, Foster, and Samuel. Their words and those of the chorus frame the completed portrait of Ayamonn Breydon.

In O'Casey's plays, miracles are wrought by action. The transformation of Ayamonn is a case in point. Satiric answers to the miracles of Lourdes and the weeping plaster saints, as well as satiric commands to those who sit around, bewail their plight, and wait for miracles to happen, are reduced to their essence in *Red Roses for Me,* as they are later in *Cock-a-Doodle Dandy. Red Roses* contains two true miracles—both of which answer prayers of the faithful. The first is the transformation of the drab, faded, and yellowed Virgin, who reflects the wear and tear of slum living. She becomes a vision "Fair as th' first grand tinge of th' dawn, . . . an' bright as th' star of the evenin' " [*RRFM,* p. 162] The Virgin's return is complete with mystical visions by two eyewitnesses, by Ursula—the ill child whose sickness cannot be removed by a new coat of paint—and by a gentleman citizen. Ursula is happy, but uncured; the adoring crowd is amazed and momentarily transported. Their sincere and joyful hymn of prayer is directed to the Virgin, resplendent in her new clothes:

> Oh, Queen of Eblana's poor children
> Bear swiftly our woe away,
> An' give us a chance to live lightly
> An hour of our life's dark day! [*RRFM,* p. 184]

Their prayer is answered by the second miracle. The gloomy scene is the "bleak, black, an' bitther city. . . . Like a batthered, tatthered whore, bullied by too long a life." Those who inhabit the "graveyard where th' dead are all above th' ground" are content to dream of the good old days gone by and to prophesy the winning horses in the next race. Their prophesies have much in common with Ayamonn's prophecy in the first act. Because of the habitual resignation and inaction of Dubliners, the three gates of their city are "castles of poverty, penance, an' pain." Ayamonn tells the "Down-and-Outs" of their city's true nature:

> She's what our hands have made her. We pray too much and work too little. Meanness, spite, and common pattherns are woven thick through all her glory; but her glory's there for open eyes to see. [*RRFM*, p. 196]

The power of the poet's word—"No-one knows what a word may bring forth"—and the light of the sun transform the scene into a vibrant and joyful exemplum of song and dance and hope. The miracle is such that the people are made radiant and are moved to praise their city of splendor in song. Ayamonn joins Finnoola in a symbolic dance of life, joy, and fulfillment. The people are moved to oaths of allegiance and oaths to take the necessary action to remove the bonds of poverty and to rebuild a perfect city. But when Ayamonn departs to lead the active strikers, his word and its power also depart: then, the colors and lights fade, the songs cease, and the singers resume their interrupted roles as dark figures in a dark city.

In both of these miracles, O'Casey explicitly contends that man's plight can be improved by man himself, that direct involvement and direct action are necessary to life in the here-and-now, that miracles—when they do occur—are the results of man's efforts and not of his complacent waiting. Whatever the Virgin meant to the poor and whatever visions accompanied her kidnapping and her miraculous return, her new splendor was calculated, planned, and paid for by Brennan o' th' Moor, a man. The miracle at the bridge on the River Liffey resulted directly from the efforts of men: the lusty song of Brennan o' th' Moor and the practical artistry of Ayamonn were directly responsible for the transformation of the "Down-and-Outs" into singing, dancing humans vowing immediate and positive action.

The third miracle, that of transforming that vision into reality, does not come to pass because the people of Dublin, O'Casey's chorus in this play, awake *from* their dream instead of awaking *to* their dream. They see the sable shawl but only half remember the red roses. They resume complacent waiting rather than using Ayamonn's Sword of Light. The new world in the womb of Finnoola is aborted as the miracle becomes a strange curiosity rather than a sought-after reality. The Down-and-Outs fail to see, as the Rector does see in the final act, that "From the clash of life new life is born." They are also unable to recognize with Mrs. Breydon that "often new life dies in the clash too."

Ayamonn's Sword of Light is the evocative power of language, the power of the word to transform fear, lethargy, and complacency into courage, energy, and action. It is not so restricted as the Fenian Sword of Light hailed by Roory O'Balacaun: patriot, zealot, and nationalist.[62] O'Casey satirizes Roory's unquestioning Catholic faith and his instant nationalistic zeal throughout the play, though no more savagely than he does the Protestant zeal of Brennan or the dedicated bigotry of Samuel, Dowzard, and Foster. Brennan's "Abuse is no equivalent for lugic—so I say . . . God save th' King, an' tae hull with th' Pope!" is countered by Roory's "You damned bigot—to hell with th' King, an' God save th' Pope!" [*RRFM*, p. 167]. Both are offset and made to seem better causes by the cowardly hypocrisy of Samuel, Dowzard, and Foster, who seek the sanctuary of the church, yet object to the daffodils, the Celtic Cross, and the Easter preparations as popery. The satire implicit in the portraits of these zealots is similar to that in the caricatures of the young idealists, the ardent communists, the uniform wearers, and the other talkers in all of O'Casey's earlier plays.

In the satiric portrait gallery that O'Casey's plays provide, his stage-nationalist (Roory O'Balacaun) and his stage-atheist (Mullcanny) have become familiar figures—usually sympathetic, but always having straight-line tunnel vision and very funny lines. By the time of *Red Roses for Me*, the gallery includes Samuel and Dowzard and Foster, whose bigotry and smoky ignorance are malignant. These characters are cowardly, support the scabs, and hide from danger. In them and in the Down-and-Outs who resume their dying after the miracle by the River Liffey are epitomized the greed, complacency, and irresponsibility that delay Ayamonn's ideal from becoming reality.

Also included on the smoky side of the gallery is Inspector Finglas, Dublin's civil authority who enforces existing laws and does nothing to encourage or raise the expectations of the people. Finglas, a Protestant church warden, pompously misquotes scripture to justify the ways of man with man and to demonstrate that God is on his team. His mounted policemen restore order "be poundin' th' riothers undher their feet," and "don't wait to ask the way you worship when they raise their arms to strike." They also shoot Ayamonn Breydon. In his various distortions, Finglas is ultimately recognized by Sheila, whom he courts, as a "dusky-minded killer of more worthy men." His "dusky" mind is blood relative to the "smoky ignorance" of Dowzard and Foster, and all three help to destroy the possibility of the single shilling's becoming either a reality or a meaningful symbol of a new world waiting to be born.

From the outset Sheila Moorneen urges Ayamonn to give up his protest, to settle down in a lucrative safe job, and help to preserve the status quo. She resents his fidelity to his role as poet and she sees his effort to paint, his devotion to Shakespeare, and his consorting with potentially dangerous people as foolish things. Sheila is necessarily forsaken by her idealist, who must act. As he tells her in Act II, "Go to hell, girl, I have a soul to save as well as you." The religious differences of the Catholic Sheila and the Protestant Ayamonn are unimportant as such, though their parents and the larger part of Ireland do object. Their religious differences do help to accent the bickering and the inane theological arguments. O'Casey, armed with his sardonic sense of humor, provides the perspective. The bickering continues as the atheist is rescued from those workers he has offended by proclaiming that the "Story of Adam an' Eve was all a cod" [RRFM, p. 165]. It continues as the impetuous men charge the strikers. It continues, and—as presented by O'Casey—is inconsequential and somewhere beside the point. The ardent spokesmen who cower somewhere away from the action present in comic relief O'Casey's contention that theological disputes are unlikely to resolve the problems of life in the world as it is.

One of the disputants, Brennan o' the Moor, is 76 years old, a survivor in the world as it is. He is a straight-talking man of action. Like Bessie Burgess (*The Plough and the Stars*), he is from Ulster and he is a compassionate Protestant singer. He spares us another rendition of "Rule, Brittania," but does sing the title song for *Red Roses for Me*. Brennan helps those in need, sometimes at the expense of those who have plenty. His Robin Hood ancestry and his miracle with the Virgin anticipate much that we see in *Cock-a-Doodle Dandy*, and he is a forerunner of Codger Sleehaun *(Bishop's Bonfire)*. The character type established by Brennan o' the Moor is increasingly important. He helps people because they need help; he does not insist that they convert to Protestantism before he helps them; he is wise and good and able to act.

Brennan, for all of his good deeds and practical wisdom, is also delightfully funny. He spends more time on his knees hiding from danger than he does praying. His arguments are not interrupted as he hides from stones and strikebreakers. He is a man of means concerned always for the safety of the bank where his money is kept.[63] For him, Ayamonn's shilling is "the root of all evil."

Red Roses for Me is a play about a poet's efforts to bring perception to the people and his attempts to move them in meaningful action. Each of the four acts of this Easter play ends in an epiphany resulting from those attempts. At the curtain ending Act I, Ayamonn is with Roory O'Balacaun, a zealous Irish Nationalist, an Irish Catholic who sees the Sword o' Light in Republican banners and the Catholic faith. His dark view is limited, but his words and his song have deeper meaning for Ayamonn, who clasps his hand and joins him in singing:

> When out to th' place where th' battle is bravest,
> Where th' noblest an' meanest fight fierce in th' fray,

Republican banners shall mock at th' foeman,
An' Fenians shall turn a dark night into day!

Ending Act II, the softly singing men and women, still awed
by the miraculous transformation of their Virgin, offer religious faith as a pat answer, while Sheila, rebuffed by Ayamonn, weeps in the background. The faith and the tears,
moving as they are, remain as inadequate as Fenianism alone
to build a new Ireland. The song of promise echoed in the
concluding lines of Act III recalls the intensity of the miracle
at the bridge and holds some promise for Ireland, but the
promise, like the new world in Finnoola's womb, is stillborn
because the people return to their former stances and do not
act.

The final scene ends on a note of prophecy and hope and
thereby keeps the play from being a tragedy. The dead
Ayamonn lies in the church on Easter Eve. Sheila's crimson
roses are on his breast, and Brennan sings the prophetic "Red
Roses for Me," indicating that though Ireland still wears the
black shawl, she also continues to hold the red roses in her slim
hand. Ayamonn's committed action, though economically
ineffective, has altered the thinking of both his mother and
Sheila. Despite the wanton suffering of the Ireland represented by Eeada, Dympna, Finnoola, and those attacked by
the troopers of Finglas, Brennan o' th' Moor still sings and
Kathleen, bleak as she is, is not without hope.

These four significant scenes all end in song. They offer in
turn nationalism, religious faith, enthusiastic vows, and idealistic dedication. Recalling Jannice's quest for the answer in
Within the Gates, this play demonstrates that no single answer
is sufficient in itself, and that no combination of answers,
without direct human action, can be effective. It is the role,
then, of O'Casey's mature poet to initiate such action, to be
where the action is, and to begin the journey toward a new
world. In Ayamonn's message to the Rector as delivered by
Finnoola, "He said this day's but a day's work done, an' it'll be
begun again tomorrow."

O'Casey's sardonic sense of humor, which he describes as
the only thing "we Irish have in full measure,"[64] underlies

every phrase of *Red Roses for Me*. The play is an album of satiric portraits. Sheila denies responsibility for immediate pleasures but ultimately shares Ayamonn's vision; the Down-and-Outs can be manipulated, but return to slothful lethargy when the strong poet leaves; the one-answer hawkers, such as the Irish Roory O'Balacaun and Freethinker Mullcanny, despite the inadequacy of their answers, are sympathetically portrayed. Dowzard and Foster are prejudiced fools whose cowardice and audacity render them humorous rather than terrifying. The uniform-conscious, ritual-conscious Samuel is close kinsman to Uncle Peter and the prancing, brightly uniformed braggart soldiers of *The Plough and the Stars*. The pomposity of Inspector Finglas, together with his essential innocence, prevent his being an essentially evil man, but, like the Bishop in *Within the Gates*, he is an instrument of evil.

O'Casey's sardonic humor extends to the action itself: Ayamonn's aim is far greater than the finite goals of Red Jim Larkin in the debacle of the General Strike in 1913. The forces which helped to destroy that historic strike are integral to Ayamonn's vision of a transformed Ireland. Nationalism, religion, lethargy, and fear of public opinion are pilloried in this prophetic play, whose cast and setting are topical, whose protagonist is largely autobiographical, but whose impact is much further reaching. Written during the blitz of London,[65] *Red Roses for Me* is O'Casey's attempt to give a picture of the present peopled by those who cause it to be what it is. An Ireland transformed by O'Casey's poet would be an Ireland (or a world) of decisive people committed to action as well as to vows, an Ireland no longer dominated by the combined forces of Priests, Politicians, and Poltroons. O'Casey viewed Ireland as untransformed as late as *The Bishop's Bonfire* and *Behind the Green Curtains*, but the seeds for transformation are planted by Ayamonn Breydon, a poet whose power and responsibility closely parallel those of Christ, as clearly revealed in the basic action and the basic symbolism of *Red Roses for Me*.

In the plays of this transitional period (from *The Silver Tassie* through *Red Roses for Me*), O'Casey looks back to characters, techniques, and themes examined and—in some cases—perfected in his Irish plays. He explores the advantages of expressionism and fantasy, becomes increasingly symbolic, and continues to assert his dismay with those who proclaim "realism" as the way, the truth, and the light. He increases the velocity and the effect of his attack on those responsible for priest-ridden Ireland's plight as he presents a gallery of priests leading toward the volatile active evil force of Father Domineer in *Cock-a-Doodle Dandy*. Her Protestants are hardly saints. They too are fomenters as well as victims of hypocrisy and fear. In short, the Protestant Sean O'Casey wrote of the world and the experiences that he knew. Never absent from his plays are the Catholic-Protestant hassles, which he reduces to some proper perspective. Never absent, then, are the causes and consequences of the divided nation wrought by the creation of the Terrible Beauty, the Irish Free State. Clearly, O'Casey did not curry favor nor seek popularity by adopting these stances. Clearly, those he speared in his satiric thrusts knew they had been speared. Increasingly, O'Casey gives way to reckless abandon and, as we see in the last plays, he has a roaring, laughing good time in the process. Those who lament his loss of Fluther Good and Uncle Peter need only re-read *The Plough and the Stars*. They are still there. The people in O'Casey's later plays are other people, though their foibles and bad habits and excesses remain human. Further, their institutions—whether church or state or business—remain repressive. So do their traditions and conventions. Consequently, O'Casey's targets—despite his massive efforts—remain intact if a bit scarred. He continues and increases the intensity of his attack. His sensitive characters—be they like Jannice or Ayamonn—continue their quests.

4

Finale and Encore

O'Casey's final period lasts from the composition of *Oak Leaves and Lavender* in the early 1940s until his death in September of 1964. During this period, he continued to experiment with expressionism, fantasy, and morality plays. He continued, also, to harangue his enemies and to put didactic, informative speeches in the mouths of his favorites. His basic themes—that the old must give way to the new, that habitual servitude must give way to joyful abandon, that lethargy must give way to action—are further developed and modified in plays that tend to focus on Ireland as microcosm. It is essentially true that O'Casey sacrificed character to theme in this period, but O'Casey would not admit the sacrifice as a weakness: for him, repetition of a legitimate theme is but a way of instruction; for him, as his prefaces and his essays clearly show, the plays themselves are best viewed as moralities and their worlds as microcosms. Virtually every play from *The Silver 'Tassie* on is, in many ways, a morality play; consequently, his specific attacks on specific individuals and situations in Ireland are at the same time topical and universal.

A legitimate argument might be made for discussing *Oak Leaves and Lavender* in conjunction with *The Star Turns Red:* both are hate-filled and splenetic attacks, both depict the essential strength and wisdom of the communist doctrine, and both trace a steady progression from despair to hope and awareness of inevitable victory. *Oak Leaves* is better drama than *The Star Turns Red*, but not as effective as *Purple Dust*, which portrays the old house that is the microcosm of England in steady disintegration and decay, augmented by the foolishness and stupidity of Stoke and Poges—the living embodiments of a graveyard. The contrast between *Purple Dust* and *Oak Leaves and Lavender* is an informative one. In the earlier play, the house was a monument to the past at whose shrine the owners and perpetuators worshipped. O'Casey's flood, not unlike Noah's, swept away the idols and the idolators, leaving the world for the people of the present who had the good sense to escape to higher ground. In the later play, the oak gives way to steel and the shades give way to the living; then, victory is possible.

The final period includes three first-rate plays (*Cock-a-Doodle Dandy, The Bishop's Bonfire,* and *The Drums of Father Ned*). All include elements of the marvelous; all attack censorship and complacency as ways of death; all suggest an honestly pagan rebirth as an antidote to the destructive poison fostered by the unblessed union of wealth and church—as that union exists in O'Casey's microcosm.

The play which begins the final period, *Oak Leaves and Lavender,* is perhaps the "most bloodthirsty play ever written by a congenital pacifist."[1] O'Casey's congenital pacifism was considerably augmented by a decisive pragmatic awareness. As described in *The Plough and the Stars* and elsewhere, the Easter Rebellion was doomed, however heroic; in *The Silver Tassie,* the war was not Ireland's war and was not made by the young men who were sacrificed on its altar. In both, as well as in *The Shadow of a Gunman* and *Juno and the Paycock,* war is a destructive external force that ravages the lives of the innocent and destroys some of the brightness of the future. In all, he condemns war. In *Red Roses for Me,* on the other hand, the congenital pacifist presents a war foredoomed, but a prophecy of hope and a call to arms are implicit in the action of the play. It is a war, as portrayed by O'Casey, that must be won if men are to live as they ought. Similarly, the war in *Oak Leaves and Lavender* must be won to preserve mankind and to preserve any hope of progress in the right direction: for O'Casey, the right direction is toward ethical humanism.

Set during the Battle of Britain, the play recalls the terrifying experiences of O'Casey and his family as they sought refuge from German bombs. As is abundantly clear in the text, it is mankind—not the British system—that must be saved. The play is a call to arms, not unlike the call to arms satirized so effectively in *The Plough and the Stars*. The English must be aided by the Russians and both must be supplied with American materials of war if the mad game is to be won; likewise, all social distinctions, hereditary obligations, and traditional obediences—insofar as they are inadequate—must give way to the more significant struggle.

The home team that must win the big game consists largely of loveable incompetents and rejects, not greatly unlike the early day New York Mets. In *Sunset and Evening Star*, O'Casey views the English girding for war as Prufrock "fitting on a steel helmet, reconciling himself to a sharp and stinging death in the midst of what he called his duty." In the war, as in *Oak Leaves and Lavender*, "The Englishman, so clever in his foolishness, was fighting for his life, and the Irishman, so foolish in his cleverness, was fighting with him."[2] As pictured by O'Casey, Churchill stood by the wireless, as Prufrock murmured, "Get us the tools, sir, and we'll do the job." The British "were measuring out life now, not with coffee spoons, but with rifle, tommygun, sling, splint, and bandage. A bitter change, but not all evil." O'Casey saw traditional worship "demolished in the fire and detonation of the struggle." He saw all political divisions disappear as war demanded a united effort:

> All classes strained themselves into activity, ready to fight in the streets, in the fields, on the hills, against the Nazi. Invasion! They meant it, too, nearly killing themselves with the preparation. . . . Sprained arms and ankles, pulled muscles, and black eyes sprouted out everywhere. In every corner, one heard the crack crack of rifles going and the explosions of hand-grenades, till it seemed that England was blowing herself to pieces. Busy people were getting ready for their own burial.[3]

Oak Leaves and Lavender, like *Purple Dust*, presents the old ghost-inhabited mansion as a microcosm of England. England, during the emergency of war, however, is able to

change as she must in order to survive. The old house in its
process of physical change from a mansion to a rest home to a
military headquarters to an industrial site creating tanks and
munitions, reflects the changes necessarily undergone by
England. Here, as in *Purple Dust*, the characters have the task
of getting the old house in order; despite the immediate
emergency and the high patriotic feelings, O'Casey presents
the bungling inefficiency of the bourgeoisie at war just as he
had earlier presented the bungling inefficiency of the bourgeoisie at peace, at play, and at work. Mary, we are told,
while "putting a blackout up in th' dark" stepped "from th'
window-sill on to a chair that wasn't there," and Tom is
"Another fool! Not able to drive a nail into wood without
shoving his hand through a window and cutting a vein open!"
Another fool, while "cloakin' a window, top of a chair, top of
another, top of a table, 'as pitched down, lookin' like 'ell's
broken back, or somethin'!" All of these, and other casualties,
create chaos instead of order as they almost turn the house
into a hospital for bungling incompetents. Feelim correctly
observes, "The foe'll do less injury to us than we're doin' to
ourselves!"[4] O'Casey demonstrates herein that fools at war
remain fools, for war itself performs no miracles in the
character of men—not even when it is a holy war in which
"Christ, Mahomet, and Budda are one."

Yeats wrote to O'Casey during *The Silver Tassie* affair: " . . .
the whole history of the world must be reduced to wallpaper
in front of which the characters must pose and speak."[5] Yeats
was wrong in his condemnation of *The Silver Tassie;* had
Yeats lived another decade, however, he could have and
probably would have levied the same charges against this
later play, which is ironically subtitled *A Warld on Wallpaper.*
Here O'Casey does treat a war that he is very much involved
in, one that threatens to snuff out his life on any given day. He
is unable to gain the necessary artistic distance because he is so
impressed by Prufrock's adaptation and by the essential
heroism of the whole English nation. Without that distance,
artistic control is impossible, as this play amply demonstrates.
The play fails because O'Casey was too much involved, had

too much firsthand and incidental information, and he—like his Home Guardsmen—is unable to choose a target. Since he cannot gain aesthetic distance from the microcosmic society of the play, he is unable to perform as critic and satirist, as he did so well in *Purple Dust*.

He does set up the now familiar straw men as spokesmen for pacifism and fascism, as perpetuators of the Ireland versus England feud, as parrots for the Protestant versus Catholic arguments, and as performing clowns in the town versus farm fuss. As easily as the straw men are set up, they are destroyed; the incessant governmental forms and reports, together with the destructive incompetents in their besieged world, emphasize the meaninglessness of old customs and hallowed traditions in the face of new and immediate dangers. They, like the ghosts of the past, are impotent in the presence of the new dangers wrought by modern technology.

Oak Leaves and Lavender is dedicated to "LITTLE JOHNNY GRAYBURN who, in his sailor suit, played football with me on a Chalfont lawn and afterwards gallantly fell in the Battle of Arnhem." Johnny's death, unlike the senseless mutilations depicted in *The Silver Tassie*, is heroic, gallant, and meaningful. In the text of this play, death is portrayed as inevitable, but somehow beautiful and meaningful when young people give their lives for a cause or for love. O'Casey's two spokesmen are Feelim, a fellow Irishman in self-exile, and Drishogue, a fellow communist dedicated to living for the moment and to dying for the brotherhood of man. This tract against fascism only incidentally sings the praises of humanity and communism; the true focus is on the war effort itself, and O'Casey's redundant praise of that effort moved Robert Hogan to read the play as "almost an ethical tract on why one should fight."[6]

O'Casey's expressionistic techniques are mechanically implemented in this play and are never as dramatically effective as they are in *The Silver Tassie*. The devices of expressionism are used early to create a mood of impending disaster. The wraithlike dancers of the minuet, the lavender seller's song, and the odor of lavender are associated with death and with a dead past. They are made integral to the play by the frequent and fearful references to the legends and superstitions associated with them. The repeated image of the swastika, the wireless, the trumpeting of "Deutschland über Alles," and the haunting repetition of "Germany calling, Germany calling" further develop the mood of impending doom and the awareness of everpresent death. So also do the clock with its purple dial, the pervading odor of lavender, and the purple light on the wireless.

The mood changes abruptly in Act III when the swastika, the trumpets, and the ever-increasing tempo of "The Ride of the Valkyries" give way to the final screen image of

> The Union Jack and the Soviet Flag crossed, and fluttering, together, while a voice speaks from the cabinet," We wage a desperate war till death seizes the evil thing born from Germany's belly, and trained to destroy the world! British people, the Red Army's with us now! To work! Tanks for us and for them; planes for them and for us; guns for us and for them! To arms! To work!

The call to arms and the singing response announce hope and prophesy the ultimate victory of the combined forces against Hitler's fascists. The impotent ghosts of the past prepare to leave the efficient industry of the newly vitalized house. The war effort will succeed due largely to the adaptability of the old house (England) as it is transformed from a museum for dead things to an industrial showplace. The symbolic change is gradual and, for the most part, the changes wrought by the workers are superficial and temporary—the implicit suggestion being that the ghosts of the past will return when the emergency of the present is past.

In this propaganda tract, O'Casey again sets up straw men to spout cliches, slogans, and idiocies. They, without exception, represent those factions and segments of mankind that have all the answers. They are the one-answer hawkers who radiate deficient vision and deficient good sense. The conscientious objector, Pobjoy—despite O'Casey's own strongly pacifistic feelings—is portrayed as a coward and a fool whose half-baked ideas are neither convincing nor acceptable. The

fascist spokesman is Mrs. Deeda Tutting, obviously the fictive
descendent of Mrs. Creda Stern.[7] As stern in her creed as her
improbably named prototype, Deeda Tutting "has something
important, very important, to say," has lost one husband to the
Russian Ogpu, and insults her listeners with her loudly inartic-
ulate prose. Further, Deeda is O'Casey's satiric view of the
tourist who knows all there is to know about Russia because
she's been there. In her eyewitness account, she describes a
"chaos of incompetence, a mass of sullen terror, a swamp of
ignorance" behind the "boasting facade of Soviet achieve-
ment." She, like the conscientious objector, is a fool, despite
her educational tour, her personal loss, and her "Em Ay."
Deeda is a fool because she, like Creda, knows that "Only
what I say, only in what I believe, is the truth."[8]

The gallery also includes Mr. Constant, who would escape
with his money and his wife to America; a spokesman who has
done little for the defense effort except to demand bomb
shelters for others like himself; Sillery and Dillery—officious
special constables who threaten, demand, and limp, but are
overawed by Dame Hatherleigh or anyone else who has real
authority; and Abraham Penrhyn—a real pacifist who never
killed a rabbit, but performs impossible deeds of valor. His
deeds are somewhat marred by his threats to drink, his
drunkenness, and his rejection of his daughter, but the contrast between him and Pobjoy is an edifying one. Basically
Pobjoy is a talker and Abraham Penrhyn is a doer.

War actively invades the premises when Abraham carries
an unexploded bomb in, when Dame Hatherleigh receives the
telegram announcing her husband's death, and when the call
for arms is answered by the image of the tank. War remains,
here as in *The Silver Tassie*, the same impersonal, destructive
machine. Its victims are the present and future generations.
Consequently, the old must make way for the new, and the
dead must make way for the living. Dame Hatherleigh
symbolically joins the earlier occupants in her quest to find
her dead husband. In the epilogue, she replaces the young Son
of Time; his knowledge of vitality and death and his memory
of things past establish the proper perspective for the new

tenants of the old house. Dame Hatherleigh has not the earnest
and warm vigor of youth, but she has accepted the necessity
for change, for adaptation, and she does recognize the only
alternative as total destruction. The epilogue, with Dame
Hatherleigh as spokesman, answers Feelim's final exclamation:
"Which is worse—th' burden of th' dead who are with us now;
or that of the living still to come!" She knows that "our end
makes but a beginning for others," that "only the rottenness
and ruin must die." She notes, as the insistent young lovers
have testified earlier, that, despite war, death, and destruction,
life goes on and will continue to go on.

The flaws in *Oak Leaves and Lavender* are numerous, most
of them stemming from O'Casey's inability to separate himself from his "Warld on Wallpaper." He employs the same
tricks of rhetoric in his call to arms that he satirizes in *The
Plough and the Stars;* he tends to overstate the moral implicit
in the necessity to adapt; and he exults overmuch in the
inadequacy of family heritage, organized religion, and national distinctions to cope with the demands of war. O'Casey's
young lovers, not unlike young lovers anywhere in similar
circumstances, seize the moment—despite the protests of
parents and elders. The child in Monica's womb is as relevant
as the prophecy of victory: life does and will go on. It would
go on just as well, however, if she and Drishogue had not been
secretly married for a month and just as well if Edgar's
talisman had not survived the fire that consumed him and his
fun-loving Jennie. The secret civil marriage satirizes the
Catholic father's unwillingness to accept the validity of any
but a church wedding; the ironic survival of the talisman
points up the inadequacy of religious tokens: both are redundant in that neither adds significantly to the plot, theme, or
action of the play.

It is significant that the overwhelming presence of the past
is not rejected by O'Casey's characters; rather, they stand in
awe of it despite the urgency of their own immediate lives.
The embodiments of the past, complete with rustling skirts
and the odor of lavender, leave of their own accord, presumably to be embraced when they return after the war is

won. The prophecy and hope of the future are embodied in Monica's unborn child—just as they are embodied in Mary Boyle's unborn child in *Juno and the Paycock*. In many ways, *Oak Leaves and Lavender* concerns time and seasons: as Edgar informs his eager Jennie when she offers all the pleasures prescribed in *The Rubaiyat*, "There's a time for everything." Jennie's provocative songs, her advice that her "girdle's easy undone," and her contention that love "is the very breath of time and space" augment the ecclesiastical note that places her apparent abandon in proper perspective.

The play is hardly a call for hedonistic abandon, Fallon and his cohorts to the contrary. Nor is its focus on political and idealistic discussions, despite Hogan's suggestion that "Had O'Casey trimmed down some of the political and idealistic discussions and concentrated more on the love story, the play might have been better."[9]   The play is a call to arms, demonstrating the unlikely prospect of Prufrock girding for battle and the predictable phenomenon that fools remain fools whether England is at war or peace. Unlike Prufrock, O'Casey does not go gently into the dark night of war. He goes screaming and protesting—even when the war is a holy one that emphasizes the inadequacies of political systems, organized religions, and family tradition.

O'Casey's next—and far better—play is *Cock-a-Doodle Dandy*. Like virtually all of O'Casey's later works, it is a morality play: its world is a microcosmic Ireland and its people are established stock characters for all who know O'Casey's earlier work. The drama itself, as O'Casey insists drama must be, is a religious experience. Its satire is a weapon directed against the knavish hypocrisy and the malignant sickness that lie at the heart of his modern society. In *Cock- a-Doodle Dandy*, as in *The Bishop's Bonfire* and *The Drums of Father Ned*, the malignant sickness is nourished by Ireland's priest-ridden plight. O'Casey's antidote combines a symbolic slaying of the old powers and an honestly pagan birth of the new accomplished through the efficacy of magic: magic associated with song, dance, love, and joy. The malignancy, due to the potent combine of religion and riches and rank, can be cured by honest youthful re-evaluation, exuberance, and courage.

Symptoms of society's illness are portrayed in the hypocritical antimaterialism of Marthraun, the puritanical puddling of Shanaar, the destructive power of Father Domineer, and the general apathy of the "Down-and-Outs," who wait for a miracle to be delivered unto them.

The villains, here as in O'Casey's earlier morality plays, are stock villains labelled with name, uniform, and action. Shanaar is a religious quack, and as David Krause records in *Sean O'Casey: The Man and His Work*, Shanaar "means Old Man in Gaelic *(Shan Ahr)*: but there is a biblical reference to Shinar, the land of confused languages where the Tower of Babel was built [Gen. 11:2, 9], which is a particularly appropriate allusion for Shanaar's confusion of superstitious nostrums, medieval exempla, and bog-Latin." His pretentious language is approached by that of Michael Marthraun, who is concerned with Mahan's not being "versed in th' endurin' promulgacity of th' gospels," as well as by the pomposity of Father Domineer's commands. Domineer, as his name clearly shows, must be the dominating force, and when his authority is defied, his rage and his violence destroy human life, as he demonstrates by killing Mahan's lorry driver when he refuses to leave his lover. One-Eyed Larry, in addition to being half-blinded, is virtually half-witted. He courts approval by lying and protects himself by cowering behind Father Domineer, whose parish, Nyadnanave, is truly a Nest of Knaves, however saintly they profess themselves to be.

Sailor Mahan, despite his alliance with the forces of evil—those forces intent on the destruction of joy and life—has some vestiges of goodness. He sings of a "Long time ago when men was men/An' ships not ships that sailed just to an' fro-o-o." He notes that "there's nothin' evil in a pretty face, or in a pair of lurin' legs," he perceives that Domineer and his militant corps of destroyers are fools, and he recognizes the bearded Shanaar as a dangerous oul' cod. It is Mahan who rescues Loreleen from the vigilantes, who attempts to protect his lorry driver from Father Domineer, and who will not be bullied by either Michael or Domineer. Due to old alliances and the prospects of continued financial gain, he is unable to leave Nyadnanave and follow the Cock, so he remains with those whose mission it is to destroy life and song and dance in the present and sings his memories of a long time ago when men was men.

The forces for good, for the preservation of life as it ought to be lived now, are led by the spectacular Cock—a poet transformed and retaining the power of the word. Though a mathematical equation would be ridiculous, there are clearly discernible elements of O'Casey himself in the sardonic Cock, and, to complete the identification of the Cock and O'Casey's poet figure, this play is dedicated to "James Stephens: the Jesting Poet with a Radiant Star in's Coxcomb." The Cock uses essentially the same kind of transforming magic as that employed by Ayamonn in *Red Roses for Me*. The Cock's followers include Maid Marion and Robin Adair—the first named for the lovely lady of Robin Hood's greenwood, a name evocative of a legendary era of hearty merriment and honest, rebellious disregard for oppression and corrupt authority. The name of Robin Adair, the minstrel, announces his eventual abandonment of Nyadnanave as it recalls its namesake, the old traditional ballad, "Robin Adair":

> What's this dull town to me, Robin Adair?
> What was't I wished to see, what wished to hear?
> Where all the joy and mirth
> Made this town a heaven on earth?
> O, They're all fled with thee, Robin Adair.

Another follower of the Cock, Loreleen, is reminiscent of *Die Lorelei*, the sirens of power and beauty whose beautiful songs lured sailors to destruction. In an O'Caseyan reversal, Loreleen is saved from destruction by a sailor who adores and would possess her charms. Loreleen's stepmother, Lorna, completes the list of those who follow the Cock and understand the power of his word, and she agrees with Marion that "th' place'll lose its brightness if th' Cock's killed."

Utilizing the transforming powers of his magic and those of his gifted followers, the Cock turns the materialistic Nyadnanave upside down and reveals, in the new view, the grotesque essence of the regimented inelasticity of Nyadnanave. The distorting process, a traditional comic device, is used here to reveal and to emphasize truth: the truth that dance, though forbidden by the church in Domineer's parish, has been throughout history and will continue to be "a sacrament of rest and joy"; and that, even in Domineer's parish, a song brings "a spray of light, now and again, into a dark place." Dance and song are presented as positive forces associated with the positive powers of Nature which the Cock somehow controls.

The efficacy of dance and song as healing and transforming rituals is demonstrated and proclaimed by O'Casey in various plays and essays. The triumphant dance in *Red Roses for Me* eliminates the poverty and misery on the banks of the Liffey; Jannice makes song and dance integral to her quest for meaning in *Within the Gates;* the healing and sacramental powers of dance and song are even more fully discussed in *The Drums of Father Ned.* In all these examples, Father Domineer's church views song and dance as institutions of the devil. Domineer, with his scowl and his limp and his demands for obedience, is a representative morality figure rather than an individual. For O'Casey, he symbolizes an historical procession of Procrustean priests whose chief concern was the size and shape of an inelastic regimented creed rather than the spirit and the capacity of man. Historically, O'Casey sees that creed as a compost of Thou Shalt Nots:

All these old boyos dreaded the dance—St. Augustine, Salimbene, Aquinas, even Abelard, . . . Even Petrarch, even he, immersed in the puritanism of the medieval Church, denounced dancing too. Even he, a poet! Says he, "From dancing we get nothing but a libidinous and empty spectacle, hateful to honest eyes and unworthy of a man; take lust away, and you will have removed the dance also."[11]

Like "all these old boyos," Father Domineer equates joy and sin, laughter and sin, song and sin, dance and sin. When the magic dance in the garden moves Mahan, Marthraun, and the Sergeant ever nearer to the ardor and abandon of Loreleen, Lorna, and Marion, Father Domineer enters from the midst of a loud, long peal of threatening thunder and "glares down at the swinging dancers" as he shouts with vicious intensity:

> Stop that devil's dance! How often have yous been warned that th' avowed enemies of Christianity are on th' march everywhere! An' I find yous dancing'! How often have yous been told that pagan poison is floodin' th' world, an' that Ireland is dhrinkin' in generous doses through films, plays, and books! An' yet I come here to find yous dancing'! . . . Th' empire of Satan's pushin' out its foundations everywhere, an' I find yous dancin', *ubique ululanti cockalorum ochone, ululo!*[12]

As Robin Adair, the messenger who provides music for the dance, tells Michael Marthraun of his religion, "Faith, your fathers' faith is fear, an' now fear is your only fun." Utilizing logic and the fact that Father Domineer's inelasticity will not permit him to understand, Robin Adair discovers to him that "the devil was often in th' street, an' as intimate in th' home when there was nor film nor play nor book." Since the rigid spokesmen of the church see black as black, white as white, and joy as evil, O'Casey ironically grants their premise that song and dance are devil inspired, has Loreleen sprout horns, has saints' pictures turn to the wall, and permits the Cock's followers to testify: Lorna says that "th' devil's not a bad fella either," and Maid Marion warns Robin Adair, "I've some of th' devil in me." And the Devilareans, with their pagan gospel of song and dance, are united in their onslaught against the entrenched powers of conformity and codified religion. Their spiritual leader, O'Casey's devil who inspires joy and laughter, is close kinsmen to Joyce's God who is a shout in the street, and he ultimately becomes Father Ned in O'Casey's later play, *The Drums of Father Ned.*

The natural rhythm of Father Ned's drums controls the action and the tempo of that play just as the Cock, in a more whimsical way, controls the action of *Cock-a-Doodle Dandy.* In both plays, the enemy is the entrenched power of the newly-rich politician and codified religion—the awesome power of state and church united against change of any kind and, therefore, against life itself. When such a union prevails, the dispensation of "Honour be th' clergy's regulated by how much a man can give," and since priests (like Domineer) cannot smile, hypocrisy, complacency, and shirking of social responsibility seem dictated by the prevailing fear of change.

The devotees of this codified religion see good and evil in terms of financial profit and loss: Michael and Mahan, for example, condemn the unchristian ethics of the workers who demand a living wage when they should be thankful to be employed at all. Michael's wealth is ill-gotten and he manages to twist that into a Christian virtue since it is his money that sends Julia to Lourdes. While congratulating himself on good business sense and trying to outfox Mahan, he spouts platitudes against materialism and simultaneously tallies his own increasing wealth. O'Casey's attack on such Christian materialism is extended on the level of pun and parody to include the politicians of Ireland, the newly powerful members of the bourgeoisie-aristocracy who are further damned by "the terrible beauty of the tall hat."

Michael Marthraun, with his new top hat, his impressive public office, and his eager anticipation of a papal visitor, is de Valera reduced to absurdity. Michael, like de Valera, belongs to the right organizations, prays to the right God, and does business with the right people. O'Casey's bitterness here is but a brief glimpse of that displayed in "A Terrible Beauty is Borneo," which is an extended examination of the fearful new nation under the fearful new leadership of an Easter Monday veteran, who was—after all—an honorable man:

> Devotion to the church's curriculum kept De Valera on the steady path, avoiding hell, and reaching heaven, and all that. His kneeling on a stage, in front of a crowded house . . . to receive the blessing of a visiting cardinal, was, to Sean, a humiliating thing for the head of a Republican State to do.[13]

Marthraun, the De Valerian, is in league with Father Domineer, and they are at oppostie poles from O'Casey's Devilarians, the followers of the Cock. Krause calls the Nyadnanavians " 'devalerian' puritans under strict orders from their politicians and priests to beware of the joyous temptations of the 'devilarian' Cock." The "devalerian" way is the way of death, the way of further increasing the compost of generations of Procrustean denials; the "devilarian" way is the way of life, the way of joy and laughter here and now. The conflict between O'Casey's De Valerians and his Devilarians provides the central action of this drama and of every play he wrote after 1950.

Cock-a-Doodle Dandy combines the universal application of the morality play with the specialized illumination of the expressionistic technique; further, it demonstrates in all three scenes O'Casey's contention that life has a lot of time for dance, laughter, and song, for each.is a part of life itself. As quoted by Robert Hogan in *The Experiments of Sean O'Casey*, the dramatist says of *Cock-a-Doodle Dandy*: "It is my favorite play; I think it is my best play—a personal opinion." And, of its possible interpretation, he states:

> Broadly it stands against everything interfering with, or hinder-
> ing, the natural joys of life, applicable to all men, but cast in a gay
> Irish mold. It shows, or tries to show—regarded in this way—that
> Ireland is the world; just as Ibsen made Norway a world and
> Strindberg made a world of Sweden.[14]

In this play, O'Casey goes beyond the surrealism and the posed distortions of *The Silver Tassie* and *Within the Gates* to use a new technique anticipated by the Liffey scene in *Red Roses for Me*. He utilizes magic and supernatural weapons to combat the lethargy, complacency, and evil fostered by Domineer and Domineer's religion. In *Cock-a-Doodle Dandy*, the magic is farcical and its immediate effects successfully reduce the materialists to ridiculous levels as they worry about the religious pictures turning to the wall, the devilish horns sprouting from the foreheads of the beautiful girls, the demonized liquor bottle, the collapsing chairs, and the hat-cock confusion. The individual episodes repeat the same theme over and over again, showing graphically that the true members of Domineer's church are fearful of and are incapable of change. Their answer to anything out of the ordinary is that it is evil and that it must be destroyed.

The mock-heroic battle between Domineer's forces and the Cock's magic permits the satirist to dissect his enemy at leisure and to reduce his enemy's mode of being to absurdity. Shanaar advises that all things unnatural and unseemly must be ignored; that evil demons—in this case the followers of the Cock—have no behinds (an interesting absurdity in view of the charges against Loreleen, Lorna, and Maid Marion); and that no demons caught out in the open air can withstand the force of Latin phrases. The stage for the mock-heroic battle is set as the Cock's miracles unfold before the awed eyes of those who try to ignore them and shout Latin incantations toward them at the same time. One-Eyed Larry, half-blind coward and obvious liar, carries bell, book, and candle for Father Domineer, who will attempt to cleanse the house of evil spirits. The superstitions of the devoted followers of Shanaar and Domineer are as ridiculous as their attempts to hold up their trousers against the fearsome wind.

Their authority and the symbols of their power reside entirely in the grim visage of Father Domineer and in the impotent guns of Michael and the comic Sergeant. The Sergeant fires his guns at the top hat and fears the hat's "unholy novelty" of either changing into the Cock or disappearing whenever the gun is fired. Michael, despite his magic charms and his false knowledge of the existence of evil, screams at Lorna,

> . . . Through our bulgin' eyes, didn't we see th' horrification of me tall-hat turnin' into th' demonised cock? Me tall-hat, you bitch, me own tall-hat is roamin' round th' counthry, temptin' souls to desthroy themselves with dancin' an' desultory pleasures! [*CADD*, p. 180]

Both of these authorities, the grim visages of the priest and the guns, are less than effective against the evil of joyous life fostered by the miraculous Cock. Domineer is magically whisked away and returned in disarray on the back of a wild duck, either a white one or a speckled one, or perhaps on the back of a barnacle goose, depending on which of Father Domineer's followers has the clearest vision. All are eyewitnesses, and all provide different accounts of the miracle which restored their priest to them. All the eye-witnesses are members of Father Domineer's church and their conflicting accounts provide, in context, yet another satiric view of the religious miracles extolled by eyewitnesses and clung to as positive proof of the power of the church. A point obscured by the bickering of the miracle proclaimers is that Domineer's return is hardly a stately one and his steed, such as it was, was not commanded by his authority.

The stern visage of Father Domineer's authority is clearly evident in the actions of his vigilantes, who throw stones at Loreleen and are praised for their noble work of beating, mauling, and robbing her; his authority is further evident as he addresses Loreleen as sinful slut, honied harlot, painted paramour, and shuttlecock of sin. The vigilantes are women far less attractive than their victim and lustful louts whose "whole nature's a tuft of villainies!" Lorna addresses one of the lustful toughs who would condemn Loreleen, "If God had given you a tusk, you'd rend asundher every woman of th' disthrict!" Robin Adair addresses Domineer as "Father, so full of pity and loving-kindness," an ironic greeting designed to bring the melee into focus. The entire episode juxtaposes, in satiric fashion, Christ's treatment of the guilty adulteress and Father Domineer's treatment of the innocent Loreleen.

Domineer, rather than forgiving and aiding, condemns her, condones the robbery and mauling, and threatens her with death if she doesn't get over the "virtuous bordhers" of Nyadnanave. He is frankly fascinated by the "rosy rottenness" of her sin, for he is a lecherous old man stuffing the minds of his followers with meanness and fear. Agreeing with the fanatic Shanaar, he teaches them the catechism that "a woman's always a menace to a man's soul. Woman is th' passionate way to hell!" Loreleen tells Domineer, "When you condemn a fair face, you sneer at God's good handiwork. You are layin' your curse, sir, not upon a sin, but on a joy." The way of Father Domineer with his flock is a thinly veiled satiric allegory of the church's way with mankind, as O'Casey sees it, a way he sees as consistently opposed to any social change.

Father Domineer and his followers resist all change and all competition as necessarily evil. Women who contradict their husbands, wear bright colors, and consider themselves as independent human beings violate what Michael Marthraun knows to be "a basic law of nature and a law of God." Lorna, his "costumed slut," breaks this law and further jeopardizes her soul by seeing avarice as evil and materialism as a way of death. This basic law of nature and of God is reaffirmed by the Sergeant, who says of women, "Th' house is their province, as th' clergy's tired tellin' them. They'll have to realize that th' home's their only proper place"; and again by Father Domineer, who orders the women into the house, "th' place, th' proper place, th' only place for th' women." This consistent attitude is further mocked by O'Casey, who portrays all the followers of the magic Cock, except Robin Adair, as women

Those who follow the authority of Domineer, O'Casey's villains, blame books for "th' woeful way we are," and they describe "minds that babble about books . . . [as] th' biggest curse of all." Loreleen's sinful mind, according to Michael Marthraun, "is always mustherin' dangerous thoughts plundered outa evil books!" Father Domineer knows books to be "Hell's bells tolling people away from th' truth," and presumably away from the basic laws of nature and of God, as he interprets them. Such being the case, the vigilantes follow their leader and confiscate two banned books after the evil spirits have been exorcised from Marthraun's house: one by Voltaire and *Ullissississies* which is "Worse than th' other one." Ardent disciple of change and avid espouser of books as one stimulus for change, O'Casey further develops his attack on book burning in *The Bishop's Bonfire* and in *The Drums of Father Ned*. For life to continue as it is and for them to remain what they are, Domineer and his followers must oppose any stimulus to change just as they must repress any evidence of life and must maintain their power at any cost.

Actually, the way of Nyadnanave is, as Lorna observes, the way of materialism and the way of death. Recognizing the social evils perpetrated by Michael's avarice, she warns, "If you want to embalm yourself in money, you won't get me to

do it." The hypocrisy of the materialistic religion of the
Nyadnanavians is perpetuated in their adoration and blind
faith in such miracles as those viewed by eye witnesses in the
"money making madness" at Lourdes. O'Casey is especially
splenetic in his comments on the miracle cures and on those
who sit back and wait for such miracles to change the way of
the world. Father Domineer sends Julia there to "fetch home a
miracle," to join the candle carrying crowds on the variously
colored trains

> that race, tirra lirra, along to Lourdes! Racing along, carrying
> their rotting crops of humanity, to where a hymn and a prayer are
> to prosper them back to health. The woe and the waste of it all!
> Lourdes, where hope is swallowed down by misery to be
> vomited up again, more miserable, and lost. Where Lazarus is
> offered a crumb, but can never crawl near enough to get it. . . .
> Where belief plays her last joke on the dying. The church's great
> sweep of misery and woe. . . . The Coney Island of misery, agony,
> and woe.[15]

O'Casey continues his harangue against the blindness of
regimented faith and faith-healing by noting that Lourdes, a
religious shrine, takes in more money than any bank can hold.
Such wealth and such energies could be more profitably
invested in a cure for killing diseases and

> the direr ills of man, sending more young to the grave than
> Lourdes can cure in an eternity of time. Disease can never be
> conquered, can never be quelled by emotion's wailful screaming
> or faith's cymballic prayer. It can only be conquered by the
> energy of humanity and the cunning in the mind of man. In the
> patience of a Curie, in the enlightenment of a Faraday, a
> Rutherford, a Pasteur, a Nightingale, and all other apostles of
> light and cleanliness, rather than of a woebegone godliness, we
> shall find final deliverance from plague, pestilence, and famine.
> [*IFTW*, pp. 383-84]

In *Cock-a-Doodle Dandy*, Julia returns from Lourdes un-
cured and destined to an early death. Her sickness, like that of
Mollser in both *The Plough and the Stars* and "A Fall in a
Gentle Wind," reflects the diseased condition of society itself,

which will not be cured by a miracle. For Julia, as for other victims fated to remain in Nyadnanave or its counterpart, the only cure is death.

Each of the scenes in this satiric play ends on a chilling note, indication enough that the main point of O'Casey's satire is more than laughter at man's folly. The villains are vicious and dangerous to life itself. Scene I ends in a mock ritual as Julia is ushered off to Lourdes by a parish priest who cannot smile, on a journey whose consequences testify to the inadequacy of faith without action. Scene II ends with the priest's symbolic murder of the lorry driver, who will not conform and will not renounce his lover. The death is presented in a hackneyed and unconvincing way, but its thematic importance is obvious on a symbolic level. Father Domineer condemns to death those who are finally disobedient, and he continues to wage active and deadly war against life, joy, song, and dance in any combination. Scene III ends with the revelers being expelled from Nyadnanave and taking with them all the song and dance, all the life, that was there. Robin Adair follows them, playing his accordian and singing; Michael Marthraun is left behind clutching his rosary, and Julia remains on her stretcher awaiting death, which is simultaneously the way of life and the only escape from Nyadnanave after the Cock is expelled.

Father Domineer is successful in driving life and joy from his parish. His influence and power, ridiculous as they are, are too strong for the natural inclinations. Lorna, Loreleen, Maid Marion, and Robin Adair are free from the destructive materialism of the community and leave it to its own end. They, like Synge's tramps and tinkers, will not be denied the joys of song and dance; like their counterparts in Synge's drama and in O'Casey's earlier plays, they know the power of the word. They cannot transform an unwilling society but they can and do leave the place "where a whisper of love . . . bites away some of th' soul," the place whose priest cannot smile and whose cowardly citizens cannot face their own failures. Unable to transform Nyadnanave, the followers of the Cock go "To a place where life resembles life more than it does here." Marthraun, who is "very lonely now," having "no one left . . . but th' Son o' God," asks, "What, Messenger, would you have me do?" The messenger replies characteristically and truthfully, "Die. There is little else left useful for the likes of you to do."

O'Casey's bitterness is more apparent in this than in any preceding play. The optimism that marks most of his other works is absent here. It is driven out with Loreleen, Lorna, Maid Marion, and Robin Adair. Nyadnanave is a monument to death—to complacency, lethargy, and blind faith. The artist's satiric advantage is marked as he combines elements from virtually every genre in this kaleidoscopic expose of society's ills. For the first time, the opposition wins a decisive victory, but their victory is a hollow one. Even in victory, they remain fools, fools who fear truth, ignore truth, spout incantations against truth, and try always to protect their positions of relative power against change of any kind. So it is that the women of Nyadnanave must stay in their appointed temples and obey their husbands, books which arouse questions or even puzzled thought must be destroyed, and evil spirits which would bring about social change must be hunted down and either destroyed or driven out. This is necessary for the continuance of life in Nyadnanave, whether the evil spirits be called Jim Larkin, Ayamonn Breydon, or Cock-a-Doodle Dandy.

This, like O'Casey's other plays, offers far more than instant entertainment. Its scope is universal and the villains are not restricted to the theatre stage; they are, as O'Casey says, all those who would

> drive the joy of life from the hearts of men; . . . It isn't the clergy alone who boo and bluster against this joy of life in living, in dance, song, and story . . . and who interfere in the free flow of thought from man to man. . . . They are fools, but they are menacing fools, and should be fought anywhere they shake a fist, be they priest, peasant, prime minister or proletarian.[16]

The three one act plays that follow *Cock-a-Doodle Dandy* (*Hall of Healing, Bedtime Story,* and *Time to Go*) share a peculiarly blended optimism and resignation. All three were

performed for the first time on 7 May 1952 in New York, the
year after they were published. They provide an interesting
mixture of O'Casey's experimental techniques and the realism
of his earlier period. His chosen kinship to Shaw in his
continuing war against poverty, in his presentation of truth as
it is rather than as we would have it be, and in his extensive
stage directions are as apparent in *Hall of Healing* as in any of
his longer plays. The stage directions themselves serve both
literary and dramatic purpose and keep this play from being
only a loud scream of protest. The bitterness of the satire is
akin to that in *Cock-a-Doodle Dandy*, but here there is neither
song, nor dance, nor a magic messiah to alleviate the methodical march to death. The only hope is in the continued
existence of such complainers as Red Muffler and Green
Muffler, complainers who refuse to accept death as a blessing
or as the wish of God, complainers who recognize injustice
and social sickness in the Doctor's manner of allocating life
and death as he enforces his rules and permits Alleluia to reign
supreme in the waiting room.

O'Casey's own experiences in the Parish Dispensaries of
Dublin and his memories of them form the basis for *Hall of
Healing*, a "sincerious farce," as censurious as it is sincere in
damning the inadequate and inhumane medical care available
to the poor in Dublin. This is perhaps the only play in
O'Casey's canon that was more effective and more censurious
than he intended, for he was unaware when he recalled the
incidents of his childhood and early manhood and wrote them
into his play, that the same conditions and the same rickety
dispensing shacks still existed and were still operative in the
Dublin of 1951. "The notorious Red Ticket that exacerbated
some of O'Casey's days, was still the method of communication between patient and doctor, and, for all one knows,
flourishes still."[17] One severe young critic so hopelessly misread O'Casey, the play, and Dublin itself, that he was able to
condemn O'Casey's "attitude of profound contempt for the
poor," to read the characters and the style as "peculiarly
unacceptable" Stage-Irishism and Irishism, and to conclude:
"The hopelessness you portray in *Hall of Healing* is out of
date."[18] Whether Patrick Galvin really believed that O'Casey

contemptuously exploited the suffering of the poor is imma-
terial; what is important is that O'Casey's poor are not
necessarily Down-and-Outs, as amply demonstrated in this
play by the presence of Black Muffler and Green Muffler. Nor
are all O'Casey's Down-and-Outs necessarily from the lower
echelon of the economic scale, as is clearly seen in *Within the
Gates* and *Cock-a-Doodle Dandy.*

The bitter irony of the play's title, *Hall of Healing,* becomes
more and more apparent as death's inevitability and death's
presence are made manifest in the lives of the poverty stricken
patients. The irony is further dramatized as the Apothecary
refers to Red Muffler, the outraged father of the dead child, as
a "cheeky boyo" and continues, "Not a grain of gratitude in
one of them for all we thry to do for them. . . . It would almost
make a man despair of humanity."[19] Alleluia's dance to the
organ music and the patient waiting of the poor for medical
aid are identified as a dance of death by Red Muffler, who
also recognizes that "Patience is only th' holy name for
suicide." Red Muffler, O'Casey's socialist spokesman, despite
his rage and his suffering, is impotent against the system
which condemned his child and the Young Woman to death.
The Doctor and the Apothecary go home on schedule, leaving
Alleluia to dance his dance and sing his song in his "fussy,
fiddlin'" way. Equally impotent is the rage of Green Muffler,
who spent his last penny on empty bottles as directed by the
officious Alleluia, empty bottles not used for his prescription.
His threats and outrage gain neither aid nor special attention
from the patient poor who wait for liniments in the same
numbing postures that they wait for death.

O'Casey's rage against the conditions permitting such poverty and such suffering is as much in evidence as ever. The
play is set in winter and the cold, falling snow is the same
snow that covers Dublin in Joyce's *Dubliners,* the snow of
death. The essential difference is that O'Casey's snow is wet
and cold; his characters are miserable in their sickness and
poverty, and he offers no romantic illusions concerning the
relationships of the present and the past. The time is now and
"Death has sometimes a kindlier touch than many a human
hand," in that it removes the sufferer from the maladies of life.

Hall of Healing is a morality play whose stylized characters are simultaneously involved in the ritual of waiting and the dance of death—a ritual that emphasizes the uncertainty, need, and resignation that comprise their lot in life and a dance whose finality is universal. The drabness of their existence is effectively symbolized by their drab, patched, threadbare clothes that cover their diseased undernourished bodies; by their flesh tones of yellow, pale grey, and white, and by their diseases—rheumatism, delirium tremens, diphtheria, and consumption. The only colors that brighten their lives are the red sign (TUBERCULOSIS: BEWARE!), the green sign (CANCER: BEWARE!), the black sign (DIPHTHERIA: BEWARE!), the colored medicines, and the colored glass bottles. Obviously, these visual diversions only heighten their constant awareness of the inevitable.

The Old Doctor, a human being who was their friend, died of cancer; the new doctor is as helpless against their poverty as he is against his own addiction to the "dhrop." His Monday hangover and his inordinate concern for his fountain pen and his rules evoke laughter and horror—the first because he is a fool, the second because the sick and the dying are dependent upon him. The juxtaposition of the Doctor's rich warm clothing and the wraps worn by the patients further magnifies the separation between his lot and theirs, as does his refusal to see the nine-year-old child of Red Muffler because he is too busy, he is hungover, and "there are thousands of kids like yours gasping for life in the city today." As the Young Woman who is dying of consumption takes her prescription of liniment and her "note to the consumption dispensary o' Charles Street," she recognizes the note as her death warrant, as did Mollser in both *The Plough and the Stars* and "A Fall in a Gentle Wind." For these services, the Doctor and the Apothecary expect gratitude, devotion, and humility from the patient poor.

They are self-appointed gods whose personal schedules, desires, and frailties are more significant than the needs of humanity. Perhaps it is too much to have Alleluia's chorus of "The Rose of Tralee" and his dance accompanied by organ music, but O'Casey's immediate target is the "blasted fomen-

ter of medicine" who permits people to die as he maintains his
schedule and enforces his rules, as he stacks the red tickets on
his desk to worry about tomorrow, and as his victims become
"something silently seen no more." His more significant target
is the social system that appoints such a person and such a
coterie to dispense life and death as they will. The naturalistic
devices in the play (juxtaposition, amassing of detail, topical
referent, etc.) point up the significance of the subtitle: the play
is not a farce, but the societal values it portrays are.

In the second of these one-act plays, *Bedtime Story*,
O'Casey draws freely from the farce, melodrama, and situa-
tion-comedy traditions for his episodic expose of the "decline
and fall into the drab and malicious menace of puritanism."[20]
Angela Nightingale is the only vital person on stage as she lives
her song of life; she combines vitality, paganism, and sense of
humor in her lucrative professions of con-artist and whore.
Angela likes to dance and sing, ignores public opinion, and
recognizes that

> Sometime or other, we have to face out of all we get into: face out
> of getting into bed with a woman no less than face out into silence
> from the glamour of prayer; face out of summer into winter; face
> out of life into death![21]

Her gull, John Jo Mulligan, is a "constitutionally frightened
chap" who will never recover from a "futile sense of sin,"
from an overwhelming fear of public opinion, and from his
sincere conviction that Angela "should be ashamed and sorry
. . . instead of feeling sinfully gay about it. It's necessary to feel
sorry for a sin of this kind." Mulligan wears a Trilby hat and is
proud that "the head of my department's a grand Knight of
Columbanus, an uncomprising Catholic. . . ." The Trilby hat,
here as in O'Casey's *Within the Gates,* identifies the wearer
with the makers and the fearers of public opinion and with the
worshippers at the shrine of the daily newspaper; just as
surely, John Jo Mulligan's actions in the presence of Angela
Nightingale identify him as a fool who is "all for go-ahead
godliness" as soon as he has completed his carnal sin on a cold
January morning "the very next day after me Novena." He

prays to Saint *Panteemalaria,* adores the Knights of *Colum-banus,* and promises only a quiet hour of poetry to Angela, a quiet hour of Yeats, as he succeeds in luring her into his rooms. Apparently the only line he read was "I will arise and go now, and go to Innisfree" before he was overcome by Angela's "dance that uplifted . . . [her] skirt out of the way of . . . [her] movements, and juggled a vision of spiritual desolation into a mirage of palpitating enjoyments."

He, like all of O'Casey's respectability-enslaved puritans, is ultimately reduced to total absurdity by the healthy vigor of an Angela Nightingale. Using blackmail like the veteran she is, Miss Nightingale ultimately departs with Mulligan's ring, his best overcoat, his umbrella, his new wallet, £18 in cash, and a check for £10. Having stripped him of these symbols of masculinity, respectability, and sanity, Angela leaves him with his Trilby hat and his second best overcoat to "face out" the winter that always follows summer.[22] The world he must face is his own element, the world of puritanical hypocrisy, ridiculous poses, and public opinion. Ironically, his landlady, Miss Massie, and his friend, Daniel Halibut, accurately diagnose Mulligan's madness and have him hauled away by a policeman, a doctor, and a nurse, while he babbles inchoherently about his wallet, his money, and Angela's lost handbag.

The world ridiculed by O'Casey is the one in which Miss Massie "sleepwalks" to her gentleman boarders "at the dead of night, with a loving look on her face,"[23] the one in which anything out of the ordinary is presumed mad. The Homburg-wearing Halibut is not as severely chastised in this "Anatole Burlesque" as is his celibate friend, for Halibut loves to dance and sing and try his way with the girls. He does not attempt to hide his appetites behind a religious facade, nor to blame them on sleepwalking. Furthermore, he chooses life itself to the canned questions of Yeats, who will "drive you nuts." Neither does he use Yeats to lure girls into his rooms, to make him drowsy, nor to explain his late hours. In the mad world inhabited by John Jo, Halibut, and Miss Massie, the only recourse when patterns are broken is to assume the violator insane; hence, Massie and Halibut have Mulligan committed while he assumes both of them to be mad. All are essentially correct, but for the wrong reasons. This superficial satire of the mores and customs of respectability is funny, does burlesque the manners of a whole segment of society, and did manage to get itself banned by the Education Council—to the great delight of O'Casey:

> . . . it was decided by this Council that this play was too saucy to be shown to the elderly audiences which might come to witness the performances during the drama trials of the Festival. So this little play has never been performed in England, as far as I know, except by the students for the students of the R.A.D.A. [Royal Academy of Dramatic Arts], for fear it might weaken the moral fibres of the elderly, bringing the land to a decline and fall into the depravity of whoredom; though this, at least, would be better and brighter than to decline and fall into the drab and malicious menace of puritanism.[24]

Angela Nightingale's song, her can-can, her escape from the permeating madness of John Jo's world, and her victory over hypocrisy are thematic and provide both structure and continuity for the play. Angela Nightingale, as her name testifies, is much too good and much too alive for the hypocrisy and the inelasticity of John Jo's respectable world of saints and Trilby hats. She passes through his life singing her song and dancing her dance, and he remains unchanged. A devotee of novenas, materialism, and respectability, Mulligan is momentarily stripped of·all his grandeur by Angela Nightingale and left with only hollow pretense and his hollow zeal for "go ahead godliness." Constantly seeking for a divine world and furtively concealing his human qualities, Mulligan, like Marthraun clutching his rosary at the end of *Cock-a-Doodle Dandy*, makes his way a way of death. Angela, like the Cock and his revelers in that same play, has moved through Nyadnanave (Nest of Fools) and moves on in her quest for the quick of life.

Time to Go: A Morality Comedy iñ One Act provides an interim capsule of O'Casey's major themes. Once again, Ireland is a microcosm of the world, and the church is allied with business. Both are supported by the police, and all three extract exorbitant profits from the populace. Once again, honesty is madness, health is sickness, and true miracles require human action. The businessmen make large donations in return for priestly silence, and the police enforce the dictums of the church. In the business as usual world of Bull Farrell and Canon Bullero and Michael Flagonson, the young leave and the harp of Tara sounds like jingling coins.

Kelly from the Isle of Mananaun and Widda Machree are blessed with honesty and the desire to conduct business honestly. Such intentions can only destroy the lucrative jingle-jingle of business in the Irish country town, whose citizens demand conformity to the local mores. When the kilt-wearing Kelly and his sister-soul, Widda Machree, do not conform, they are adjudged insane, public menaces, and real threats to the status quo. This is precisely their value: they do threaten the status quo as they dance, sing, and wish to promote honesty among the daylight robbers, the rogues, and the gulls of the country town. The only solution is to have Kelly "cured into seein' things as we all see them" and to take the widow where her "poor mind'll be mended."

The young couple who stop for nourishment and are driven away by high prices and poor offerings are symptomatic, for the town's own "young are going who aren't already gone. . . . there's ne'er a one, lad or lass, in th' disthrict between seventeen and thirty."[25] The town itself is just recuperating from the heavy and lucrative business of a fair which provided both the clergy and the businessmen with their usual inordinate profits. Flagonson is surprised at "How lonesome an' woebegone the decorations look now the crowd's gone." The blasted trees with their withered limbs symbolize the way of death taken by the town, as does the tune of "Jingle Bells" in the background as profits are totalled up. This "butt-end of an Irish town" is ruled over by the triumvirate of Business, Clergy, and Polis'—the last because the Polis' are "th' only ones to put th' fear o' God in" the children.

Despite several prophetic warnings from the kilted Kelly and Widda Machree, the town's citizens pursue their hypocritical way of confusing the jingle of cash profits "with the gentle jingle of the Mass bell." Following his escape from Sergeant Killdooey, Kelly further demonstrates his magic— magic similar to that practiced earlier by Ayamonn on the Liffey and by the Cock in Nyadnanave. As if to show what life could be, Kelly transforms the town: the blasted trees flower and bloom and glow, the archetypal argument concerning the fair price of cattle ceases, Bull and Flagonson "fall on their knees," and the performers of the miracle are acclaimed saints. The spell is broken by Mrs. Flagonson's, "Come in, Michael, an' help me tot up th' takin's." Flagonson obeys, and the marvel is dismissed as "an halleelucination."

The transformation was a fleeting one because no real change is possible without effort by the communicants, whether the miracle is on the River Liffey or in a country town. The madness of society, which sees all change as dangerous and all who initiate change as mad, is emphasized here by distorted and incoherent language, by the public's insistence that the miracle workers have a warrant for their actions, and by the foolish consistency that is the hobgoblin of their little minds. This village, like Nyadnanave, is condemned to death when its potential saviors decide that "it's time to go." Life and hope for life depart with the magic of honesty and song and dance; in the village, after the "halleelucination" it's business as usual as all the vigilantes of materialism rush to fulfill Kelly's prophecy: "Soon yous'll all be no more than these two barren deadened trees. Then when yous are silent stiffs, others will count your coins."

The Bishop's Bonfire: A Sad Play Within the Tune of a Polka once again presents a microcosmic Irish village as the site for the continuing battle between life and death. Here, as in *Cock-a-Doodle Dandy and Time to Go*, those out of sympathy with Mullarkey, Burren, and Reiligan are expelled and leave behind them willing captives performing in a Punch and Judy show whose inevitable end is death. As portrayed by O'Casey, the hapless puppets are controlled by church officials dedicated to power, money, and the status quo. The conflict and the ultimate victory won by the church-state combine lead up to the final scene—the exit of all affiliated with the forces of life and joy and the remainder of the rest before the increasing brightness of the bonfire awaiting the triumphant arrival of Bishop Mullarkey.

The forces for life are nurtured by O'Casey's version of an ideal priest, Father Boheroe. In Gaelic, his name means "Red Road";[26] in anagram, he is Boyo-Hero. Considered heretical by the faithful and the mercenary, Boheroe sees drinking as an attempt "to glimpse heaven through the wrong window," and says of making love that "a man in a woman's arms may indeed be close to God." He believes that

> All places are sacred, . . . the church we pray in, the homes sheltering us, the shops where we get the things we need to go on living, the halls we dance in; yea, the very place we walk on is holy ground. Work, too, is holy, but only when it's reasonable. . . .[27]

Boheroe, despite the church's pietistic reverence for work and for prayer, warns that "too much work misfits a soul for heaven and for here" and that "too much formal prayer . . . sometimes makes a soul conceited." He contends that man does not do his part when he waits for God to perform miracles, that "God is unhappy when we don't do what we can with what He gives us," and that "when we have problems, . . . ourselves are the saints to solve them."

Like O'Casey's ideal poet, his ideal priest relates his artistry to the nature and needs of life, is aware of and involved in life, and is dedicated to understanding and assisting other human beings. Though loved by the people of Ballyoonagh, Boheroe is constantly warned and reminded by his superiors—both Burren and Reiligan—that he is only a curate and not the parish priest. For Boheroe, religion must be more than a showpiece, must do more than take time and make money, and must accept and extoll the beauty of life here and now. By his last line, "Oh, to hell with the Bishop's Bonfire," it is obvious that such a priest as Boheroe can no more survive in the church of Ballyoonagh than the Cock's spirit can survive in Nyadnanave, for Boheroe is opposed to the money-church power combine that rules and will continue to rule the microcosmic village.

Codger Sleehaun, an 84-year-old man devoted to joy and song and production in life, is a thinly disguised Sean O'Casey in a vicarious return from exile. Like his creator, Codger Sleehaun is at the same time wise and foolishly proud, aged and delightfully young at heart, respected for his abilities and expelled for his attitudes. Despite his age, his wisdom, and his joy of life, Codger is totally lacking what the citizens of Ballyoonagh might call dignity. He, like the workmen in *Purple Dust*, does his best to reduce the festival preparations to a shambles: he brings the gin keg, crashes through the picture window, dumps the cement on the new carpet, urges Prodical not to take the pledge, and returns for the confiscated bottle. He sings and dances—though his dance with Foorawn is a goosestep to the grave—and he knows that Bill Mullarkey is Bill Mullarkey, whatever his new title is. He and the Prodical are the "oul' butties" who bring the curtain down on this play, as Captain Boyle and Joxer brought it down in *Juno and the Paycock*. They exit, bottle in hand, the Codger singing the "merrily mournful" tune of his dead Bonnie—who, like Foorawn, will never return.

The relationship between the young Father Boheroe, the old Codger Sleehaun, and the dead priest, Manus Moanroe, is a close and important one. All are alive and all recognize life as it is to be a monstrous joke, a Punch and Judy show, an affliction to be cured rather than endured. When Codger is discharged and ordered out of the village, Manus decides to leave, and so does Boheroe who goes in "an opposite direction" from the bonfire so that he can "at least . . . walk under the stars." All three have recognized the decay and march toward death implicit in the church-controlled Ballyoonagh, whose church is—in turn—controlled by Reiligan. Boheroe's comment on the professionals of the church who fear public opinion is equally true of all the citizens of Ballyoonagh, "We are dead people, and must learn to lie circumspectly in our shrouds" [*BB*, p. 80].

Manus Moanroe's growing disgust with "god-frighted people" and his cynical attitude toward the construction of temples which must be ever "higher and higher till the shouting of heavenly pride encases and hides the growling-grumble of men" mark him as opponent of the Reiligan-Rankin-Roman combine, whose pietistic materialism seeks effectively to destroy life itself. Manus's frustrated love for Foorawn (who has vowed eternal chastity), his devotion to Codger (who is expelled from Reiligan's garden after long and devoted service), and his bitterness at being alive after his suicidal heroism in the British Air Force are all involved in his decision to right some wrongs by "stealing a little from a lot stolen from many" [*BB*, p. 117]. His rage at the chastity-bound Foorawn as a "mournful, empty shell of womanhood" is, by extension, his rage at the restrictive demands of the church which has her vow of obedience and from which he has been expelled. Her death, on a symbolic level, is her total commitment to the church and his total rejection of it. As depicted by O'Casey, her death is the responsibility of the church which denied her life, pronounced Manus a "dead priest," devoted itself to the collection of large sums of money, and ignored the humanity of its victims.

Foorawn's suicide note effectively frees Manus from suspicion: her life's blood, like Minnie Powell's (*Shadow of a Gunman*), makes Manus a poltroon free of suspicion, but guilty of murder. While he "goes slouching away out of sight . . . the Bishop's Bonfire flames higher and more brightly, and the cheers are heard a little more clearly." The bonfire is, of course, the central symbol of the play. As the church's way with dissenters and dissenting literature, Mullarkey's bonfire casts eerie shadows during the concluding action of O'Casey's "sad play within the tune of a polka." It means different things to different characters, and each is ultimately identified in terms of his relationship to and his attitude toward the welcoming fire: Manus's "words are like the words in the books that will burn to ashes in the Bishop's Bonfire," according to Foorawn; Rankin prays that "it may light such a blaze in all the hearts in Ballyoonagh that men may no longer think of women, or women think of men. . . ." Father Boheroe rejects it and goes away, and the Prodical—having vowed once more never to drink again—notes with more perception and more censure than he knows, "We're all part of the Bishop's Bonfire, flaming up with feelin's, of welcomin' good-will. I wouldn't like the Bishop to catch me noddin' " [*BB*, p. 90].

Several earlier O'Casey plays anticipated this thematic and titular use of the bonfire, whose church saints remain Columbanus, Panteemalaria, and Casabianca. The evil spirits remain those banished in *Cock-a-Doodle Dandy* ("Kissalass, Velvetthighs, Reedabuck, Dancesolong, an' Sameagain") and those exploited and expelled in *Time to Go* (Youth and Honesty). The church officers (Reiligan, Burren, and Mullarkey) are— like One-Eyed Larry—half-blind cowards who destroy what they cannot grasp. The victims include not only Boheroe, Moanroe, and Codger, but also Keelin, abandoned by Daniel who feared her father; Foorawn, chastity-bound parody of total commitment; Rankin, Puritanical hater of "the evil Eves who send men sidling into sin"; and the Prodical, alternating drunkard and vower of abstinence. Rankin's obsession with ever present sin, his death's skull, and "his high falsetto voice of a man unmade" clearly identify him as a victim; he literally spits in the face of life, but readily succumbs to the manipulative artistry of Canon Burren. His prayers, whining, and smugness are comic devices, but—like Shanaar—he is a dangerous fool. The Prodical vacillates between the songs and invitations of the Codger and the threats and insistences of Rankin, Reiligan, and the Roman Monsignor. Though he exits last with the Codger, he will probably continue to vow and to dance in the light of the fire.

The real power behind the church in Ballyoonagh is Reiligan. His name, while a legitimate name, is also an anagrammatic *Religion;* he, in his pomp and glory, with his riches and his top hat, serves many satiric functions for O'Casey. His attitude toward profit is implicit in his dismissal of Codger, "I'm sorry at losin' the Codger, but he must be nearin' his end anyhow," and in his desire to keep Manus Moanroe, "his right hand man," on his payroll. His appointment as Papal Count, his financing of the elaborate preparations for Bishop Mullarkey's visit, and his desire to match his daughter in marriage with the Bishop's brother further indicate his relationship to the established church. Reiligan is perhaps the most representative figure in this play, for, with his great wealth, his gauche tastes, and his black hat, he is also the bourgeois Irish politician of de Valera ilk. His class is satirized in his selection of and great concern for rugs, tapestries, tables, piano, prayer stools, and ducks. Reiligan, with his papal association, his political and economic power, is the religion of Ireland, as viewed by Sean O'Casey. Keelin is a virtual slave in her father's house, while Foorawn "belongs to God, an' is separated from menial work." The Monsignor—adept manipulator that he is—takes care not to offend Reiligan, who has the power to buy, sell, hire, and banish men. As identified by Codger, and by the text of the entire play, Reiligan owns all the land, all the businesses, and all the people of Ballyoonagh; he is "a menace to the world."

Lieutenant Michael Reiligan, in full military regalia, is the son—the only son—of Reiligan. His profession, his being in charge of the Guard of Honor to meet the Bishop, and his remarkable jeep plan to combat "tens of thousands of Russian paratroopers"[28] identify the father-son relationship of Church and Army and the remarkable foolishness that enslaved people will listen to if the speaker is in uniform. His claim of authority is "I'm an Army Officer; I know these things";[29] however, he must compete with the welcoming festival for his father's money. He needs only enough to keep up his "stattus in the Officer's Mess" and resents the vast expenditure for the Bishop's welcome.

O'Casey uses various devices and techniques to satirize his chosen targets. His characters' names frequently identify their true natures and their thematic functions: Canon Burren, promoted to Monsignor when his patron becomes Papal Count Reiligan, burns books to welcome Bishop Mullarkey; the Prodical returns again and again and again and again; and Rankin is rank enough to spit in the face of beauty. O'Casey reduces the workers to absurdity: they argue that bricklayers don't carry bricks and don't pluck ducks, and they do very little work. Reiligan blusters, when he discovers so much talking and so little working:

> From this out, there's to be no talkin'; and if anyone does talk, everybody is to listen to nobody. Anyone—no one—mind you! Damn it, are yous listenin' to me? [*BB*, p. 59]

This ridiculous command, his great concern for the new carpet and for his Catholic piano, together with his consternation at the unplucked ducks reveal him to be as absurd as any of his workmen, the essential difference being that he is more ostentatious about his own absurdities than the workmen are. Reiligan's desire for Keelin to marry the 56-year-old farmer brother of Bishop Mullarkey, who prefers his pipe to the company of any woman, renders Reiligan a mad fool. This series of absurdities in the burlesque picture of the newly-rich, hat-wearing politician Reiligan proves once again that "O'Casey will commit any outrage on a character short of giving him dull lines."[30]

In the burlesque sequence involving St. Tremolo, the Bookineeno, that hollow plaster saint is given the power to utter piercing noises heard only by a sinner in his presence. This variation of "The Emperor's New Clothes," when combined with the basic honesty and guilt feelings of the laborers, provides some slapstick comedy and a rather cynical view of the adoration of plaster saints. The prayer cushion and the brandy are also reserved for the eminent Bishop, as is the music of the piano, and the caustic O'Casey reveals the great void behind the facades of Reiligan's pretense and his religion. He, the elaborate preparations, and the hierarchy of the church are all reduced ultimately to the absurd level of the unplucked ducks and St. Tremolo's fearful shrieks.

The Bishop's Bonfire does not end well for anyone: Foorawn is dead, killed by Manus, who leaves; Codger is out of work; Keelin will probably marry Farmer Mullarkey; the peasants cower; the bonfire rages. The episodic action of the play is incidental and is not substantial. O'Casey was "by no

means satisfied" with the play, but thought it was good.[31] His
scathing attack on his critics in "Bonfire Under a Black Sun"[32]
does little to illuminate his intent in the play, but Codger
Sleehaun, with his lantern and his keg and his concern for the
meadows and the geranium, is certainly the most positive
voice in *The Bishop's Bonfire*. He, as O'Casey's vicarious
spokesman, and Father Boheroe, as O'Casey's perfect priest,
attempt to show the way to regeneration and life. Reiligan's
followers defeat them, for their bonfire is destructive rather
than life giving. The village forces of Church and State drive
out or destroy any threat of life. Even the Codger's dance is a
goosestep to the grave, and the ash tree—like its counterparts
in *Time to Go*—is not a tree of life; Reiligan's garden, empty
as the curtain falls, will have no roses on its new brick wall as
Ballyoonagh, like Nyadnanave, takes the shortest way with
dissenters, whether they are young women, old codgers, dead
priests, or boyo-heroes.

In "O'Casey's Drama Bonfire," the artist says of his *Bishop's
Bonfire*:

> The play tries to symbolize the conditions, the superstitions, the
> frantic obsession with sex. . . , the fleeing from their country of
> the young . . . , and the dreadful fear now stifling the Irish writers
> of saying anything critical about the serious things of life.
> Fortunately, so far . . . there is no official censorship over plays, as
> there is on books, and so it is possible to put in a play what one
> cannot put in a novel—that is, of course, if one can get the play
> performed.[33]

When it premiered in Dublin's Gaiety Theatre and ran for five
weeks to packed houses, its combined bitterness and caustic
superiority kept the vigilantes of the Irish press occupied for
several months, and perhaps set the scene for the debacle of
1958, when Dublin's International Theatre Festival was ultimately cancelled due to the efforts of the Archbishop of
Dublin.[34] In his usual uncanny way, O'Casey had anticipated
in *The Bishop's Bonfire* the·fate of his later play, whose
repetitive theme and comic characters are much less scathing,
whose religious leaders are more foolish than vicious, and
whose ironic fate was a more telling blow against the regimen-

tation of Irish Catholicism than its performance could ever
have been. O'Casey anticipates the Archbishop's "withdraw-
ing permission for any religious ceremony to inaugurate the
Dublin Tostal," a festival that was to feature a dramatic
version of Joyce's *Ulysses* and, of course, *The Drums of
Father Ned.* The Most Reverend Dr. McQuaid specifically
forbade "any religious ceremony,"[35] including the celebration
of Mass. Bishop Mullarkey, bonfire and all, was not more
effective.

In *The Bishop's Bonfire,* while no one is undamaged, the
clowns do survive. But not even one of them survives with the
verve echoed in O'Casey's conclusion to "Bonfire Under a
Black Sun":

> . . . He laughs, lads, he laughs. Laughs as Cuchulainn did, even
> when his shadow rises up to meet him, showing that the day is far
> spent, and the night is at hand. It is the right thing to do, for it is
> part of man's right and part of God's pleasure.
>
> Laugh, for the time is brief, a thread the length of a span.
>
> Laugh, and be proud to belong to the old proud pageant of
> man.[36]

In *The Drums of Father Ned,* O'Casey anticipates and
accepts his Irish countrymen's charges against his high priest
of life and joy. So doing, he makes Father Ned the namesake
of Old Ned, and his symbolic drums throb as the human heart
does, in exact tempo to the pulse of life. Father Ned is Father
Boheroe three years later, an ideal priest who "says that
through music, good books, an' good pictures, we may get to
know more about th' mysthery of life."[37] Father Ned never
appears on stage, but he is as omnipresent as Bishop Mullarkey in the preceding play. Here, as elsewhere, O'Casey's
satiric deck is stacked: the regimented church is represented
by the Reverend Doctor Fillifogue, a blustering fool, and by a
collection of pious materialists who really rule the church as
they conduct business as usual, "only pure business . . . uncon-
taminated with any smidereen of friendliness" [*DFN,* p. 21].
Binnington and McGilligan are outraged at the hypocrisy
of the common people, who refuse "to realize that when they

work for us they're workin' for God." Business is business and
must realize a profit; these two and Father Fillifogue are
against the Tostal Festival because it does not make money
and because it saps the energies of the workers, who could be
more gainfully employed.

The play begins with a PRERUMBLE set during the troubles of
1920-1922. The brief scene sets the mood for the ensuing play
and isolates the pettiness and the personal hatreds that become the chief targets of the artist's invective. The play itself
is "A Mickrocosm of Ireland" and the costume-wearing businessmen, the new DeValerian politicians of the later acts, are
anticipated by the hate-filled captives of the Black and Tans
in the PRERUMBLE. Ireland is burning and the Irishmen are
divided by personal hatreds. These two Irishmen were born
the same year in the same town, live on the same street, court
and eventually marry sisters, attend the same parochial school
and the same church, and conduct profitable business with
each other. Their "perfect hate casts out fear" and the Black
and Tans spare their lives, for "these two rats will do more
harm to Ireland living than they'll ever do to Ireland dead"
[*DFN*, pp. 8-10]. The PRERUMBLE device was used earlier and
less effectively in *Oak Leaves and Lavender,* again as a kind
of flashback—the essential difference being that in the earlier
play the flashback was from a time of war to a time of
distantly remembered peace. The pretentions of the two
haters who crawl off in opposite directions gain fuller development in the more opulent surroundings of their later riches.

The pompous grandeur of Alderman Aloysius Binnington
and Councillor McGilligan is rendered comic by their elaborate costumes, the elaborate furnishings of their elaborate
homes, the etiquette lessons afforded their wives, and their
attitudes toward business. Each strives to have the biggest
palm trees, the largest piano, the most elegant wife, and the
largest bank account. "Business, patriot, and pietist," Binnington "loves himself more than anything else living or dead." So
far as he's concerned, " . . . it is a dereliction of good taste for a
Deputy Mayor to wear a more gorgeous gown than the
Mayor." The business ethics of these two Irishmen who hate

each other are based invariably on expedience and profit, as were those of Poges, Reiligan, and O'Casey's other successful businessmen. They, too, figure prices, scold the young, and complain that "This appalling materialism's spreadin' everywhere."

The play within a play sequence testifies to O'Casey's dramatic dexterity, as it restates the basic themes of the outer play: that it is time for a change, that those who demand change are guilty of "high treason against this realm and the realm's law," and that "our chapel's on fire," set ablaze by the yeomanry. Here, as in the PRERUMBLE, and as in Ireland, the Irishmen do mechanical and wary battle with each other while the chapel burns. Fittingly, the play rehearsal is interrupted by the Reverend Fillifogue, who also interrupts and interferes with all of the other preparations for the Tostal. Fillifogue's comments on the play within a play and on the chorus rehearsal are thematic, and anticipate his ultimate paralysis and that of his followers. At the same time, his comments reveal his stand against change, against what O'Casey calls life:

> So your play babbles about the rights of man. What with your rights of women, rights of children, rights of trade unions, rights of th' laiety, an' civil rights—youse are paralysin' life! . . . [*DFN*, pp. 34-40]

The Drums of Father Ned, while satirizing the personal battles and personal hatreds of individual Irishmen, wages a pitched battle for change and for action against the complacent lethargy and the entrenched power of Fillifogue, Binnington, and McGilligan. The terms of the battle are clearly stated by Nora, who runs for public office against Binnington:

> [We are fighting]—not against our fathers! We're fighting what is old and stale and vicious: the hate, the meanness their policies preach; and to make a way for th' young and thrusting. [*DFN*, pp. 81-82]

When informed that it's easier said than done, Nora retorts, "Everthing said, Michael, is easier than anything done. It is a fine fancy to say brave things; better to do them." Nora sets out to do brave things that O'Casey says his play is about:

To snatch from Erin's back the sable shawl,
And clothe her as she was before her fall;
In Cloak of green as bright as spring's young call;
. . . . [*DFN*, p. x]

Doonavale is the Nyadnanave and the Ballyoonagh of this play. On the battlefield of Doonavale, as background for the Life versus Death conflict, the Orangeman from Ulster argues politics and religion with his Catholic counterparts, while the pietistic vigilantes are commanded by Father Fillifogue, who tells them:

I'll do th' thinking for youse; I'll say th' things that should be said; an' youse'll do th' things I'll tell youse to do. Now go ahead, an' burn th' atheistical timber, or something may happen to our town. . . . Burn it as a reparation to God for landing atheistical timber on th' holy wharf of Doonavale.

Father Fillifogue attempts to use the old hatred for the northern counties to manipulate his Southern flock to do his will; he threatens and dismisses his adversaries from appointive posts. He wields his obviously symbolic umbrella as a threatening weapon until his organist, Mr. Murray, sends him away after a ludicrous wrestling match, and as the play ends, the Ulsterman and Mr. Murray take the umbrella away for good. Fillifogue, without the support of capital and without the blind following he's accustomed to, becomes ridiculous, impotent and paralyzed: he has suffered what O'Casey diagnoses elsewhere as a "purelytic seizure."[38]

The main action of *The Drums of Father Ned* is much embellished by occasional and continuing slapstick comedy as pretense is reduced to absurdity: McGilligan warns Skerighan that "a Protestant tune's no fit thing to be played on a Catholic piano"; and every workman and visitor who enters Binnington's house drinks freely of his liquor, recalling the audacity of the workmen in *The Bishop's Bonfire* who drank the Bishop's brandy. Mrs. Binnington, never successful in her attempted

pirouettes, which are so necessary for the wife of the ostentatious mayor, sums up her confusion and her frustration in her
much repeated, "God damn it!" Father Fillifogue's brilliant
capacity for reducing everything to a capsule cause and effect
relationship interprets the reading of banned books, the
importing of Red lumber, the confusion of Doonavale, the
communistic tendencies of the workers, and the love affair
between Nora and Michael as direct results of "th' College
lettin' th' students wear jeans" [DFN, pp. 98-99].

Bernadette notes early in the play that "in Doonavale, near
everything said or done is dangerous. We're tired out at feelin'
afraid of a word or a look bringin' courage or affection into
our lonely souls!" The reversal of fortune and the salvation of
Doonavale is possible, however, only after Nora tells the
Reverend D. Fillifogue:

> You see, Father, we're fed up bein' afraid our shaddas'll tell what
> we're thinkin'. One fool, or a few, rules th' family life; rules th'
> school, rules th' dance hall, rules th' library, rules th' ways of a
> man with a maid, rules th' mode of a girl's dhress, rules th' worker
> in fields and factory, rules th' choice of our politicians, rules th'
> very words we try to speak, so that everything said cheats th'
> thruth; an' Doonavale has become th' town of th' shut mouth.
> [DFN, p. 98]

Bernadette Shillayley is a saucy vital wench, twin sister to
the whore in *Bedtime Story* whose antics and success she
duplicates. Her victim is just as fearful but more alive than
John Jo Mulligan; the Orangeman from Ulster, far from
promising to read Yeats for a quiet hour, wants a kiss "just as a
fine beginnin'." Bernadette, who "can guess only dimly at its
meanin'" when Skerighan accuses her of "twutterin' your
luddle bum," succeeds in frightening him into paying a few
pounds blackmail, forgives the "poor sinful man" for "th'
dhreadful harm you have done to a poor innocent counthry
girrl," promises to pray for him, and leaves him half terrified
and fully stunned by her duplicity. Father Fillifogue further
confuses the victimized Orangeman when he says of Berna-

dette, "That sly little vixen schatters occasions of sin everywhere she goes" [*DFN*, pp. 58-68].

Bernadette Shillayley, as her name suggests, is as bold as a
bear and as subtle as a cudgel in her attempts to live naturally,
to dance, to sing, and to enjoy the results. Her indecorous way
of life is an exemplary foil for the respectability and the
decorum proffered by Fillifogue and fellows. She echoes her
counterparts in *The Purple Dust* as she agrees with Tom that
one day, she and he must fade and fall:

> Yes, yes, when all that could be done is done; not be a wild
> grab at life, but a sturdy, steady livin' of it; when all our deeds
> and joys'll be as many as the leaves on an ash or th' blossoms
> on a three of hawthorn. Then we can fade in quietness, and
> fall with the carelessness of satisfaction. [*DFN*, p. 51].

The mood of the whole play is permeated by the frenzied
activities of those involved in the Tostal. The drums, periodically sounding in the background, the rough renditions of
Adeste Fidelis, the play rehearsal, and the choir rehearsal all
look forward to and anticipate the Tostal celebration. All the
people are actively involved and, as a result, Doonavale is
transformed into a living town, a transformation possible for
Ireland when the Irish people follow the lead of Nora,
Michael, and Bernadette.[39] As the tempo of the action increases and more and more of the trappings are removed
from the ostentatious homes of the Binningtons and the
McGilligans, the old changes into the new. O'Casey's forces
win a resounding victory as the decorations are distributed to
conceal the drabness of Doonavale behind splashes of color,
as the door of Fillifogue's house is painted "a flamin' red;
redder than th' reddest sun a frosty sunset ever seen," as
Fillifogue's clerk and macebearer drop dead, "Plonk plonk—
just like that!" and as the forces of life assemble on the Hill of
Three Shouts to determine the election of new officers.[40] As
life's victory becomes more evident, Father Ned's drums
increase in tempo, playing the Death March for the symbolic

death of Fillifogue's power, for it—like his clerk and his macebearer—is dead.

Father Ned, like Joyce's God, is a shout in the street:

> It might be a *shout for freedom*, like the shout of men on Bunker Hill; shout of th' people for bread in th' streets, as in th' French Revolution; or for th' world's ownership by th' people as in th' Soviet Revolution; or it might just be a drunken man, unsteadily meandhering his way home, shouting out Verdi's "Oh, Le-on-or-a."[41]

In any case, the music of Father Ned's drums is the music of life, and "Dee moosic of life is scarin'." Fillifogue, Binnington, and McGilligan, the apostles of discord and fear and materialism. They are paralyzed and are unable to move out of their chairs, however violently they try. They are symbolically dead, and O'Casey's dead cannot rise and walk. The steadily increasing tempo of Father Ned's drums is matched by the new and abounding life in Doonavale. Even Oscar McGunty contributes to the new confusion by playing his trumpet version of "Boots and Saddles," fitting funeral music for the paralysis and death of Fillifogue and his flock.

The satiric burlesques and invective of *The Drums of Father Ned* reduce the social and religious hierarchy of Doonavale to ashes, even as their spokesmen are symbolically dead. Ironically, "The Dead March" and "Boots and Saddles" become the rally music for a united Ireland: Orange does join Green; youth will win the election; inevitable change will be neither feared nor avoided; song and dance will become as natural and as healthy as a shout in the street so "that mobled minds may all new courage grow, and miser'd hearts be merry."[42] All in all, the play is "but an idle, laughing play/About the thorns encumbering Ireland's way."

Prior to the Archbishop's refusal to permit any religious ceremony in conjunction with the Theatre Festival of 1958 and the consequent cancellation of that festival, O'Casey had written

> The intelligent and educated Irish are, I believe, becoming impatient with, and resentful of, the interference of priest and

bishop in every phase of their life. Some of them have spoken out, and even de Valera (Ireland's present Taoiseach—Prime Minister) has publicly repudiated the Bishop of Galway on a question of religious intolerance. I try to show this awakening, this thrust forward in thought, this new resolution, in my latest play, *The Drums of Father Ned*.[43]

ENCORE

The Green Crow was justifiably outraged by the entire Tostal proceedings, and his next play, *Behind the Green Curtains*, begins where *The Drums of Father Ned* leaves off: the "Dead March" continues to play, and it could be the death knell for the rigid controls of the church, except for public cowardice. The public funeral of a Protestant benefactor is overlooked by a portrait of Parnell and virtuously ignored by a couple of worn-out hawkers, who wonder which saint the portrait honors. The intellectual leaders of Ireland—the journalist, poet, actor, and senator—are "jittering at the gate" but do not attend the memorial service because they fear clerical reprisals if they commit the grave sin of attending a Protestant funeral.

The first scene establishes the mood of the play and identifies the leaders of Ireland, who cower, in the second scene, behind the pulled drapes—the green curtains—to think their brave thoughts. The masked vigilantes whom they fear are also cowards, as their masks and actions prove. The battle between life and death continues, but in this play Nyadnanave is called Ballybeedhust, and O'Casey's accent is on the last syllable, as he sings of the death of Ireland.

This play is a bitter song sung by a poet in exile as he laments both his own loneliness and the literary void of Erin, as Erin consistently drives away talent and crowns mediocrity. In his prefacing comments, O'Casey identifies journalists as writers who are dangerous, more dangerous than other writers, if they do not walk "within the shadow of truth, courage, and sincerity." The literary cult in this play represents the Yeatsian hangers-on, those without talent or means who derive glory and income from their associations with each other and with the Irish Academy. Their names and their actions clearly identify them: Wycherley McGeera, the dramatist, debunks Yeats on general principles, and has one volume of plays published at Chatastray's expense; McGeelish, the gossip columnist, complains of his hard life, cowers, and has spent the money given him by Chatastray to finance his novel—a novel he has never written and will never write; Bunny Conneen, the actor, is a rabbit who reads his press clippings and believes himself to be "an artist of a wide fame"; Leslie Horawn, the poet, lives by the creed that

> Th' writer's place is th' cool contentment of quiet, in a corner where no voice comes; no car drives by; no child's laugh disturbs; no touch from a woman to ruffle th' stillness of thought; only birdsong and th' gentle ripple of a rose on its own bush.[44]

These are the great minds of Ireland; all are Catholic and all refuse to attend the funeral of a Protestant patron for fear of gossip and retaliatory action. Their living patron is Senator Chatastray, who is as cowardly and as confused as his sycophants. His plush library is fully stocked with Gaelic books, but he can't read Gaelic. Hidden away in a lower drawer of a sideboard, he keeps Renan's *Life of Jesus* and a photo of a nude, much to the delight and the horror of his followers, who alternately envy him and condemn the "leader of piety and upright conduct."[45]

Christy Kornavaun is a "squinting prober" for *The Catholic Buzzer* and is a combination Judas goat and jackal, as he snoops, leads the vigilantes, and writes for *The Buzzer*. He, as representative of his church's power, is the real villain, the hypocrite, the lecher, the suspicious paranoid whose fruitful imagination fills in the details of Noneen's sex life "when darkness hides things, and th' flimsy frills of night are worn, [and] behind green curtains th' handling sport begins." When his direct advances are thwarted by Noneen, she ceases to be "damned pretty before, behind, an' below," and becomes a "painted doll," a "festhered lily," an "ignorant, impudent little arcadian tart," and ultimately is physically punished by Kornavaun's vigilantes.[46] Nominally, Noneen's punishment is for consorting with an unmarried man; ironically, it is for rejecting Kornavaun, the blackmailer and the lecher, and for throwing a drink in his face.

Kornavaun is much feared by the respectable and cowardly artists, who all submit to his threats; he is suitably treated and identified only by Beoman as "this viper-fool" and by Reena, who addresses him as, "you bordher-line lunatic, you full-feathered hypocrite, you mouldy crumb of life, ..." Kornavaun and his church gain their power from the fear that overwhelms Ballybeedhust, and they are powerless against those who do not fear. Reena describes Ireland as "a huddled nation frightened undher th' hand of fear," and therein states the basic thesis of *Behind the Green Curtains*. Reena also informs Senator Chatastray, the poet patron, that fear and seclusions are not legitimate answers to the problems of life, but that one must be involved in life in order to live: "No one and nothing can be left alone in this world. As long as you're alive, you'll have to bear being touched by th' world you live in." Chatastray himself, in a brief moment of lucidity, which results from his conversation with Reena, identifies the marchers as

> Th' groggy gang of hypocrites! Cowardly minds an' spent-out lives trudge along on unsteady feet to th' rhythm of th' *Marseillaise*, without any idea of the singing revolt in its melody. [*BGC*, p. 61]

Momentarily there is hope for Chatastray as he defies his sycophants and Kornavaun, but he is ultimately overcome by his own fears and his own hypocrisy and joins the marchers, symbolically choosing comfortable death rather than threatening life as he chooses conformity and the status quo.

Basically, the play is a study in the progressive deterioration of those afflicted by cowardice. After a given point, a moment of decision, all is lost. All the writers and actors except Chatastray are lost when the play begins. Though no flowers fill his vases and his green drapes are drawn, he is still potentially a living man; his potential is not so much as Sailor Mahan's in *Cock-a-Doodle Dandy*, but is more than that of Keelin's young Daniel in *The Bishop's Bonfire*. His copy of Renan's *Life of Jesus* and the photo of the nude (both hidden from view) identify him as a hypocrite, but as one with more capacity than his friends have. When he dons the symbolic uniform and joins the processional, he is lost in "an army with banners marching in th' wrong direction"; he will continue to live behind curtains and to "move be candle-light when the sun is out," for he lacks, as Reena tells him, "Guts," and, thereby, he lacks life. Such being the case, he joins "th' third Ordher of th' Brothers Repentant" and marches under the banner ironically proclaiming "Free Thought in a Free World." After a brief flurry of life, he succumbs and rejoins the regimented followers of the Bishop, who "said that no writer can become great unless he always does it prosthrate on his belly before God."

The aptly named saints honored by the Bishop's religion are St. Sinfoilio, St. Ishkabaheen, St. Stepaslide, St. Touchnrun, St. Dubudont, and St. Goslow. True followers are impressed by miracles and have no difficulty understanding what the plaster Virgin of Syracuse is weeping about: she obviously weeps because a suppliant "woman was weepin', an' she was weepin' because her husband was a Communist"; this greatly amuses Beoman, O'Casey's spokesman, who suggests that the saint may be weeping because the woman is not a communist. The Bishop's religion keeps the true followers fearful and at the same time ashamed of their fear. Fear is the way of life for the artists who do not attend Lionel Robartes's funeral because "o' th' risk: Catholics at a non-Catholic religious service may incur excommunication." The fear is compounded as Bunny corrects this interpretation by noting that such Catholics "incur it automatically." [*BGC*, p. 18]

The bickering continues as the age old Catholic versus Protestant question dominates the conversation of the devoted Catholic friends of a dead Protestant benefactor. The bickerers and their comments are reduced to the proper perspective by O'Casey's sardonic Beoman, who sings:

So th' old flute was doomed, and its fate was pathetic.
'Twas fasten'd an' burn'd at the stake as heretic.
While the flames roar'd round it, they heard a strange noise;
'Twas the old flute still whistlin' "Th' Protestant Boys!"[47]

Beoman is O'Casey's confident workman blessed with ability and common sense; he sees through sham, frightens the vigilantes, proclaims Parnell a better man than either St. Joseph or St. Peter, and snorts "at a faith that has th' Christian world sizzlin' with miracles!" Beoman leaves Ireland with Reena and Noneen to get away "from this dead place," the dead place which reflects its character by banning and burning "filthy literature that corrupts Irishmen and makes them ripe for Communism." [*BGC*, p. 14, p. 84]

The death of Ballybeedhust is clearly reflected in the Catholics who fear to attend a Protestant benefactor's funeral, in the punishments administered by the vigilantes, and in the closing of the factories to protest a marriage between a Catholic girl and a Protestant man. All of these, together with solemn processionals protesting against communism by marching under banners proclaiming "Free Thought in a Free World," are emblematic proofs that Ballybeedhust is a dead place.

The bitterness of O'Casey's satire is due in large part to personal experiences other than the stillborn festival of 1958. He was invited to join the Irish Academy of Letters when it was created by Yeats, an invitation signed by George Bernard Shaw. "Shaw was asking a favour from Sean; the first favour ever asked," and O'Casey had to refuse because he

> didn't like institutions powered to decide what was good litera-
> ture and what was not good; they had made too many mistakes
> before. They were inclined to look kindly on those who flattered
> their own work.[48]

Pictured in the inept poet of this drama is O'Casey's view of the ultimate evil of the Academy, that members of such an Academy might become an exclusive mutual admiration society and thereby stifle, rather than encourage, creative writing. O'Casey also believed that Yeats led a protected and an essentially unseeing life "behind velvet curtains." O'Casey's marriage to a Catholic girl, the resulting protests, and his series of clashes with the Catholic hierarchy contribute some bitterness to his portrayal of the continuous conflict between Protestants and Catholics and to his view of the inelasticity of the religion which demands total conformity. Concerning the marriage which closes the shop in this play, O'Casey's own oft-expressed view was that all marriages should be mixed: each should consist of one man and one woman.

There is no real movement and no real change for the citizens of Ballybeedhust, though the scene of action moves from a public park fronting on a burial ground to the confines of Senator Chatastray's home to the processional protesting against communism. As the scene-title indicates, the great minds of Ireland are "jitterin' at th' gateway" in Scene I just before they succumb to the threats of Kornavaun; they are protected from light and life by the thick green curtains shrouding Chatastray's home in Scene II; they move from one darkness into another in Scene III, "The Day of the Marching Souls," as they fall into line amidst the regimental hierarchies of honored groups. The demonstration shuts off light and enforces the separation of the marchers from involvement in life just as effectively as Chatastray's green curtains do. The Brothers Repentant take great pride in their unfurled banner and recognize no irony in its proclamation, FREE THOUGHT IN A FREE WORLD.

"The green curtains of the title . . . symbolize the obscurantism and humbug of Irish Catholicism . . . ,"[49] and the artificial blinders worn by those who prefer not to question and not to'jeopardize either their immediate or their eternal security. More than that, they symbolize the constitutional blindness of O'Casey's ostrich-like Irishmen, who continue to assert that one can unthink anything simply by ignoring it, that one can eliminate a church-proclaimed evil by chanting Latin phrases at it, and that one can shut out fear and life by drawing one's own blinds.

The satiric bitterness of this play cannot be discarded as the result of splenetic old age, since O'Casey's main theme for three decades was that Ireland's way is a way of death. The alternatives in this play are not essentially different from those offered in the preceding plays: the young and those who wish to live out of the shadow of fear can follow Joyce, O'Casey, Beoman, Noneen, and Reena into exile and thereby save themselves and perpetuate Ireland's mediocrity and accelerate her march toward death. The alternative (an Ayamonn miracle) would involve thought and action independent of the Procrustean mold, a cessation of internal bickering, and a sustaining faith in the magic and the power of vital people.

The second play in O'Casey's last volume of plays is *Figuro in the Night,* a morality play satirically "*dead*icated" to

> *The Ferocious Chastity of Ireland* . . . in the abiding hope that all, North and South, will combine against, fight, and destroy this communist and insidious effort to overthrow the age-long virtue of the Irish People; to prevent this rock-built chastity from corrosion, so that it may outlive all redlike attempts to frighten or weaken its determination by a godless and ruthless ridicule. Amen.[50]

The setting is Dublin and the morality figures of the first scene maintain their rock-built chastity, do not tarry nor marry, and piously praise themselves for their good sense. They are the walking dead and their world is a darkly silent one of gloom and desolation.

The young girl sings a song of love, "O Dear, What Can the Matter Be?", the improvised lyrics being O'Casey's own answer to the sterile plight of Ireland and the song itself becoming thematic as the play progresses. The old woman's antiphonal answers to the young girl's love song are based on memory—a barren memory, for she "never heard a birdsong to disthract me from me higher thinking." The mother and the father that she and the old man listened to in their youth "are but cracked china figaries on the mantelshelf of memory." The blue ribbons given her by the old man in his youth are yellow with age and have never been worn. The old couple meet, stir up half-forgotten memories, and depart in opposite directions, both decrepit and leaning on their canes, both much concerned with public opinion and reputation. Blue ribbons and birdsongs and unbridled youth are recognized and feared by both as occasions for sin. In fact, she remembers and embroiders the memory of her youthful beauty and the blue ribbons offered by one young man, "gay ribbons fit only for a girl's ringlets, or for decorating dainty pieces shelthering the pleasant and secret parts of a lassie's virgin form. . . ."

The old woman, in a brief moment of envy and lucidity, defends Adam's tying a "blue ribbon on the bonnie brown hair of his Eve," for "The poor man got tired looking at her dressed only in her innocense; he needed her to look gayer to him and feel gayer herself, for the heady juice of the apple they'd eaten jollied them into a jostle together." The high thoughts, the obeyed parental commands, and the resulting barrenness of her youth are in violent conflict with the thoughts and the essential fecundity of Adam and Eve. The old woman's ambivalent responses to life are too late. She is no longer a young girl, and, for the pagan purposes of this play, she is no longer alive.

The birdsong, the crow's caw, the Adam and Eve tale, and the continuing search of the young girl during the initial scene anticipate the transformation and the avid enthusiasm of the second scene, which is a pagan hymn to pagan joys. The old people remain old and impotent, but are secretly lecherous and envious. Their puritanical comments are suggestive and impotently obscene, while the natural antics of the young are essentially innocent and potent. The impotence of the old is emphasized as one has a bandaged head, one wears his arm in a sling, one is deaf, one is blind; all are out of place in a world where "Everything seems wonderful to eyes that see and ears that hear."

O'Casey briefly revives what Krause has called his *cock ex machina* with its spirit of youth and joy;[51] it is present in both the Figuro and the Birdlike Lad and soon becomes the dominating spirit of the play. The transformed world is one of bright color, light, flowers, and song. The old symbolize public opinion (bowler hat), deValerian politicians (top hat and tails), hypocrisy (envy of those they condemn), and death (imposed self-denial and reverence for the status quo). The young in their pagan song and dance represent thrusting life and promise for a future as they ignore and symbolically tear to tatters the prevailing public opinion and fear of change.

The morality play context remains intact as the fearful young man, who is praised by the old man for protecting his "decent dangling accessory" from "them bitches of girls,"[52] moves from fear through questioning toward understanding of the mysterious mood of the transformed Dublin. He asks of the old men, "Every living thing goes in couples, so why shouldn't lads and lassies do the same?" He identifies the old men who fear the evil import of "silk-sinisthered legs" as "holy buckoes, groping and rowdying about in the spare parts of the crowd, looking for what you couldn't get even if you got it!" Inspired by the Birdlike Lad, who testifies that the same transformation has occurred all over Ireland and that "the Bishops are seated at a Round Table in the Senate Room" singing love songs, the young man tells the old, "To hell with the lot o' yous—I'm for the thrust and throe of Figuro!" He takes bonny blue ribbons to his Alice and, like Adam, emerges with the golden apples of the sun. Unlike the old people in the first scene, the young man has learned about life before it is too late.

O'Casey tells his reader that the two scenes of *Figuro in the Night* are "eloquently and humorously related," and they are: the first presents the aridity of negation and the second presents the joys of involvement. The Figuro, with his "Peek-a-boo," his "Sight Enthrancing," is the venerable poet's answer to the screams of St. Tremolo in *The Bishop's Bonfire,* and the raucous dance of youth is O'Casey's answer to the plight of Ireland, whose decreasing population is due to the emigration of the young, the increasingly late age of marriage, and the Puritanical yokes of conservative Catholicism and conservative Protestantism.

The satire is not masked as O'Casey dissects his homeland and ridicules the hypocritical piety that he reveals there. Much of the humor of this poetic morality play is due to the salacious use of language by the old and the inverted situation of the young wenches dragging down any male in sight. The element of fear continues, however, as the Catholic journalists, one deaf and one blind, are ordered back to their "airless little office, to write your scraps of gossip, and try to tell your shrinking little world that the world outside is changing." All the while, the dance of life continues in the streets of Dublin, and, according to the Birdlike Youth, throughout Ireland.

Obviously, this unperformed play is not one of O'Casey's better efforts, but the aged satirist did enjoy flaying his old enemies, and his Young Man does come to grips with the joy of life, thereby affording at the same time a victory and a prophesy. O'Casey's people must leave the everlasting lullaby of Eden, and in order to do so they must be "too human to be unafraid, but too human to let fear put an end to us!"[53] If the result of leaving Eden is death, then it is "Death for this man, death for that woman, but greater life for all." Eden, whether it be called Dublin, Nyadnanave, or Ballybeedhust, is a way of death if it does not admit change.

The fair mentioned in the thematic song, "Oh Dear, What Can the Matter Be?", is used in essentially the same way that the fair in *Time to Go*, the homecoming in *The Bishop's Bonfire*, and the Tostal festival in *The Drums of Father Ned* are used: it is a joyous time of gaiety and frivolity, but leaves in its wake desolation and unfulfilled dreams. To go to the fair is to escape from reality; O'Casey's answer is to make life itself a perpetual fair so that the young may never experience the desolation and drab loneliness endured by the old people in Scene I, so that blue ribbons can be worn and enjoyed while they are bright and new, so that the young—once they become old—will have something other than fear and chastity to remember.

The setting of *The Moon Shines on Kylenamoe* is also a dead town inhabited by the very old, "th' lot o' them, man an' woman, if not there already, is on th' top o' 70."[54] It is "a dark and lonesome land" whose somber midnight mood is emphasized by Sean Tomasheen's singing a song of death, "I Dreamt That I Dwelt in Marble Halls." Kylenamoe is a town unaccustomed to having the train stop. The symbolic red light surprises Andy O'Hurrie, and utter confusion reigns so long as the train is stopped.

O'Casey's chief targets in this farcical episode are the pretensions of little men who have some authority and the ludicrous overspecialization that makes a change of hats and badges necessary before Tomasheen can perform his various chores. The inefficiency recalls the incident when O'Casey first journeyed to Coole, as Lady Gregory's guest, carrying the first suitcase he'd ever owned. The Galway Express was to leave Dublin at 8:00 A.M. and the sleeping ticket salesman refused to heed the demands of the crowd before that magic hour. In the confusion enforced by the sarcastic guard and compounded by shrill blasts from the engine, O'Casey defied the uniformed authorities and boarded the train without the required ticket. The crowd followed, and all reached their destinations in spite of the rigidly enforced rules.[55]

The Irishmen of the play are the stage Irishmen of *John Bull's Other Island,* who kibitz and call names and hurl insults at each other, but united against the ludicrous English intruder who is clad in a burlesque of the official parliamentarian's uniform, is impeded by an attaché case and an umbrella, and is named Lord Leslieson of Otterry St. Oswald. He is a parody of the stage Englishman, and it is delightful to contemplate his arrival at his destination in a donkey-drawn creel cart.

The moon does shine on Kylenamoe, as is evidenced by the presence of the young lovers and the essential kindness of the Conroys. The silver apples of the moon sought and found by Eve in Eden and by Alice in *Figuro in the Night* are suggested by the transient presence of Mave Linanawn and her lover who would rather own her "than own all of Ireland, without division." It is a wise choice for him to make, so far as O'Casey is concerned, but the lovers, like the young of Ireland, are threatened and ordered off the property for violating the rules.

Behind the Green Curtains, Figuro in the Night, and *The Moon Shines on Kylenamoe* were written following the death of Niall, a loss which sent O'Casey hurtling into prodigious writing activity. They restate his basic themes and include the same devices of fantasy and expressionism used in the other plays of his final period. While not as effective as *Cock-a-*

Doodle Dandy, or *The Bishop's Bonfire,* or *The Drums of Father Ned,* these plays argue rather forcefully that Sean O'Casey did not lose his touch, and did resent the stranglehold that was stifling Ireland. Further, he did envision a better life which could come to pass whenever his countrymen were willing to make a conscious choice, to demand change, and to take off the symbolic straitjackets worn as badges of tradition and complacency and fear. Despite the significant and oft-repeated theses, O'Casey's Finale neither begins nor ends very auspiciously, but between *Oak Leaves and Lavender* and *The Moon Shines on Kylenamoe* are several excellent examples of a significant satirist at work.

5

PostRumble

Sean O'Casey's drama, like his vision, is satiric, becoming increasingly so from the incidental satire in the tragicomic plays of his Irish period to the universal implications of the satiric fantasies of his last period. The dramatist who calls his plays tragedies may, as the best do, include the most hilarious comedy and the most revealing satire without de-emphasizing the dimensions of human loss or human suffering. The time of the troubles *(Shadow of a Gunman)* and the time of the Irish Civil War *(Juno and the Paycock)* were times of pain, fear, and senseless death. O'Casey's microcosms reflect this. They were also, like all moments of human history, times when human foolishness and selfishness and vanity would not be kept down by a few bullets or bombs or knockings on the wall. O'Casey's satire in his early plays is incidental, his main thrust, as his title pages indicate, being toward the tragic and the enduring.

His satire, though incidental, is incisive. We can laugh at the pretenses and the antics of the tenement dwellers; we can delight in the capers and shenanigans of Joxer and Captain Boyle, as O'Casey clearly does. The fact that they evoke laughter makes them and us human; it does not make their values, their fears, and their occasional sacrifice of basic human decency acceptable. The human capacities to be the fool and to laugh at the foolish do not lessen the horrors of raids in the night or bullets in the breast, nor that of a drunken boistrous paycock whose son is dead, whose daughter is pregnant, whose world is in a terrible state of chassis.

In *Shadow of a Gunman* and *Juno and the Paycock*, Dublin's playgoers were made aware of the madness that methodically infringed upon and destroyed the lives of the characters on stage, for it was the same madness that still raged outside the theatre itself. Just as they were aware of the human strengths and capacities of Juno Boyle and Minnie Powell, so also were they aware of the strong ironic bite of O'Casey's topical satire directed at the Auxiliaries, the Black and Tans, and the argumentative civilian populace.

O'Casey's satire in *The Plough and the Stars* is even more incisive than that in *Shadow of a Gunman* and *Juno and the Paycock*. He uses sound more dramatically as the orator's rhetoric provides background for the pub scene and for the bloody war that follows, and as the sounds of battles and looting provide background for the human tragedy that is enacted on stage. He uses color effectively as the drabness of the slums is relieved by the colorful costumes and the brave sounds that hide the fear of the cowards. The brave old world of the strutting militants and the pretenders who follow them collapses as it must, for their dedications and proclamations are false.

The rioting and looting, though less deadly, are just as real as the English artillery. The looters are as much a part of the populace as the Easter Week soldiers are. More of them survive. Easter Week is no less deadly as portrayed by O'Casey than its original enactment was. O'Casey emphasizes the fact that it was deadly, that carnival atmosphere relinquished the stage to mayhem, that the innocent and well-meaning were the real casualties of that as well as of more recent terrible beauties.

O'Casey's hilariously, perhaps instinctively, funny characters do survive the bloodletting. Fluther Good is intact. His life and the Covey's and Rosie's will go on, essentially unchanged except for memory. Nora's baby, Nora's health, and Nora's husband are casualties, but the greatest loss is Bessie Burgess, the hymn singing oul' Orange bitch.

The observations of the dramatist opposed to the rising were no more popular in 1926 than they were in 1916. The riots in the Abbey clearly demonstrated that. O'Casey did contain his bitterness and his rage sufficiently enough that no reader or viewer of *The Plough and the Stars* can argue convincingly against its merits as great theatre. The 1926 performances and riots mark the end of the most successful era in the continuing history of Dublin's Abbey Theatre. It is further appropriate, I think, that "at 10:15 on the evening of 17th July, 1951, the curtain fell at the conclusion of a brilliant performance of *The Plough and the Stars*," the last play to be performed in the old Abbey Theatre, for the theatre was destroyed by fire that night.[1]

O'Casey's departure from Dublin, his marriage to Eileen, and his completion of *The Silver Tassie* mark the beginning of a new life for him and the beginnings of a rapid decline in the fortunes of the Abbey Theatre. Too much has already been written about O'Casey's exile and too much made of the fact that from *The Silver Tassie* on, O'Casey wrote in exile from his people, his characters, and his theatre. The usual aim of such criticism is to demonstrate O'Casey's decline as a playwright. O'Casey knew, if his critics did not, that the artist sees more clearly if he gains some distance from his subject, that his effectiveness as artist is enhanced if he gains new perspectives.

In *The Silver Tassie* and the colorful plays that follow, O'Casey frankly experiments with assorted dramatic techniques, with changing perspectives, and with making the teacup into a microcosm. Having read and understood assorted efforts of August Strindberg and O'Neill, O'Casey did not discover expressionism by reading the second act of *The Silver Tassie*, though several of his critics apparently did, and certainly thought O'Casey did. In his scream against war in *The Silver Tassie*, O'Casey's attitudes toward the wanton destructiveness of war have not greatly changed since Bessie's murder in *The Plough and the Stars;* for that matter, they aren't all that different from the dramatist's personal convictions surrounding the death of Minnie Powell in *Shadow of a Gunman,* or the execution of Johnny in *Juno and the Paycock.* The wars remain wars, though they change names and gain momentum and become increasingly devastating. The people who make war and are destroyed by war remain human, usually Irish, but the victims are no deader and no more mangled than their predecessors during the Rising, the Troubles, or the Irish Civil War.

At the same time that O'Casey's surrealistic, biblical, and cacaphonic experiments on stage establish the destructive madness of war and the impersonal sterility of Surgeon Maxwell's hospital ward, they also reflect the deep personal changes of O'Casey's war casualties. All are war casualties and all are changed utterly. Life does go on—for the living. The final scene of *The Silver Tassie* insists on that. Such experiments and such accomplishments anticipate the fantasy and the magic that momentarily transform Dublin in *Red Roses for Me*, the devastating portrait of Nyadnanave as the Cock's followers abandon that nest of fools, and set the stage for the transformation of yet another microcosm in *The Drums of Father Ned*. Even in the bitterest of Sean O'Casey's satires, the thrust of life goes on.

The morality play figures in *Within the Gates* epitomize the human frailties and human fears that Everywoman must confront, if she is to live. All the characters are fragmented; none has a complete understanding; each sees through his own blinders. The education of Jannice consists of her being instructed by assorted representatives of assorted world views. Her hopes for joy and fulfillment, like those partial views of the fragmented characters she comforts, are thematically basic to virtually all of O'Casey's plays that follow.

The existence of expressionism, fantasy, and morality play features in O'Casey's earlier works ably refutes the customary and arbitrary cataloging of his plays as naturalistic, realistic, expressionistic, or fantastic in any neatly chronological sequence. Such labels tend to obscure, rather than to illumine, the plays of either period.

As the plays become progressively more satiric, the settings become progressively more universal. By the last period, each setting (however specific) is microcosmic, each character type (however Irish) is representative of some aspect of mankind, and the poet's satiric weapons (however destructive) are directed toward the improvement of the comic world he portrays. O'Casey's penchant for burlesques and his willingness to reduce his villainous straw men to absurdity (to depict them not as individuals but as type characters, and to endow them not with dialogue but with poisonous platitudes) are offset by his equal willingness to reduce his heroes to absurdity by utilizing essentially the same techniques. The result is that in many of his satiric portraits of society, the viewer sees the two opposite extremes (perhaps the two lunatic fringes) between whose boundaries lies the saner and more meaningful way.

It is not necessary to be a clever whore to be a vital personality, but Angela Nightingale is the only vital personality in *Bedtime Story* and Jannice is the only vital personality in *Within the Gates;* it is not necessary to wear a uniform to be a villain, but virtually all of O'Casey's evil men do wear either clerical, political, or military uniforms. O'Casey's satire juxtaposes the good and the evil components of his comic world, and in the juxtaposition illuminates, by distortion and by example, the problems that confront mankind. He does not solve the problems, but does suggest an active approach toward their solution. The plays rarely, if ever, offer hedonism or escapism as an answer to man's problems; rather, they insist on involvement and calculated action. Occasionally, as in *Cock-a-Doodle Dandy* and *Time to Go,* when involvement is pointless, the calculated action is abandonment so that the pursuit of life and joy can continue. Characters like Ayamonn Breydon and Father Ned[2] state or exemplify O'Casey's basic theme so clearly and make the association between the box stage and the world outside so obvious that none can miss the author's intent: man must act, must correct his own follies and those of his world, and must forge his own miracles; if he does not, he must accept death as the consequence of his inactivity and his refusal to join the living.

O'Casey's people exist in a world ruled by clearly defined and easily recognizable authorities. The people must—in order to survive—recognize their relationship to that authority and find their assigned roles in the society ruled by such authority. If they are weak or fearful of change, they obey the laws, respect those in power, and try to keep the ships of faith and State and business from rocking. When this occurs, as it does in the majority of cases, their priests and bishops are Domineer, Fillifogue and Mullarkey, and they are in league with the politicians and the landowner to keep a good thing going—good for them. This need to know one's relationship and responsibility to authority is hardly unique in O'Casey's canon. Stephen Dedalus wends his way through *Portrait of the Artist as a Young Man* and *Ulysses* trying to recognize and then to modify or to escape such traditional patterns when they seem repressive. O'Casey's poets, laborers, dancers, and singers question and seek to better the best of all possible worlds.

The authority figures in O'Casey's "dying worlds" are most often the appointed leaders of the church, the emergent successes of lucrative business, and the elected politicians of the community. Their combined efforts perpetuate the usual and prevent any threat to the way things are. The fathers in his plays symbolically join with the entrenched powers and pose—by their very presence—barriers against growth and fulfillment. Captain Jack Boyle embraces the way of the church and those in power as soon as he believes he has money. He becomes an authority on the evils of the world that must be corrected. For reputation and appearance he rejects his daughter and the curtain falls on his drunken revelation that "th' whole worl's . . . in a terr . . . ible state o' . . . chassis!" The Bishop in *Within the Gates*, while a growing and maturing man, refuses to acknowledge his relationship to Jannice and can't keep eyes or hands off her knees. Abraham Penrhyn, in *Oak Leaves and Lavender*, does heroic deeds, but he cannot accept Monica's marriage to Drishogue, nor give her fatherly assistance when she needs it. Loreleen ultimately abandons her father (*Cock-a-Doodle Dandy*) as he abandoned her and Lorna for the preferred riches of his bog. Even Feelim O'Morrigun (*Oak Leaves and Lavender*), perhaps the best father of the lot, is not too happy with the civil marriage and

he states, "The gettin' o' children should be done accordin' to
rule!" In *The Bishop's Bonfire*, again, a young girl chooses a
father other than her own: "oh, Codger, dear Codger, I wish
to God that you were me Da!" Finally, in *The Drums of
Father Ned*, Michael and Nora lead an orderly revolt against
the power of their fathers—both of whom are motivated by
hate and greed.

O'Casey's satiric portraits of inadequate fathers are much
augmented by the everpresent fathers of the church—most of
whom are also selfish, arbitrary, domineering, and essentially
unaware of what their children really need. O'Casey's real
priests, like real fathers, are more sensitive, more aware, and
more willing to work for meaningful change. Further, such
priests and such fathers are mavericks, occasionally outcasts
or rejects feared by the very societies they would improve.
The roster is an impressive one: the Protestant Reverend E.
Clinton *(Red Roses for Me)*; the Brown Priest *(The Star Turns
Red)*; the much loved, but finally exiled, Father Boheroe *(The
Bishop's Bonfire)*; the omnipresent, but never seen, Father
Ned *(The Drums of Father Ned)*. The values and sensitivities
of these enlightened authority figures help us to understand
Jannice's need and her quest for a real father *(Within the
Gates)*; Monica's appeal to Feelim O'Morrigun *(Oak Leaves
and Lavender)*; Keelin's stated wish to have the Codger as
father *(Bishop's Bonfire)*; and the constructive action of the
young in *The Drums of Father Ned*.

O'Casey's real mothers, like his real fathers, are practical,
down-to-earth human beings. They take charge when male
authority is inadequate or absent and try to reestablish order,
to restore the values of humanity, and to respond to needs of
the moment. Juno Boyle *(Juno and the Paycock)* more than
compensates for the deficiencies of her husband as she
mourns a dead son and cares for a living daughter. Bessie
Burgess *(Plough and the Stars)* functions as mother in caring
for the needs of those around her. Her selfless courage and her
great concern for Nora do much to restore sanity in the midst
of the madness. Mrs. Breydon *(Red Roses for Me)* is the
loving and devoted mother of O'Casey's first mature poet.

Ultimately, she shares his vision just as she earlier shared his rehearsals for the Shakespeare performance. As virtually every critic has written, such women are close kin of O'Casey's own beloved mother.

Not all the mothers in O'Casey's canon are primarily concerned with feeding, nurturing, and healing. Not all subscribe to the basic values of humanity. Mrs. Gogan, who begets children according to the rules and the boundaries, takes her baby to the pub and virtually abandons her dying Mollser. Elvira Binnington and Meeda McGilligan (*Drums of Father Ned*), sisters in every possible way, amuse themselves learning the movements and arts befitting their place in society. In their pursuit of superficial polish, they are hangers-on who support their husbands, maintain the status quo, and bar any meaningful change. As presented by O'Casey, they are laughable, ignorant puppets in an artificially enclosed world. Their children set out to change that regimented world of etiquette lessons and uniformed authority.

While the parent metaphor is certainly the most basic metaphor of authority in O'Casey's works, the clothing metaphor is also significant and—on occasion—the two are not separable, for O'Casey's characters are identified by the clothes they wear. His priests, soldiers, and successful businessmen are suitably costumed. Whenever a character takes himself too seriously or assumes the symbolic value of his costume to be overly impressive, he is comic. Hence, the soldiers who hide their fears behind the gaudy costumes of the Foresters and the Irish Citizens Army (*Plough and the Stars*) are as foolish as those who wear the formal attire and the top hat of the DeValerian politician (*Cock-a-Doodle Dandy, Bishop's Bonfire, Drums of Father Ned,* etc.). O'Casey bitterly satirizes the wearers of Trilby hats and bowlers as reflectors of and worshippers of public opinion, as a sick society's leaders, and as its touchstones of success (*Within the Gates, Cock-a-Doodle Dandy, Behind the Green Curtains,* etc.).

Those who transform the world (especially in *Cock-a-Doodle Dandy* and *The Drums of Father Ned*) are also suitably and elaborately dressed in brilliantly colored costumes, as they make free use of paint, flowers, song, and magic to dress up a drab world. His laborers don Shakespearean garb over their work clothes and are themselves transformed by the magic of the word. O'Casey's contempt for the drab dress of the Catholic clergy offers an interesting contrast to his own preference for the drabbest kind of work clothes, a preference reinforced by his presentation of such figures as Red Jim Larkin, Ayamonn Breydon, and the Old Codger. Further, the essential goodness of the Brown Priest is at least partially symbolized by the color of his habit and its contrast to the colorful habit of the materialistic and greatly powerful Purple Priest. The seeming paradoxes and the apparent inconsistencies, rather than distressing O'Casey, seemed to give him pleasure.

The same O'Casey who refused to dress for receptions of first-night performances and condemned the soldiers of the Irish Citizen Army for adorning themselves in expensive, colorful, easy-to-see uniforms, loved the pomp and splendor of parades and processionals. Holloway records that O'Casey wore the green sack of the Foresters on one occasion and participated, during a thirsty friend's absence, in the annual Parnell procession, a participation that ultimately resulted in his joining the Gaelic League.[3] This is the same O'Casey who uses the pomp and the splendor of parades in both *The Plough and the Stars* and *Behind the Green Curtains* as facades for cowardice, the participants themselves marching and acting for fear their fears will be discovered. O'Casey's own choice of the laborer's clothes earned him much criticism from other members of the Gaelic League, for he attended meetings "untidily dressed, and was once asked to wait outside as he was not suitably clad to appear before the Dean of St. Patrick's."[4] Perhaps O'Casey hoped the Gaelic League would be a working league and he dressed accordingly. Perhaps he viewed the Abbey Theatre as a working theatre and dressed accordingly. Certainly, he brought a new group of viewers to the Abbey—a group he hoped would be more concerned with seeing than with being seen.

Like O'Casey himself, and like characters in Greek theatre, O'Casey's creations wear masks and costumes to tell us who they are and what they are about. When their costumes reflect their joy in living and singing and loving, they are healthful signs of vitality and continuing life. The workman attired for honest labor is as relevant and significant as Ayamonn's Shakespearean costume when he rehearses or performs Shakespearean drama. When Mary Boyle is more concerned with what ribbon to wear than with the strike itself, she is as foolish and immature as Sheila *(Red Roses for Me)* and Julia *(Star Turns Red)*. Consistently, O'Casey's characters who focus on their own attire or their own shadow as having substance or meaning in themselves are ridiculous—perhaps foolishly so as Mary and Sheila and Julia exemplify; perhaps fatally so as the richly accoutred soldiers in *The Plough and the Stars* demonstrate. Whenever the costumes signify authority, whole authority, and nothing but authority, they identify the wearers as chosen targets.

Like Jonson, Swift, and Twain before him, O'Casey recognized that society's authorities— whether chosen, ordained, or imposed—enforce the boundaries that can become repressive or destructive, reject questions that threaten those boundaries, and question those who persist in questioning the unquestionable. The chain of authority ultimately includes those at the bottom who accept without question, who embrace a single partial truth as the total truth, and who seek to dominate all those seen as somehow less authoritative or less experienced. Consequently, O'Casey's targets include those who openly accept eyewitness accounts as bonafide fact—without being concerned about the credentials of the viewer. Tourists like Creeda Stern, who has seen Russia, and shoppers, like the distressed woman in *The Plough and the Stars,* qualify.

So do his one-answer advocates who—like Emerson's monsters in *The American Scholar*—are not whole men: their views are partial whether they call themselves Atheist, Bishop, Poet, Communist, or Fascist. The more insistent a character is that his view is clear and that his answer is right, the more ridiculous and potentially dangerous he is. In O'Casey's world, hollow poses and empty facades, like hollow statues and empty promises, are to be laughed at rather than adored—ridiculed rather than endured.

The same O'Casey who exiled himself from Ireland, who had the Cock and Maid Marion lead the procession of living people out of Nyadnanave and leave that hamlet to Death *(Cock-a-Doodle Dandy)*, who had Kelly and the Widda Machree demonstrate the efficacy of truth and honesty and then abandon an Irish town to continue in its vicious practices *(Time to Go)*, argues again and again that man and nation must be adaptable and flexible enough to continue life in any situation; that if man and nation cannot adapt, the best will leave the worst to the fates of Nyadnanave and death. The microcosmic mansion in *Purple Dust* is destroyed because its masters can not adapt to momentary emergencies; Ayamonn and Father Ned insist that people must forge their own miracles and right their own worlds. Those who wait for miracles live sterile and disappointed lives.

O'Casey's adoration of Walt Whitman, "another emotional fool,"[5] is apparent in his desire to believe that the basic evils of society are man made and will be corrected when the common man attains the position that he is entitled to within that society. Like Whitman, O'Casey is dismayed when his common men attain wealth and cease to be common men. In O'Casey's plays, such men don rich clothes, buy big houses, display ornamental wives and own pianos. In other words, they adorn themselves so that we can know them and know what they are about as they become pompously complacent. His offered solution is the destruction of their miasmic affectation and the revelation of their basic follies. O'Casey's attacks on regimentation, materialism, and anything else whose inelasticity would deny individual man's identity and would prevent him from ennobling and enriching "the star we stand on"[6] are barbed attacks using revelation, recognition, and laughter as weapons. It is laughter that simultaneously reveals and destroys the sham and hypocrisy of the arbitrary way of the world fostered by those who have reason to fear laughter and joy. Among O'Casey's villains,

Laughter is allowed when it laughs at the foibles of ordinary men, but frowned on and thought unseemly when it makes fun of superstitions, creeds, customs, and the blown-up importance of brief authority of those going in velvet and fine linen.[7]

It is true that O'Casey's didactic voice is increasingly heard in his increasingly satiric canon. It is also true that he lost patience with those forces responsible for the deaths of Nannie and Bessie, Jannice and Ayamonn. O'Casey's antiheroic characters, at the outset, are richly comic, and we share his laughter at their antics. The energies of O'Casey's antiheroes in *Red Roses for Me* and *Cock-a-Doodle Dandy* and *The Drums of Father Ned* are increasingly directed to reforming or replacing the societal framework that causes and condones human suffering. O'Casey loses patience with his fools and sits with us as we laugh *at* them. He did learn from the inexcusably bad *The Star Turns Red* and the excusably bad *Oak Leaves and Lavender* that the didactic voice does not work nearly as well when it goes on and on and on as it does when it provides only the incremental refrain as the ballad tales tell themselves. He learned the lesson so well that Father Ned does not appear on stage in the battle that his words and wisdom make inevitable.

From first to last, O'Casey was a critic of his society; from first to last, he was didactic. His way with his villains is often Swiftian, as are his manipulations of the reflectors of society's values and traditions. O'Casey the satirist hardly replaces O'Casey the comic genius that we know paradoxically first by his three tragedies—*Shadow of a Gunman, Juno, and the Paycock,* and *The Plough and the Stars.* That paradox *is* O'Casey, who was a satirist from first to last. His sympathies, alliances, and resources change. His villains grow and accrue power until they become a threat to all that is good in human life; his antiheroes and his textbook heroes change and develop so that they can cope with the encompassing threat.

What remain constant, together with his capacities to create theatre, are O'Casey's laughter and his ability to make us laugh. Laughter is O'Casey's shared joy. When he directs our laughter, it becomes his weapon against evil. With laughter,

O'Casey—without apology—puts human values into meaningful perspective. With laughter, after ample warning, he
does seek to modify and—failing that—to destroy those
responsible for denying life in the present.

Notes

CHAPTER ONE

1. David Worcester, *The Art of Satire* (New York: Russell and Russell, 1960), p. 6. Worcester writes that "in theory the satirist is a sober, slogging fellow. When he shows a spark of liveliness or reveals a polished art, he is apt to be called a humorist."

2. Northrop Frye, *Anatomy of Criticism* (Princeton: Princeton University Press, 1957), p. 224. See also Matthew Hodgart, *Satire,* World University Library (New York and Toronto: McGraw-Hill, 1969).

3. As quoted by James Sutherland, *English Satire* (Cambridge: University Press, 1957), p. 224.

4. George Bernard Shaw, *The Quintessence of Ibsenism* (New York: Brentano's, 1929), p. 186.

5. *Purple Dust, Collected Plays,* III (London: Macmillan, 1962), 92, 100.

6. *Juno and the Paycock, Collected Plays,* I, 86.

7. *The Silver Tassie, Collected Plays,* II, 64-65.

8. *Ibid.,* p. 102.

9. *The Green Crow* (New York: George Braziller, 1956), p. 238.

10. Rod Nordell, "Cock-a-Doodle Casey," *New Leader,* XLI (3 November 1958), 21.

11. *Ibid.,* p. 20.

12. R. M. Fox, "Civil War and Peace," *The World of Sean O'Casey,* ed. Sean McCann (London: Four Square Books, 1966), p. 49. Fox quotes A.E.

13. *Purple Dust, Collected Plays,* III, 44.

14. *Ibid.,* p. 100.

15. Letter from Sean O'Casey to Walter C. Daniel, dated 16 March 1961, as quoted in "Patterns of Greek Comedy in O'Casey's *Purple Dust,*" *Bulletin of New York Public Library,* LXVI, 612.

16. *The Green Crow,* p. 227.

17. *Under a Colored Cap* (London: Macmillan, 1963), p. 141.

18. "The Green Crow Caws," *Under a Colored Cap,* p. 76.

19. *The Drums of Father Ned* (London: Macmillan, 1960), p. x.

20. "The Power of Laughter: Weapon Against Evil," *The Green Crow,* p. 226.

21. *Behind the Green Curtains* begins with "The 'Dead March' in Saul, played on the organ," the music of those who cannot join in life as it ought to be, one of the Dead Marches that ends *The Drums of Father Ned.* In theme, character, and setting, *Behind the Green Curtains* is the sequel and constitutes O'Casey's prophecy of what will continue to be if the seeds of hope planted in the earlier play do not grow.

22. B. L. Smith, "O'Casey's Satiric Vision" was published, with minor modifications, in *James Joyce Quarterly,* Vol. 8, No. 1 (Fall 1970), 13-28.

CHAPTER TWO

1. William A. Armstrong, "History, Autobiography, and *The Shadow of a Gunman,*" *Modern Drama,* IV, 4 (February 1960), 417-24.

2. *Collected Plays,* I (London: Macmillan, 1963), pp. 96, 131-32. Further references to this edition of *The Shadow of a Gunman* will be cited parenthetically in the text [*SOG,* p. 132]. O'Casey's preferred title, *On the Run,* could not be used because, according to Lennox Robinson, there was already a play called *On the Run.* See *The Letters of Sean O'Casey,* I, ed. David Krause (New York: Macmillan, 1975), pp. 101, 105.

3. *Inishfallen, Fare Thee Well* (New York: Macmillan, 1960), p. 65.

4. *The Green Crow* (New York: George Braziller, 1956), pp. 170-73.

5. *Inishfallen, Fare Thee Well,* p. 229. The receipts were £13 for the first night, £30 for the second, and £50 for the third.

6. *Ibid.,* p. 230.

7. *Kathleen Listens In, Tulane Drama Review,* V, 4 (Summer 1961), 36. This is part of O'Casey's prefatory comment. The other accessible and useful publication of *Kathleen Listens In* is in Robert Hogan's *Feathers from the Green Crow* (Columbia, Missouri: University of Missouri Press, 1962).

8. O'Casey satirizes the same factions (Sinn Fein, Free State, and Labour) in his short story "The Seamless Coat of Kathleen." The seamless coat represents the unity of Ireland. In the story, as in *Kathleen Listens In,* the satire is not subtle, as is suggested by a thematic statement from the story: "The poor little coat is beginning to show unmistakeable signs of many and many a struggle, torn by those trying to keep it on and rent by those trying to take it off." The story is reprinted in Hogan's *Feathers From the Green Crow,* pp. 244-47.

9. *Kathleen Listens In, The Tulane Drama Review,* V, 4 (Summer, 1961), 36.

10. Hogan, *Feathers From the Green Crow* (Columbia, Missouri: University of Missouri Press, 1962), p. 295. I used this edition of the play rather than *The Tulane Drama Review* because it is more accessible and more widely known.

11. *Ibid.,* p. 296.

12. *Ibid.,* p. 279.

13. *Ibid.,* p. 284.

14. *Ibid.,* p. 282.

15. *Ibid.,* p. 290.

16. *The Tulane Drama Review,* V, 4 (Summer, 1961), 36.

17. As quoted by Robert Hethmon, "Great Hatred Little Room," *The Tulane Drama Review*, V, 4 (Summer 1961), 51-52.

18. *Inishfallen, Fare Thee Well*, pp. 231-32.

19. As quoted by Elizabeth Coxhead, *Lady Gregory* (London: Macmillan, 1961), p. 198.

20. *Collected Plays*, I, p. 8. Further references to this edition of *Juno and the Paycock* will be cited parenthetically in the text [*JAP*, p. 8].

21. The pre-Homeric Zeus is described by Edith Hamilton, *Mythology* (New York: New American Library Mentor Book, 1961), pp. 19-20.

22. This is a rather important point in any serious study of O'Casey. In all the plays of the Irish period, all of his youthful idealists—whether they be socialists, communists, laborers, poets, or what have you—are too immature and inexperienced to be effectual. They tend to do a great deal of talking and very little of anything else.

23. In "Ideals and Idealists," the second chapter of *The Quintessence of Ibsenism*, Shaw establishes and defines the categories (Philistines, Idealists, Realists) to be used in his discussion of Ibsen's plays.

24. This is discussed at length by O'Casey in *Drums under the Windows* and *Inishfallen, Fare Thee Well*. Both de Valera and his supporters are caustically satirized in *Cock-a-Doodle Dandy* and elsewhere as the "deValerians." See also David Krause's *Sean O'Casey: The Man and His Work* (New York: Macmillan, 1975), p. 196.

25. Hethmon, "Great Hatred, Little Room," *Tulane Drama Review*, V, 4 (Summer 1961), 52.

26. O'Casey's rejection of a lucrative offer from Hollywood for the film rights to *Juno and the Paycock* is indicative of his own opinions concerning his play:

> My works wait there for any film company that may desire them—for an arranged price, of course; and I'm not concerned overmuch with what they may do with them. But when it was said that the figure of "Captain Boyle" was to be all important (probably to the great joy of Barry Fitzgerald), relegating the other characters to insignificance, it was high time for O'Casey to say, ah, no, be God!
>
> In spite of powers thrusting big money before an author for work he doesn't want to do, and little or nothing for what his own will wishes to create, it is better for him to go his own way, even if it be with a limp. It is not a happy way, but it is his only way if he wishes to remain true to himself and right with God. ["No Flowers for Films," *The Green Crow*, p. 196].

27. *Inishfallen, Fare Thee Well*, p. 234. Gabriel Fallon records in *Sean O'Casey: The Man I Knew* (p. 31) that O'Casey was "thinking of calling it *Irish Nannie Passes*," that it was set in a Dorset Street place well known by O'Casey who "used to drop in at night sometimes for a glass of milk," and that the role of Joe—"a great old Dublin character"—was intended for Fallon.

28. *Nannie's Night Out* was first performed on 29 September 1924, following the main feature, Shaw's *Arms and the Man*. It was produced on

31 March 1961, by the Lafayette Little Theatre at Lafayette, Indiana; it is published in Hogan's *Feathers From the Green Crow*, pp. 299-335.

29. Hogan, *Feathers From the Green Crow*, p. 321.

30. *Drums under the Windows*, pp. 96-113. See also William A. Armstrong's "Sean O'Casey, W.B. Yeats and the Dance of Life," *Sean O'Casey*, ed. Ronald Ayling, *Modern Judgements* (Nashville, Tennessee: Aurora, 1970), pp. 131-42.

31. Hogan, *Feathers From the Green Crow*, pp. 329-30. See also Ronald Ayling's "Nannie's Night Out," *Modern Drama*, V (September 1962), 154-55.

32. *The Plough and the Stars, Collected Plays*, I, 180. Further references to this edition of this play will be cited parenthetically in the text [*P&S*, p. 180]. My essay, "Satire in *The Plough and the Stars*" was published in Ball State University's *Forum*, X, 3 (Summer 1969), 3-11. See also *The Sean O'Casey Review*, 2, 2 (Spring 1976), a special issue commemorating the fiftieth anniversary of *The Plough and the Stars;* David Krause, "Some Truths and Jokes About the Easter Rising," *The Sean O'Casey Review*, 2,2 (Fall 1976), 3-23.

33. *Drums under the Windows*, pp. 334-35.

> We will be rebels; worse—we will be traitors, even terrorists to England, and she will strike without stop or mercy. It is for us, as far as we can, to force her by dodgery to strike oftenest at the air. If we flaunt signs about of what we are, and what we do, we'll get it on the head and round the neck. As for a uniform—that would be worst of all. We couldn't hope to hide ourselves anywhere clad in green and gold, or even green without the gold. Caught in a dangerous corner, there would be a chance in your workaday clothes. You could slip among the throng, carelessly, with few the wiser. In uniform, the crowd would shrink aside to show you, and the enemy will pounce. In your everyday rags you could, if the worst came, hang your rifle on a lamp-post and go your way. But you couldn't take your uniform off, for, even if you did, a man walking about in his shirt would look as suspicious as one going about in a uniform—that is, if any of you has a shirt [p. 339].

34. Act II of *The Plough and the Stars* is O'Casey's earlier one-act "The Cooing of Doves," which was rejected by the Abbey Theatre at the same time *Kathleen Listens In* was accepted. See *Inishfallen, Fare Thee Well*, p. 164.

35. Stephen Gwynn, *Irish Literature and Drama in the English Language: A Short History* (New York: 1936), p. 21. P.S. O'Hegarty, "A Dramatist of New-born Ireland (1927)," *Sean O'Casey: Modern Judgments*, ed. Ronald Ayling (Nashville, Tennessee: Aurora, 1970), p. 65.

36. W. A. Armstrong, "The Sources and the Themes of The *Plough and the Stars*," *Modern Drama*, IV (December 1961), 240. Armstrong has meticulously worked out the specific sources for the unseen orator's words. The first speech (I, 193-94) except for the first sentence—"It is a glorious thing to see arms in the hands of Irishmen"—comes from Pearse's "The Coming Revolution," delivered in 1914. The second (I, 195-96) comes in part from Pearse's "Peace and the Gael," delivered in 1915. The third (I,

202-03) is composed of selected sentences from "Peace and the Gael." The fourth and final speech is O'Casey's adaptation of Pearse's graveside oration for the Irish patriot, Jeremiah O'Donovan Rossa, in July of 1915. Armstrong contends that O'Casey, by his artistic selection, makes his speaker "even more dogmatic in tone and oracular in attitude than Pearse"; O'Casey's orator's final speech is infinitely more "confident about the outcome of the insurrection that he is advocating" (I, 234-36).

37. Krause, *Sean O'Casey*, p. 74.

38. Rod Nordell, "Cock-A-Doodle Casey," *New Leader*, XLI (3 November 1958), 20.

39. Coxhead, *Lady Gregory*, pp. 203-04.

40. *Inishfallen, Fare Thee Well*, pp. 395-96.

CHAPTER THREE

1. See my essay, "From Athlete to Statue: Satire in Sean O'Casey's *The Silver Tassie*," *Arizona Quarterly*, 27, 4 (Winter 1971), 347-61.

2. Critics for the most part have concentrated on the correspondence between O'Casey and Yeats, Shaw's involvement in the incident, and the fact that the Abbey Theatre never regained the stature after O'Casey left it that he brought to it with his five Irish plays. Among the more lucid treatments of the incidents are: David Krause, *Sean O'Casey: The Man and His Work* (New York: Macmillan, 1975), and, of course, *The Letters of Sean O'Casey*, Volume 1 (New York: Macmillan, 1975); Robert Hogan, *The Experiments of Sean O'Casey* (New York: St. Martin's Press, 1960); Mary C. Bromage, "The Yeats-O'Casey Quarrel," *Michigan Alumnus Quarterly Review*, LXIV, 14 (1 March 1958), 135-44; and Eileen O'Casey, *Sean* (New York: Coward, McCann & Geoghegan, 1972).

3. *Rose and Crown* (New York: Macmillan, 1961), pp. 42-43. This fifth volume of O'Casey's autobiography covers the years between 1926-1934, with occasional leaps toward the future and frequent excursions back through the Irish period. "The Silver Tassie" and "The Friggin Frogs" are the two chapters most specifically concerned with the *Tassie's* rejection, reception, and renascense.

4. The role is quite obvious in Yeats's letter dated 20 April 1928, and addressed to "My dear Casey." Yeats informs Casey [sic] " . . . you are not interested in the great war; . . . the whole history of the world must be reduced to wallpaper in front of which the characters must pose and speak . . . . [As for the play] . . . it is all too abstract, after the first act; the second act is an interesting technical experiment, but it is too long for the material; and after that, there is nothing." Allan Wade, *The Letters of W. B. Yeats* (New York: Macmillan, 1955), pp. 740-43.

5. See Bernard Benstock's chapter "A Covey of Clerics" in his *Paycocks and Others: Sean O'Casey's World* (Dublin: Gill and Macmillan, 1976), pp. 239-58.

6. *The Silver Tassie, Collected Plays*, II (London: Macmillan and Company, 1964), p. 31. Further references to *The Silver Tassie* will be cited parenthetically in the text [*ST*, p. 31].

7. *Lady Gregory's Journal*, pp. 110-11. The passage from Shaw's letter is entered under the date of 28 June 1928. Shaw's letter to Lady Gregory is in Krause's *Letters of Sean O'Casey*, I, 285-96.

8. Ronald G. Rollins, "O'Casey's *The Silver Tassie*," *The Explicator*, XX, 8 (April 1962), item 62.

9. *Ibid.*, The letter quoted is included in Rollins's *Explicator* essay.

10. Winifred Smith, "The Dying God in the Modern Theatre," *Review of Religion*, V, 3 (March 1941), 275.

11. G. W. Brandt, "Realism and Parables: From Brecht to Arden," Stratford Upon Avon Studies 4, *Contemporary Theatre*, ed. John Russell Brown and Bernard Harris (London: Edward Arnold, 1962), p. 37.

12. O'Casey does in *The Silver Tassie* what he recognizes as O'Neill's accomplishment in *The Hairy Ape*, a play recommended to O'Casey by Jim Larkin. ". . . This was a play that gave more than a facsimile of life; it brought the inward outward through symbolic distortion. . . ." Personal letter quoted by Ronald G. Rollins, "O'Casey, O'Neill and Expressionism," *Bucknell Review*, X, 4 (May 1962), 365.

13. Sean O'Casey, "The Cutting of an Agate," *The Flying Wasp* (London: Macmillan, 1937), p. 48.

14. Gabriel Fallon, *Sean O'Casey: The Man I Knew* (Boston: Little, Brown, 1965), p. 140.

15. "The Cutting of an Agate," pp. 48-49.

16. Sean O'Casey, *Blasts and Benedictions*, ed. Ronald Ayling (New York: St. Martin's Press, 1967), p. 115.

17. *Within the Gates, Collected Plays*, II, 129. Further references to *Within the Gates* will be cited parenthetically [*WG*, p. 129].

18. *Blasts and Benedictions*, p. 115.

19. Hogan, *Experiments of Sean O'Casey*, pp. 71-76.

20. Rod Nordell, "Cock-a-Doodle Casey," *New Leader*, XLI (3 November 1958), 21.

21. *Blasts and Benedictions*, p. 115.

22. Sean O'Casey, "Out Damned Spot," *Under a Colored Cap* (New York: St. Martin's Press, 1963), p. 260. O'Casey's target at the end of the essay was, of course, the flood of drama and criticisms that he began to attack in *The Flying Wasp*, and continued to attack in his *Within the Gates* essay, his autobiographies and elsewhere through his final publication.

23. *Rose and Crown*, pp. 268-77. The whole incident from the play's opening in London to O'Casey's specific denunciations of his critics is included here. He reduces the objections to absurdity, understands why Shaw has "never yet met an intelligent Jesuit," praises the Harvard, Radcliffe, Wellesley, and Tufts students who protested the banning, and is more convinced than ever that *Within the Gates* is effective satire, that "what splashed from the play over the Jesuits wasn't filth in any form, but hyssop, purifying hyssop, though the clerics didn't like the sting of its cleansing criticism."

24. Lecture by Kasimir Edschmid, cited in Richard Samuel and R. Hinton Thomas's book *Expressionism in German Life, Literature and the Theatre*. As quoted by Robert Hogan, *Experiments of Sean O'Casey*, pp. 56-57.

25. Nordell, "Cock-a-Doodle Casey," pp. 20-21.

26. Rollins, "O'Casey, O'Neill and Expressionism in *Within the Gates*," *West Virginia University Philological Papers*, XIII, 77.

27. *Windfalls* (London: Macmillan, 1934), pp. 57-118. These stories are republished in *The Green Crow*, pp. 253-303.

28. *Windfalls*, p. vii.

29. George Webbe Dasent, "The Husband Who Was to Mind the House," *Folk Tales and Fables*, I, selected and arranged by Eva March Tappen (New York: 1907), pp. 280-82. This tale, usually Dasent's version, is included in dozens of anthologies.

30. *The End of the Beginning, Collected Plays*, I, 268.

31. Robert Lowery, "Premieres and Casts of Sean O'Casey's Plays," *The Sean O'Casey Review*, 2, 1 (Fall 1975), 22-37.

32. *Collected Plays*, I, p. 308.

33. Guy Boas, "The Drama of Sean O'Casey," *College English*, X, 2 (November 1949), 80.

34. "Purple Dust in Their Eyes," *Under a Colored Cap*, p. 261.

35. The whole incident is described in some detail in *Sunset and Evening Star*, pp. 161-62.

36. "The Cutting of an Agate," *The Flying Wasp*, p. 49.

37. Krause, *Sean O'Casey*, p. 161. Krause also includes (pp. 358-59) a long excerpt from Agate's enthusiastic review of *The Star Turns Red*, a review printed in *Sunday Times*, 17 March 1940.

38. George Bernard Shaw, "Preface for Politicians," *John Bull's Other Island* (New York: 1907), p. xv.

39. Hogan, *Experiments of Sean O'Casey*, pp. 101-02. Hogan notes this as a distinction between Shaw's refusal to set up straw men and O'Casey's willingness to use a stacked deck. He continues the metaphor of the card game by noting that O'Casey sometimes refuses to let the opposition take even a single trick, as in *The Star Turns Red* and *Red Roses for Me*.

40. "Purple Dust in Their Eyes," *Under a Colored Cap*, p. 262.

41. *Sunset and Evening Star*, pp. 162-63.

42. *Purple Dust, Collected Plays*, III, p. 44. Later references to this play will be parenthetical (*PD*, p. 44).

43. Robert Gellbert, "Dumb Show," *New Statesman*, LXIV, 1641 (Friday, 24 August 1962), 237.

44. "O'Casey at Your Bedside" *Tulane Drama Review*, II, 2 (February 1958), 59.

45. Letter from Sean O'Casey to Walter C. Daniel, dated 16 March 1961, as quoted in "Patterns of Greek Comedy in O'Casey's *Purple Dust*," *Bulletin of New York Public Library*, LXVI, p. 612.

46. *Ibid.*, p. 603. Daniel quotes O'Casey's *New York Times* article of 21 October 1934, p. 22. The essay is also included in *Blasts and Benedictions*, pp. 111-17.

47. "A Whisper About Bernard Shaw," *The Green Crow*, p. 198.

48. *Inishfallen, Fare Thee Well*, p. 222.

49. Boas, "The Drama of Sean O'Casey," *College English*, X, 2 (November 1948), 84.

50. O'Casey's association of the color purple with death and decay is a consistent one, most obvious perhaps in *Purple Dust, The Star Turns Red,* and *Oak Leaves and Lavender.*

51. *The Star Turns Red, Collected Plays,* II, 271.

52. *Ibid.,* p. 339.

53. Herbert Coston, "Sean O'Casey: Prelude to Playwriting," *Tulane Drama Review,* V, 1 (September 1960), 105.

54. Pat M. Esslinger, "Sean O'Casey and the Lockout of 1913: Materia Poetica of the Two Red Plays," *Modern Drama,* VI, 1 (May 1963), 53-63.

55. *Ibid.,* p. 61.

56. Eileen O'Casey, *Sean* (New York: Coward, McCann & Geoghegan, 1972), p. 193.

57. Esslinger, "O'Casey and the Lockout of 1913," pp. 53-63.

58. Hogan, *Experiments of Sean O'Casey,* p. 88.

59. Krause, *Sean O'Casey,* p. 164.

60. Hogan, *Experiments of Sean O'Casey,* p. 91.

61. *Red Roses for Me, Collected Plays,* III (London: Macmillan, 1950— reprinted in 1962), p. 131. Henceforth, I will cite this play parenthetically [*RRFM,* p. 131].

62. *An Claidheamh Soluis (The Sword of Light)* was the official organ of the Gaelic League. Edited by Pearse, the publication sought to establish Irish unity, Irish pride, and Irish brotherhood. As indicated in *Red Roses for Me* and elsewhere, O'Casey held the nationalistic opportunism of Pearse, Arthur Griffith (Sinn Fein and Irish Volunteers), and Tom Clarke largely responsible for the failure of the strike (1913-1914).

63. In *Sean,* Eileen O'Casey cites two sources for Brennan: an old man who regularly "buttonholed Sean, pouring out his troubles. His constant worry was his money in the bank. Was the bank to be trusted." He was also a property owner, a rent collector never deterred by "wet or fine, hail or storm." The other source cited was "an old man who played the fiddle, "sang hymns, then in an aside as the children gathered around him, he would say, "Go away, you little bastards" (pp. 166-67).

64. "St. Pathrick's Day In the Morning," *The Green Crow,* p. 219.

65. *Sunset and Evening Star,* p. 208.

CHAPTER FOUR

1. Vivian Mercier, "Decline of a Playwright—the Riddle of Sean O'Casey," *The Commonweal,* LXIV, 15 (13 July 1956), 367-68. Mercier's thesis, with which I disagree, is that O'Casey was on the "wrong track" from 1928 on, and that the decline was due to the Abbey's rejection of *The Silver Tassie.* Mercier dismisses other suggested reasons for O'Casey's decline: that Lady Gregory wrote his earlier plays, that an unidentified school teacher helped O'Casey in the writing of his Irish plays, and that living in England destroyed his art. To substantiate his thesis, Mercier describes *Purple Dust* as "embarrassingly bad, class-conscious," and dismisses *Cock-a-Doodle Dandy* as "having an absence of genuine conflict" and a "lack of logical development."

2. *Sunset and Evening Star* (New York: Macmillan, 1961), p. 189. O'Casey describes the coming and the presence of the war and England's adapting to her emergency in four chapters suitably entitled "Heavily Hangs the Broad Sunflower," "Orphans of the Storm," "Red Laugh of War," and "In Cellar Cool."

3. *Ibid.*, pp. 191-92.

4. *Collected Plays*, IV (London: Macmillan, 1958), pp. 13-14. Further citations of this text will be parenthetical [*OLAL*, pp. 13-14].

5. *The Letters of W.B. Yeats*, ed. Allan Wade (New York: Macmillan, 1955), pp. 740-43.

6. Robert Hogan, *The Experiments of Sean O'Casey* (New York: St. Martin's Press, 1960), p. 201.

7. Mrs. Creda Stern was one of "The Dree Dames" who called on O'Casey in his home to bring him THE TRUTH about Russia and Communism. As portrayed by O'Casey, she was irrational and on the verge of hysteria by the time she dismissed him as a fool and his twisted Irish mind as "utterly irresponsible." As quoted by O'Casey, her very important message included: "I tell you, Irishman, the Nazis are far superior, and more to be preferred, than your savage comrades in Moscow!" *Sunset and Evening Star*, pp. 125-34.

8. *Ibid.*, p. 131. Robert Lowery informs me that "Creda Stern is Freda Utley, a former prominent intellectual in the British Comunist Party" and directs me to her autobiography, *Lost Illusions*, published in London (1949).

9. Hogan, *Experiments of Sean O'Casey*, p. 201.

10. Sean O'Casey, "Merrical of Miracles," *Under a Colored Cap* (New York: St. Martin's Press, 1963), p. 208.

11. *Rose and Crown* (New York: Macmillan, 1961), p. 258.

12. Collected Plays, IV, p. 184. Further references to *Cock-a-Doodle-Dandy* will be parenthetical [*CADD*, p. 184]. My essay, "Satire in O'Casey's *Cock-a-Doodle-Dandy*," was published in *Renascence*, XIX, 2 (Winter 1967), 64-73.

13. *Inishfallen, Fare Thee Well* (New York: Macmillan, 1960), pp. 215-18. For Krause's discussion of "devalarians," see his discussion of *Cock-a-Doodle-Dandy* in *Sean O'Casey: The Man and His Work* (New York: Macmillan, 1975), pp. 187-202.

14. Hogan, *Experiments of Sean O'Casey*, pp. 122, 125.

15. *Inishfallen Fare Thee Well*, pp. 382-84.

16. David Krause, *Sean O'Casey*, pp. 201-02. This *New York Times* essay is reprinted as "Cockadoodle Doo" (1958) in *Blasts and Benedictions*, pp. 142-45.

17. *Sunset and Evening Star*, pp. 316-17.

18. *Ibid.*, pp. 318-20.

19. *Collected Plays*, III (London: Macmillan, 1967), p. 272.

20. *Under a Colored Cap*, p. 54. My essay, "The Hat, the Whore, and the Hypocrite in O'Casey's *Bedtime Story*," was published in *Serif*, IV, 2 (June 1967), 3-5.

21. *Collected Plays*, IV, p. 235.

22. Angela Nightingale offers John Jo Mulligan the same chance for life that pretty Alice, in her more jaded way, offered Jack Avreen in "I Wanna

Woman." In both of these and in *The Drums of Father Ned* (when Bernadette Shillayley profits exorbitantly from the lust of Alex Skerighan, the Ulsterman), O'Casey contrasts the essential freedom that honesty provides with the everpresent fear that accompanies hypocrisy; in all cases, the hypocrites are greatly concerned for their reputations. In all cases, the concern reduces them to absurdity and deprives them of material wealth. They, in turn, gain nothing for their efforts except shame and fear.

23. *Collected Plays*, IV, p. 252.

24. *Under a Colored Cap*, p. 54.

25. *Collected Plays*, IV, pp. 264-65.

26. Hogan, *Experiments of Sean O'Casey*, p. 124.

27. Sean O'Casey, *The Bishop's Bonfire* (London: Macmillan and Company, 1961), p. 25. Further citations of the play will be parenthetical [*BB*, p. 25].

28. *Sunset and Evening Star*, pp. 303-11. The entire jeepsie-walkie-talkie scene is included here, in some cases verbatim. The chapter, "Outside an Irish Window," also includes the voyeur's view of the house's religion, its costumed bourgeoisie, its method of driving away children, its pretense to learning, and its way with a fire. Much of the material is included in *The Bishop's Bonfire*, as well as in O'Casey's other plays. Here and in *The Bishop's Bonfire* the view is a particularly voyeuristic one.

29. *The Bishop's Bonfire*, p. 55. Those who have served with the Lt. Reiligans who prosper in the military might argue eloquently that neither the character nor his jeep plan is satiric—that both, in fact, are realistic portrayals of what is.

30. Phoebe Lou Adams, "The Play's the Thing," *Atlantic Monthly*, 196 (October 1955), 96.

31. Hogan, *Experiments of Sean O'Casey*, p. 129.

32. *The Green Crow* (New York: George Braziller, 1956), pp. 130-59.

33. "O'Casey's Drama Bonfire," *Blasts and Benedictions* (London: Macmillan, 1967), p. 140.

34. Krause relates the history of incidents leading up to O'Casey's own ban of all his plays from Ireland on the stage and on Radio Eireann. Samuel Beckett placed a similar ban on all his plays, and five years earlier, Sean O'Faolain had responded to the banning of some of his works by the Censorship Board: "I think my reader will have begun to understand the difficulties of writing in a country where the policeman and the priest are in a perpetual glow of satisfaction." Krause, *Sean O'Casey*, pp. 202-21, 360-66.

35. *Ibid.*, pp. 214-15.

36. *The Green Crow*, p. 159.

37. *The Drums of Father Ned* (London: Macmillan, 1960), p. 19. Further references will be parenthetical [*DFN*, p. 19]. In *Cock-a-Doodle Dandy* also, the devotees of life and joy agreed with the charges against them to the effect that if *evil* is the only alternative to the offerings of Nyadnanave, then evil they were.

38. *Sunset and Evening Star*, pp. 294-95. ". . . St. Preservius, a most holy man of great spiritual preprotensity . . . passed to his rest through a purelytic seizure the day he tried to read the first few lines of Joyce's damnable *Ulysses*."

39. The transformation, involving the efforts of men who have reason and volition to act, recalls the transformations of the Virgin and the Liffey scene in *Red Roses for Me*, the transformation of the village in *Time to Go*, and the incapacity of Nyadnanave *(Cock-a-Doodle Dandy)* and Bally-oonagh *(The Bishop's Bonfire)* for transformation. In neither of the preceding cases was the transformation a lasting one. *The Drums of Father Ned* gives O'Casey's formula for a lasting transformation.

40. "Folly th' crowd, an' youse won't lose your way, for people are on their way from th' Glen of th' light, from th' Meadow of Knowledge, an' from th' Gap of Courage . . . to th' Hill of th' Three Shouts" [p. 101]. *Three Shouts on a Hill* was "a wild thing" which included "a shout at the Gaelic League, a shout at Sinn Fein, and a shout at Labour." O'Casey asked Shaw to write a preface for it, but Shaw refused because, as he noted, O'Casey ought "to go through the mill like the rest of us," *Inishfallen, Fare Thee Well*, p. 31, *Green Crow*, p. 171. To the best of my knowledge, this reference is the closest that *Three Shouts on a Hill*, which O'Casey wanted £25 for, ever came to publication.

41. *The Drums of Father Ned*, p. 92. Murray informs Fillifogue earlier (pp. 42-44) that "When we worship Mozart, we worship God; . . . Mozart's moosic can be as dee murmur of a river's first flow among dee forget-me-nots an' dee meadow sweet; as gay as a dance of boys an' girls at a fair, an' no priest present!" Murray is an interesting exception to O'Casey's usual pattern of using speech defects to symbolize moral or spiritual decadence. In this play, Murray is obviously a follower of life and a devotee of Father Ned, while Fillifogue's villainy is amplified in his mockery of Murray's lisp. Murray's lisp may be modelled on Lady Gregory's, one that always fascinated O'Casey and one which he attempts to imitate in *Inishfallen, Fare Thee Well*, pp. 176-99. O'Casey's imitation, in both cases, while intended to capture the charm of personality, is ineffective and does render a strong character somewhat absurd.

42. *The Drums of Father Ned*, p. x. The Ulsterman episode, complete with theological arguments and the various shouts in the street that are God, exists in a slightly different form in *Rose and Crown*, pp. 290-97.

43. "O'Casey's Drama Bonfire," *Blasts and Benedictions*, p. 141. In his version of the Tostal incident, Gabriel Fallon includes excerpts from comments by O'Casey, Alan McClelland, and Samuel Beckett, as well as paraphrases and explanations of the Archbishop's decree. Fallon tacitly admits that the Archbishop had not read O'Casey's play or *Bloomsday*. He asserts that it was probable that McQuaid had read *Ulysses* and did know of "Sean's flamboyant gestures of camaraderie to Communism and its leaders." Fallon thinks O'Casey was probably right in his statement that McQuaid's "objections were against the authors, not the plays." As presented by Fallon, the Archbishop's action in no way constituted a ban; the banning—and the consequent embarrassing publicity—were O'Casey's doing, O'Casey's and Beckett's.

44. *Behind the Green Curtain, Figuro in the Night, The Moon Shines on Kylenamoe: Three Plays by Sean O'Casey* (London: Macmillan, 1961), p. 1. Horawn's creed is essentially the same as the Bishop's in *Within the Gates* and Davoren's in *Shadow of a Gunman*. The real difference is that he is condemned, while they are not.

45. *Ibid.*, p. 29.

46. *Ibid.*, pp. 33-34. The vigilantes here, as in the other plays and in real life, insist that the world conform to their patterns, use threats and violence to achieve their goals, and are much more evil and more reprehensible than their chosen victims. As portrayed by O'Casey, they rule through fear.

47. *Ibid. Beoman*, like his Anglo-Saxon near-namesake *Beowulf*, is a folk hero. Unlike Beowulf, he emigrates when the hopeless fear that dominates the actions of the citizens of Ballybeedhust makes disaster inevitable. He lives, and in O'Casey's humanistic view, the living Beo*man* has greater potential than Beo*wulf*.

48. *Sunset and Evening Star*, pp. 254-55.

49. *Behind the Green Curtains*, p. i.

50. *Figuro in the Night*, p. 87.

51. Krause, *Sean O'Casey* p. 262. Krause laments the absence of a "symbolic or mythic equivalent of the *cock-ex-machina* in *The Bishop's Bonfire.*"

52. *Figuro in the Night*, p. 107.

53. *Drums under the Windows*, p. 274.

54. *The Moon Shines on Kylenamoe*, p. 144.

55. *Inishfallen, Fare Thee Well*, pp. 172-75.

CHAPTER FIVE

1. Lennox Robinson, *Ireland's Abbey Theatre* (London: Sidgwick and Jackson, 1951), p. 183.

2. Though Father Ned does not appear on stage, he is the spirit which moves others toward involvement in life, and it is his thematic gospel that ultimately isolates the complacently powerful in their lethargy and leaves them and their miasmic doctrines symbolically dead, as the young and vital prepare for the future.

Nyadnanave is deserted by the Cock and his followers in *Cock-a-Doodle Dandy*, for the miracle of life is impossible there. The desertion is itself a quest for life in much the same way that Joyce's exile and O'Casey's exile were quests for ways of life impossible in Ireland.

3. Saros Cowasjee, *Sean O'Casey: The Man Behind the Plays* (Edinburgh and London: Oliver and Boyd, 1963), pp. 9-11. Further, it is on record that "O'Casey himself supported the motion that uniforms should be distributed to the ICA, though from *The Story of the Irish Citizen Army*, it would appear that O'Casey was against the distribution of uniforms," p. 21.

4. *Ibid.*, p. 11.

5. "The Green Crow Caws," *Under a Colored Cap* (London: Macmillan, 1964), p. 78.

6. "The Lark in the Clear Air Still Sings," *Under a Colored Cap*, p. 40.

7. "The Power of Laughter: Weapon Against Evil," *The Green Crow*, (New York: George Braziller, 1956), p. 227.

Index